ALONSO DE SANDOVAL, S.J.

Treatise on Slavery

Selections from

De instauranda Aethiopum salute

ALONSO DE SANDOVAL, S.J.

TREATISE ON SLAVERY

Selections from

De instauranda Aethiopum salute

Edited and Translated, with an Introduction, by

Nicole von Germeten

Hackett Publishing Company, Inc.
Indianapolis/Cambridge

13 12 11 10 09 08   1 2 3 4 5 6

For further information, please address:

Hackett Publishing Company, Inc.
P.O. Box 44937
Indianapolis, IN 46244-0937

www.hackettpublishing.com

Cover design by
Text design by
Composition by
Printed at

Library of Congress Cataloging-in-Publication Data

Sandoval, Alonso de, 1576–1652.
  [De instauranda Aethiopum salute. English, Selections]
    Treatise on slavery : selections from De instauranda Aethiopum
salute / by Alonso de Sandoval ; edited and translated, with an
introduction, by Nicole Von Germeten.
      p. cm.
    Includes bibliographical references and index.
    ISBN 978-0-87220-929-9 (pbk. : alk. paper) —
    ISBN 978-0-87220-930-5 (cloth : alk. paper)
    1. Blacks—Missions—Early works to 1800. 2. Jesuits—Missions—
Early works to 1800. 3. Slaves—Religious life—Latin America—Early
works to 1800. I. Germeten, Nicole von. II. Title.

BV3500.S2513 2008
266'.208996—dc22

                                                          2007039794

The paper used in this publication meets the minimum requirements
of American National Standard for Information Sciences—
Permanence of Paper for Printed Library Materials, ANSI Z39.48–1984.

CONTENTS

ACKNOWLEDGMENTS

Over a period of ten years, many people have helped this project come to fruition. Ronald J. Morgan first suggested I look at Sandoval's work during a seminar at the University of California, Santa Barbara, led by Sarah Cline. He has continued to foster a community of Sandoval scholars. After I spent a few years away from Sandoval, Albert J. Raboteau mentioned the need for an English version of *De instauranda Aethiopum salute,* while I had a postdoctoral grant at Princeton University's Center for the Study of Religion. I revisited my translation while in residence at the Oregon State University Center for the Humanities, with the encouragement of the director David M. Robinson. Thanks go to Paul Farber of the Oregon State University History Department for his generous support of my research and publications. William B. Taylor and Ben Vinson III were among those who supported the publication of the translation by Hackett Publishing Company. I am also very grateful for the enthusiasm and professionalism of Rick Todhunter at Hackett. I was inspired further after spending time at Sandoval's *colegio* in Cartagena, Colombia, enjoying the hospitality of Padre Tulio Aristizabal S.J., the director of the museum at the Convento de San Pedro Claver. I hope he can take pride in the publication of this book. I appreciate the suggestions made by Daniel Reff, Robert Nye, John Thornton, and the very helpful, knowledgeable, and thorough anonymous reader for Hackett, although I am responsible for all the errors that remain. Thank you to Jacob Bolotin for reproducing the frontispiece of the original 1627 edition. My husband, Brent Ayrey, has supported me and my work in many tangible and intangible ways for the last eleven years. In the case of this book, completed mainly during my summer breaks from teaching, he worked hard to provide me with the best possible work environment. Without his efforts, I would not have been able to complete this project.

INTRODUCTION

Alonso de Sandoval's Biography

Alonso de Sandoval was born in Seville, Spain, in 1577. His father, Tristán Sánchez, was born in Toledo, Spain, in the 1530s. Sánchez went to the Americas as a young man in the mid-1500s, working as a government official in the Spanish bureaucracy, including as a treasurer and a notary in the viceroyalty of Peru. His work took him to the regions of South America that are now Chile and Bolivia. Sandoval had eleven siblings, born from relationships his father had with three different women. In 1555, while he was in the viceroyalty of Peru, Sánchez fathered a child whom colonial documents describe as mestizo, meaning his father was of European ancestry and his mother was an indigenous woman. Sánchez did not marry the mother of his first child; however, he did marry an American-born Spanish woman before going back to Spain in 1573, taking his wife, his illegitimate son, four other children, his mother-in-law, two servants, and a slave with him. His first wife must have died en route to Spain or in Spain soon after, because he married another woman in Spain. This second wife gave birth to Alonso and several of his siblings.

When Sandoval was around seven years old, he set sail for Lima with his family to accompany Sánchez on another bureaucratic assignment. Sandoval received much of his education in this city, the capital of the viceroyalty of Peru. As the Catholic Church was an important arm of Spanish bureaucracy, many well-off Spaniards living in the viceregal capitals of Lima and Mexico City educated their sons in prestigious religious institutions. Six of Sandoval's siblings joined religious orders, and two of his brothers achieved important positions of power, one in the Mercedarian order and the other as a Dominican friar. Sandoval studied in the San Pablo Jesuit College, one of the best schools in the Americas at that time. Throughout his life, Sandoval benefited from San Pablo's large library and what he learned from his Jesuit mentors there, although he was considered to have been an average, not superb, student. He officially joined the Company of Jesus in 1593 and was sent to Cartagena in 1605. He worked in Cartagena for the rest of his life, other than some time he spent doing research in the Jesuit library in Lima and participating in missions to Amerindians living outside the city. He was made rector or head administrator of the Cartagena Jesuit College in 1624.[1] His colleagues described him as both very strict and very charitable. Although most supported his work with Africans, Sandoval had a few

---

1. Juan Manuel Pacheco, *Los Jesuitas en Colombia*, Book I (Bogotá: Editorial "San Juan Eudes," 1954), 264.

conflicts with his superiors in the Company of Jesus, including one that involved his allowing male students at the Jesuit College to wear women's clothes in a theatrical play and another involving fundraising. His attempts to attain the fourth level of Jesuit vows, by which a Jesuit would be entrusted to directly obey papal directives, failed. He died in an epidemic that hit the city in 1652.

CARTAGENA DE INDIAS

Cartagena de Indias, a city on the coast of Colombia founded in 1533, was an important Caribbean bastion of Spanish military, religious, and economic power in colonial South America. Spaniards first exploited this region in the 1530s, when they asked the king for permission to use African slaves to help them dig up treasure buried in indigenous tombs along the coast. By the end of the 1500s Cartagena became a major slave-trading port and the outlet of much gold and silver from South America.

In the early 1600s Cartagena had about three thousand residents of European ancestry and about seven thousand Africans or people of African descent, free and enslaved, living in the city. About 135,000 slaves passed through the port of Cartagena from 1595 to 1640.[2] Many continued their journey inland to agricultural areas or to the cities of Quito or Lima, or they ended up in the Chocó to the west of Cartagena or as pearl divers on the coast. Cartagena did not have a population numbering in the hundreds of thousands like the Spanish capitals of Lima, Peru, and Mexico City, because there were very few Amerindians living in the city. Lima and Mexico City had large indigenous populations who had either settled there before the conquest or were drawn from the surrounding regions. As Sandoval points out in the text, the indigenous peoples in some areas of the Americas had suffered a severe demographic decline by his lifetime, which was the case for Cartagena and its immediate surroundings.

Cartagena was an important stop for the Spanish fleet coming from Seville and also for ships heading back to Spain after a stop in Porto Belo, Panama. At the very end of this book, Sandoval describes the mercantile function of the Spanish American empire, which he would have seen in action in Cartagena. His city was populated with merchants who traded in merchandise, including slaves, brought by Spanish and Portuguese ships and purchased with American gold mined in the Chocó region, and silver from Andean mines. Pirates were drawn to the city: the French raided Cartagena in 1544, and English pirates destroyed the city in 1580. The Spanish slowly built huge fortifications around Cartagena. It remained safe from foreign military

---

2. Enriqueta Vila Vilar, "Introduction," Alonso de Sandoval, *Un tratado sobre la esclavitud* (Madrid: Alianza Editorial, 1987), 18, 27–31.

invasions for most of the 1600s, guarded by a permanent military battalion.
   Cartagena boasted all of the major Spanish Catholic institutions, including
several hospitals, catering mainly to lepers and travelers and sailors sick from
their voyage to the port, and churches and convents for both men and women.
The Jesuits received royal approval to open a college in Cartagena in 1603. In
1604 five Jesuit priests established themselves in cramped quarters near the center of the city. Very soon they began teaching Latin to local residents. In the
1630s the large Jesuit convent that still exists today was built, with the walls of
the building forming part of the city's defensive walls.
   From 1610 Cartagena was also the seat for an inquisition tribunal. Only two
other inquisition high courts existed in Latin America, one in Lima and one in
Mexico City. The inquisition court functioned as another fortification against
the influx of foreign non-Catholics who invaded the city, although not as dramatically as the English and French pirates did. In the 1600s the tribunal's crucial function was in many ways to repress Cartagena's large non-Spanish
population. For example, Portuguese merchants suspected to be secretly practicing Judaism were prosecuted by the inquisition. Protestant sailors, pirates, and
slave traders also came before the court. Of course, Africans thought to be
witches or sorcerers or Muslims were common targets of the tribunal.
   While the reader can learn about some aspects of the lives of Africans and their
descendants who lived in seventeenth-century Cartagena from carefully reading
De instauranda, other colonial documents reveal that Sandoval neglected to report
on a great deal of the Afro-Cartagenan experience. Afro-Cartagenans were
involved in almost every part of the day-to-day functioning of the city. They also
rebelled against colonial society and created their own towns outside Cartagena.
Beginning in the mid-1500s, runaway slaves founded rebel towns called palenques
outside the city walls. Especially in the late 1600s, the Spanish authorities sent
military expeditions to weaken the independence of the largest palenques.
   Not all Afro-Cartagenans who lived within the city were slaves. Many free
and enslaved people were married, and other individuals of African descent
owned property and businesses in the city. They served in the military and professions, although this upward mobility did not come without challenges. In the
1630s the inquisition court accused a surgeon called Diego López, whom the
Spanish authorities described as a mulatto, of witchcraft. The inquisition also
accused several African and mulatta women of involvement in López's supposed
coven. As indicated by inquisition court inventories of their goods, some of
these women owned homes, slaves, jewels, and expensive clothes.[3] Different

   3. "Inventario y almoneda de los bienes secuestrados a varias mujeres negras, reconcilia-
das por el tribunal de la Inquisición." Cartagena, 1634. Archivo Histórico de la Nación,
Spain, Inquisición, 4822, exp. 2.

kinds of social barriers persisted throughout the colonial era: in 1765 Cristóbal Polo de Águila needed special permission from the king to continue working as a lawyer, due to his "condition of being a mulatto."[4]

Sandoval points out that court cases involving masters abusing slaves frequently came before the judicial authorities in Cartagena. Because these cases were decided at local courts, generally this documentation has disappeared. However, other criminal cases survive involving slaves and free people of African descent in Cartagena. Slaves and freedmen had judicial status in the Spanish colonial system, so they could testify as witnesses in criminal cases involving defendants of European descent. The authorities used their testimonies as legitimate evidence to punish wrongdoers. It was illegal for nonwhites to carry weapons, so Africans, slaves, and freedmen were called before the authorities for knife fights and other public violence. In one case from 1642, the owner of a female slave accused another man of raping her. Although the owner may have been motivated to protect what he viewed as his property, he also felt some paternalistic feelings of protecting the woman and supported the prosecution of her attacker.[5] In a similar case in 1788, a man accused of deflowering a slave woman defended himself by casting aspersions on the victim's honor.[6]

Sandoval briefly mentions African festivals, parades, and celebrations in Book 3, highlighting the variety of African involvement in the Catholic Church, beyond his descriptions of their baptisms, confessions, and catechisms. These public festivities, involving dance, music, and costumes, were a lively part of street life throughout colonial Latin America, especially in cities such as Cartagena in the 1600s, where thousands of Africans from different ethnicities lived together. Sandoval refers to Afro-Catholic religious organizations in Book 1. Africans adapted Catholic fiestas and institutions to suit their spiritual, charitable, and social needs, sometimes with the encouragement of colonial religious authorities such as the Jesuits, sometimes angering them. From 1605 the Jesuits sponsored an African brotherhood in Cartagena.[7] Sandoval provides insights on

---

4. "Concesión para q. Don Cristóbal Polo de Águila pueda usar el titulo de abogado sin que el cabildo de Cartagena y los demás abogados le obstaculicen por su condición de mulato." Cartagena, 1765. Archivo General de la Nación, Colombia (hereafter AGN), Reales Cedulas, Tomo 61, 659–64.

5. "Causa seguida a Juan Carillo de Albornoz, por asalto a la casa de Pedro Soto de Altamirano y estupro de Agustina, negra esclava del dueño de casa." Cartagena, 1642. AGN, Criminales, 192, 351–562.

6. "Pablo Cano, condenado por la desfloración de una esclava de Manuel Morera, representa en defensa de su inocencia en el asunto." AGN, Criminales, 217, 495–502.

7. Angel Valtierra, S.J., *Peter Claver, Saint of the Slaves*, trans. Janet Perry and L. J. Woodward (Westminster, MD: Newman Press, 1960), 59.

how African religious brotherhoods, at least nominally Catholic, were divided by African language groups and ethnicities. As Sandoval says, these brotherhoods cooperated to honor the dead and give their members decent funerals. By going beyond the main themes and evidence in *De instauranda,* we can learn more about how Afro-Cartagenans actively worked to survive and prosper in the hierarchical, paternalistic Spanish society.

THEMES IN ALONSO DE SANDOVAL'S WORK

Starting in the late fifteenth century, numerous publications in several different European languages tried to reveal, explain, categorize, and judge the peoples encountered outside Europe and justify European domination by creating an image of non-Europeans as naturally inferior to their new or potential rulers and enslavers. The idea of race as an immutable biological characteristic that blotted out human individuality had not yet hardened into the rigidity of the nineteenth and twentieth centuries, but sixteenth- and seventeenth-century writers, including Alonso de Sandoval, helped formulate and verbalize the contours of these later developments.

Modern ideas of race originate in the early modern era. From the 1400s to the 1600s, the kings of Spain and Portugal had ambitions to gain influence over the people and to access to the material resources of Africa, Asia, and the Americas, as well as to challenge Islamic empires in North Africa and the eastern Mediterranean. On the home front, monarchs in Spain solidified their rule with a reputation as the most "Catholic" monarchs, persecuting and eventually expelling Islamic as well as Jewish residents. In the same era, Europeans began to take advantage of African slave labor for use in New World mining and capitalist agriculture. The Portuguese first sent African slaves to work on sugar plantations on the islands off the coast of Africa and then extended this system to Brazil. The Spanish also used African slaves in their American colonies. When the English, French, and Dutch gained control of regions of the circum-Caribbean,[8] they eagerly imitated their Iberian predecessors.

Before the fifteenth century, Europeans had not created an ideology of Africans as the most acceptable slaves due to ideas of racial difference. The concept of enslaving other humans developed before modern racism. Those marked as slaves often practiced another religion than their captors but may or may not have had the same skin color. Gwendolyn Midlo Hall argues that "in medieval Spain and Portugal, dark-skinned people were often identified as conquerors and rulers rather than as slaves." As indicated by the root of the word "slave"

---

8. The circum-Caribbean encompasses the islands of the Caribbean Sea, as well as coastal regions of Mexico, Central America, Colombia, and Venezuela.

(*slav*), Eastern Europeans were seen as more likely to be slaves before the emergence of the Atlantic trade.[9] As the Atlantic slave trade increased in the 1500s, Europeans no longer enslaved Christians or other whites in Europe. Not long after, enslaved populations became numerically dominant in the circum-Caribbean, including many American-born slaves. Because these Creoles could no longer be described as Africans, their skin color defined their place in society. European elites feared rebellion among Africans and their descendants in the New World, and their economy and social hierarchy grew dependent on a racist ideology that privileged whiteness. The harshest prejudices and dehumanization grew in response to fears of rebellion or social and economic disruption. By the mid-1500s black skin was more closely linked with enslavement than it had been a century earlier. These concepts would become more and more indivisible over a period of centuries, as the Atlantic slave trade grew.

The sections of Alonso de Sandoval's work, originally titled *Naturaleza, policia sagrada i profana, costumbres i ritos, disciplina i catechismo evangélico de todos etíopes* (The Natural, Sacred, and Profane Customs and the Rites, Discipline, and Evangelical Catechism of All Ethiopians—often referred to as *De instauranda Aethiopum salute* or *On Restoring Ethiopian Salvation*), that have been selected and translated for this volume represent the Spanish, Catholic perspective on Africans and African slaves brought to the Americas in the 1600s. Sandoval perceived his work as encouraging a humane and just inclusion of Africans into the Catholic Church, despite the fact that his words indirectly contributed to formulating racist ideologies. When Sandoval articulated a broad mission for his colleagues in the Jesuit order by labeling almost all non-Christians around the world *Aethiopians* (Ethiopians), this label at the same time distinguished all non-Europeans as targets for European colonial domination.

While Sandoval promotes Catholic and European imperialism, provides a window into seventeenth-century ideas of race, and does not unequivocally reject African slavery, his work is unique and valuable in its focus on the early modern black Atlantic[10]. Firmly rooted in ideas of Christian destiny, European superiority, and fascination with what was perceived as barbarous and exotic, Sandoval begins his work in Africa and engages with African political, cultural, and linguistic divisions, however judgmental his descriptions are. By starting his narration in Africa, not America or Europe, Sandoval acknowledges that African

---

9. Gwendolyn Midlo Hall, *Slavery and African Ethnicities in the Americas: Restoring the Links* (Chapel Hill: University of North Carolina Press, 2005), I.

10. The idea of the black Atlantic privileges the African diaspora experience, not the histories of nation states in the Atlantic basin. See Paul Gilroy, The Black Atlantic: Modernity and Double Consciousness (Cambridge, MA: Harvard University Press, 1993), 19.

slaves had a history and a culture before they came in contact with European slave traders. In this book African history and contemporary events affect the rest of the world. By reading the entire book from start to finish, one perceives how Sandoval moved from the very specific (a focus on African ethnolinguistic groups in Book 1) to the general (the umbrella label of "Ethiopian" over virtually the entire non-European world in Book 4). However, careful readers will find that this progression is far more complex: even the penultimate chapter of Book 4 highlights how African constructs of local identity influenced life in America.

Readers can also trace the fluctuations in Sandoval's conception of racial difference, especially noting how he oscillates from recognizing the individuality of African slaves to imposing generalized negative characteristics on all Africans. Sandoval certainly sympathizes with the slaves' suffering, but it is debatable if he ever empathizes with them. If he perceives Africans as nothing more than victimized objects playing a role in his vision of Christian redemption, what characteristics does he grant to these supposed objects? Or does he portray slaves as subjects with a sense of self-perception and a desire to control their own destinies?

Sandoval's Christian paternalism and charitable impulses disguise a desire to force cultural and religious change on African slaves. Recently, scholars have reinterpreted Bartolomé de las Casas as an "ecclesiastical imperialist" who advocated for improved treatment of indigenous Americans while promoting the right of the Spanish king to rule over them.[11] In his criticisms Las Casas targets abusive colonists, while Sandoval attacks slave masters, careless priests, and slave traders. Both Las Casas and Sandoval, despite their writings and, in Sandoval's case, day-to-day charitable acts, never perceived another choice for non-Christians than accepting Christianity. This meant that, in their opinion, the inhabitants of two continents had no right to continue the way of life they had known before violent contact with Europeans. Charity, paternalism, and advocating reform in fact only serve to strengthen a repressive system, even if the charitable impulses go completely unfulfilled.[12]

DE INSTAURANDA AND THE INTELLECTUAL TRADITION OF THE JESUITS

In *De instauranda* Sandoval draws from his personal experiences of Jesuit education and training, as well as the intellectual and ideological traditions of the

11. Daniel Castro, *Another Face of Empire: Bartolomé de las Casas, Indigenous Rights, and Ecclesiastical Imperialism* (Durham, NC: Duke University Press, 2007).

12. For a similar argument in the case of U.S. slave historiography, see Walter Johnson, "A Nettlesome Classic Turns Twenty-Five: Eugene D. Genovese, *Roll, Jordan, Roll*," in www.common-place.org, vol. I, no. 4 (July 2001).

Jesuits. This background affects Sandoval's vision of Christianizing Africans. Jesuits valued balancing "the interior life with action in the outside world."[13] Founded by Ignatius Loyola, a former soldier from the Basque region of Spain, the Company of Jesus rejected many of the traditions and organizational structures common to other religious orders in the 1500s.[14] They did not wear any particular robe or habit and officially declined ecclesiastical offices and church incomes. They were funded by European monarchs and private donors, not tithes, so they often developed their own money-making ventures. Unlike older monastic orders, they did not chant the prayers of the divine office at regular intervals throughout the night and day, nor did they follow the typical religious practices of long hours of prayer or regular fasting, penitence, and contemplation. Members of the Company were meant to spend their time in active charitable tasks directed at prisoners, those condemned to death, the sick, and people who lacked the means for a decent burial. Early Jesuits believed their goal was to travel the world proselytizing non-Christians in imitation of the New Testament apostles. Jesuits traveled to the Americas, Africa, India, China, and Japan, to spread Christianity and become "fishers of men."[15]

Loyola's *Spiritual Exercises,* a four-week meditation process designed to bring participants closer to Jesus Christ, are the basis for the Jesuit conception of internalized Christianity. All Jesuits participated in the *Spiritual Exercises* as part of their training as novices. Loyola's writings emphasize emotion and feeling in internal prayer, especially "consolation," a comforting feeling derived from spiritual closeness to God. Loyola advised Jesuits to pursue this feeling for themselves and those they encountered in their missions.[16] Due to this emphasis on the "interior life," Jesuits believed that they had to slowly educate and persuade non-Christians to willingly accept baptism. Their ideals of internal Christianity argued against superficial mass baptisms. The Jesuits also emphasized the Catholic sacraments of confession and penance. New Christians had to deeply repent their sins, "in keeping with the great importance placed by the Jesuits on the interior, emotional experience of Christianity."[17]

In terms of intellectual influences and sources, Sandoval's work resembles a book written by another Spanish Jesuit born in the 1570s. Andrés Pérez de

13. Sabine Hyland, *The Jesuit and the Incas: The Extraordinary Life of Padre Blas Valera, S.J.* (Ann Arbor: University of Michigan Press, 2003), 37.

14. Pope Paul III officially approved the foundation of the Company of Jesus in 1540.

15. John O'Malley, *The First Jesuits* (Cambridge, MA, 1993), 6, 15, 68, 70, 112–13.

16. Ibid., 19, 45, 83–84.

17. Hyland, *The Jesuit and the Incas,* 43. Hyland shows how practice often veered from these ideals: the Jesuits used violence to literally force native Andeans to confess (59).

Ribas published *History of the Triumphs of Our Holy Faith amongst the Most Barbarous and Fierce Peoples of the New World* in 1645. Daniel T. Reff describes Pérez de Ribas as

> of two minds. . . . The same author who at one moment privileges empirical observation and the rational subject the next moment privileges an invisible reality (e.g., devils, angels), preferring formal and final causes (God's plan/will) over material or efficient causality. . . . The history Pérez de Ribas recounts is as much about God's often mysterious handiwork and the operation of the Holy Spirit as it is about the heroic efforts of Jesuit missionaries.[18]

Both Pérez de Ribas and Sandoval were missionaries and ethnographers, and their "particular values, beliefs and signifying practices" were influenced by Jesuit discourse, the Renaissance, and the Counter-Reformation.[19]

Scholars view sixteenth- and seventeenth-century Jesuit missionary writings as a form of early cultural ethnography, where an observer reports on another group of people while participating to some degree in their societies. Pérez de Ribas devotes large sections of his work to describing the cultures of indigenous Americans in northern New Spain, where he worked as a missionary. For his empirical evidence, Sandoval relates his experiences working with slaves in Cartagena when he describes methods for Christianizing Africans. He refers to reports and letters that other Jesuits sent from Africa, and he speaks of interviewing slave ship captains in Cartagena. Sandoval also spoke to African slaves in Cartagena about African ethnic divisions, culture, rituals, and beliefs about the supernatural. Some of this information may be incorporated into *De instauranda*. He specifically mentions that Africans told him about their suffering on slave ships.

Along with these contemporary sources, Sandoval draws on his education in the Jesuit intellectual tradition, with an emphasis on ancient Latin and Greek authorities, the Bible, and the writings of early Christian saints and medieval Christian authorities. In the Spanish version of *De instauranda*, Sandoval references literally hundreds of scholarly works, from classical sources such as Homer, Pliny the Elder, and Aristotle to Christian writings including the works of Jerome and other early biblical commentators. Sandoval's Jesuit training meant that the philosophies of Augustine (born in 354) and Thomas Aquinas (born approximately 1225) played the most important role in his

---

18. Reff, "Critical Introduction," in Andrés Pérez de Ribas, *History of the Triumphs of Our Holy Faith amongst the Most Barbarous and Fierce Peoples of the New World*, trans. Daniel T. Reff, Maureen Ahern, and Richard K. Danford (Tucson: University of Arizona Press, 1999), 12.

19. Ibid., 11.

thinking about humanity and Christianity. The Jesuits encouraged a reempha-
sis on Augustine's and Aquinas's philosophies in the 1600s. Augustine believed
that God showed his presence constantly in every aspect of daily life. In his
Spiritual Exercises, Loyola, influenced by Aquinas, "had his followers meditate
at length on how Satan and his legion of demons set snares throughout the
world, enticing people to sin."[20] This philosophy argues that humans may be
influenced by the devil, but they have the free will to choose Christianity and
save their souls.

Jesuits, and most other literate Catholic men and women of the time,
devoured biographies of ancient and medieval saints. As was the case in the lives
of the saints, Sandoval's text indicates he believed that "God and the devil played
a dynamic role in the lives of Jesuit missionaries."[21] By far the most important
saint in *De instauranda* is Francis Xavier.[22] In 1619 Sandoval published a translation of a biography of Francis Xavier and a history of the Jesuits in India, both
written in Portuguese by João de Lucena. Sandoval frequently refers to Xavier as
his mentor and inspiration to promote his own missionary work. In *De instauranda* Sandoval repeatedly tries to prove that his Cartagena mission is modeled
after Xavier's activities in Asia and carries out Xavier's missionary goals and that
therefore it represents the Jesuits' most important endeavor.

Sandoval worked within a tradition of Jesuit missionary accounts that presented Jesuit activities in widely dispersed areas of the world ranging from
China to Mexico. His most obvious direct influence was José de Acosta's *De
procuranda Indorum salute* [On Procuring Indian Spiritual Health], written in
1576 and published in 1588, the first Jesuit book written in the Americas.[23]
Although Acosta (1540–1600) was born a generation before Sandoval, both of
their works show the influence of "Greek philosophy, Latin rhetoric and

---

20. Daniel T. Reff, *Plagues, Priests, and Demons: Sacred Narratives and the Rise of Christianity in the
Old World and the New* (Cambridge: Cambridge University Press, 2004), 22, 132.

21. Reff, "Critical Introduction," 13, 15.

22. Both Xavier and Loyola became official Catholic saints in 1622, exactly when Sandoval was writing *De instauranda.* Francis Xavier was born in 1506 to noble parents in a
Basque-influenced area of Navarre, now a province of northern Spain. He shared a room
with Ignatius Loyola at the University of Paris and later took the original Jesuit vows in
1534. While they were working in Portugal in 1540, King John III asked the Jesuits to
help bring Christianity to his new subjects in Asia. Xavier spent the rest of his life on
Jesuit missions in India and the islands of the Indian Ocean. In 1552 Xavier died of an
illness on Shangchuan, an island just off the coast of China. His body was buried in the
Jesuit church in Goa.

23. Claudio Burgaleta, *José de Acosta: His Life and Thought* (Chicago: Jesuit Way, 1999), 80–
81, 132–37.

Christian theology . . . at the intersection of classical scholarship and new discoveries."[24] Both authors combine the use of classical and medieval sources with personal experience and reports from people who had personally taken part in events related to their work. Both works epitomize the literature and worldview of the Spanish Baroque, with their authors "rooted in the traditions of scholasticism and Renaissance humanism" while trying to "make sense of very different peoples in a heterogeneous New World context."[25] Fundamentally, both authors agree that Jesuits must learn as much as possible about those they wish to Christianize.

Sandoval applied Acosta's arguments about Christianizing Amerindians to Africans. Both Acosta and Sandoval believed that Native Americans and Africans were difficult to teach but that the effort was worth it when they became good Christians.[26] Acosta notes the huge diversity among the Amerindians, similar to Sandoval's lists of African ethnicities in Book 1, Chapter 1. Sandoval follows Acosta in his presentation of a historical background and preparation that predestined Africans for Christianity, even before Europeans became involved in the fifteenth century. Acosta also gives practical guidelines for teaching Indians about Christianity, advising priests to be very flexible and pragmatic in their work. Although Sandoval focuses on Africans, he uses arguments similar to those of Acosta in discussing the topics of preparing the Indians for baptism with a simple, direct catechism, demanding that they willingly consent to baptism, hearing their confessions in their own languages, and encouraging them to take communion. Both books also serve to deflect criticism that Jesuits spend too much time working only with the elite. Acosta was censored for criticizing the abuses of Spanish rule and the methods used to baptize indigenous people in the Americas, so modern readers should not expect Sandoval to take an overly critical stance toward colonialism or slavery.

Sandoval does describe the slaves' experiences on ships during their Atlantic passage. His criticism of the slave trade was preceded and influenced by several other works.[27] Bartolomé de Albornoz, a Dominican friar who taught at the University of México, passionately denounced slavery in 1573, claiming, as an expert in jurisprudence, that all slaves were most likely illegally enslaved and that being a slave did not improve Africans' lives. Not surprisingly, the Inquisition added this book to its list of prohibited reading and forbade any new

---

24. Walter Mignolo, "Introduction," in José de Acosta's *Natural and Moral History of the Indies* (Durham, NC: Duke University Press, 2002), xix.

25. Margaret M. Olsen, *Slavery and Salvation in Colonial Cartagena de Indias* (Gainesville: University Press of Florida, 2004), 22, 59.

26. Ibid., 48–53.

27. Vila Vilar, *Un tratado,* 22–23.

editions.[28] The Dominican Tomás de Mercado published a book discussing slavery in 1569. Mercado described the conditions aboard slave ships and argued that slavery corrupted African leaders, but he did not criticize the institution of slavery itself. Lastly, the 1614 work of the Jesuit Luis de Molina had a great influence on Sandoval. This book also focused on the slave trade, as opposed to the institution of slavery itself. Molina argued that slave traders committed serious sins when they abused slaves.

Sandoval's work fell into oblivion much more rapidly than did Acosta's books or other treatises that dealt with Amerindians. Sandoval's book was not reissued in any form until 1956, when the Bogotá city government supported a new edition in a moment of Colombian prosperity and nationalism and in recognition of the 300th anniversary of Pedro Claver's death. Olsen argues that the fact that the Iberian monarchs, the colonial elite, and the Jesuits themselves were making huge profits off the slave trade might have had something to do with the lack of interest in *De instauranda*.[29] This accounts only for why the Spanish did not promote the book, not for why it was ignored by the rest of Europe, unlike many other contemporary treatises written in Spanish.

The fact that it was not an effective propaganda tool for Spain's enemies, in contrast to Las Casas's enormously famous *Brief Account of the Destruction of the Indies by the Spanish,* might explain why *De instauranda* was never translated or popularized in Europe. Las Casas's book, an unequivocal denunciation of Spanish colonists based on their abuses of American natives, was published in Spanish in 1552, in French in 1579, and in English in 1583.[30] Spain's Elizabethan and Dutch enemies leapt at the chance to spread negative propaganda and an anti-Catholic bias toward Philip II and his immense empire. But *De instauranda* did not attract European interest, as many nations were eager to exploit Africa and trade in African slaves without worrying about Christianizing the slaves. It has been argued that non-Iberian nations engaged in the slave trade had a more dehumanized vision of Africans than did Sandoval and other Iberian commentators. According to Robin Blackburn, the British, eventually a major slave-trading country, "transform[ed] what it meant to be a slave and a Negro . . . narrowing down and flattening the baroque features of Spanish notions of race and slavery."[31]

---

28. Reff notes that late sixteenth- and early seventeenth-century Jesuits were especially wary of enraging the Spanish monarchs and losing funding by criticizing any aspect of Spanish government in the Americas. See "Critical Introduction," 25–27.

29. Olsen, *Slavery and Salvation,* 7, 58.

30. See Philip Wayne Powell, *Tree of Hate: Propaganda and Prejudices Affecting United States Relations with the Hispanic World* (New York: Basic Books, 1971).

31. Robin Blackburn, *The Making of New World Slavery: From the Baroque to the Modern, 1492–1800* (London: Verso, 1997), 156.

Stories of abuses in the slave trade and neglect of African slaves' Christianity were simply not as compelling in the seventeenth century as were denunciations of Spanish ill-treatment of Amerindians in the sixteenth century.

THE JESUITS AND THEIR IDEAS ABOUT RACE

The large corpus of publications, letters, and reports produced by sixteenth- and seventeenth-century Jesuit missionaries around the world significantly contributed to developing European perceptions of race. The early modern Jesuits were not racists in the modern sense; they did not believe that a person's non-white skin color meant that he or she had inherited a set of immutable negative characteristics. They were instead intolerant of any non-Christian beliefs around the world. As Catholic missionaries, they asserted their belief in the superiority of their religion and civilization. This kind of thinking could easily evolve into using skin color as a simple shorthand for ranking the targets of European imperial expansion.

Jesuits, most notably Acosta, formulated a hierarchy of the world's populations, whom they targeted for Christian proselytization. In his book *Historia natural y moral de las Indias,* published in 1590 in Seville, Acosta judged and ranked non-European civilizations around the world according to his understanding of their writing systems, customs, and government.[32] Among those he considered barbarians, Acosta ranked the Chinese just below Europeans. The Jesuit approach to Christianizing in China and Japan differed greatly from missions in other areas of the world. Chinese and Japanese leaders threatened or rejected the Jesuits, so the order had to attempt "cultural accommodation" and fit into local styles of dress, language, and manners. The Jesuits viewed the Chinese as superior to other non-Europeans, but the Chinese saw themselves as vastly superior to Europeans. It was impossible for the Jesuits to "civilize" the Chinese and Japanese according to the methods used in the Americas and Africa.[33]

Acosta ranked the "chiefdoms" of the Mexica (Aztecs) and the Inca empire in the Andes below the Chinese, because he did not credit them with a writing

32. See Anthony Pagden, *The Fall of Natural Man: The American Indian and the Origins of Comparative Ethnology* (Cambridge: Cambridge University Press, 1982), 179, 197–99; Sabine Hyland, "Conversion, Custom, and 'Culture': Jesuit Racial Policy in Sixteenth-Century Peru" (Ph.D. Diss., Yale University, 1994), 272–73; and Sabine MacCormack, *On the Wings of Time: Rome, the Incas, Spain, and Peru* (Princeton: Princeton University Press, 2007), 164. Hyland focuses on changing Jesuit regulations about allowing mestizos into the Company, historicizing Jesuit attitudes to race.

33. Dauril Alden, *The Making of an Enterprise: The Society of Jesus in Portugal, Its Empire, and Beyond, 1540–1750* (Stanford: Stanford University Press, 1996), 67–69.

system, although he appreciated their monarchical governments. Partially due to their respect for the Incas, the Jesuits temporarily allowed sons of Andean native women and Spanish men to join the Company. Acosta put nomadic, hunter-gatherer societies on the bottom level of his rankings; the Spanish Acosta clearly saw social hierarchies as a sign of an advanced civilization. However, he did believe that, especially under Jesuit tutelage, these "inferior" civilizations could improve, with the essential condition that they became Christian. Sandoval shares these attitudes in his approach to African slaves in the Americas and Africans who still lived in their homeland. Throughout *De instauranda* he makes judgments on many African cultures, focusing on their government, social customs, and religion. Sandoval does not rank African polities exactly according to Acosta's system, but he shares Acosta's sense of European superiority.

By titling his work *De instauranda Aethiopum salute,* translated in the introductory matter as "on *restoring* salvation to the Ethiopians," Sandoval highlights his version of world history and the future. He places his Cartagena mission within an international Jesuit missionary program targeting "Ethiopians," or any nonwhites around the world. Using the Bible as his source, Sandoval observes that the Christian apostles preached in Africa, and he believes that the Jesuits, as new apostles, must help Africa return to its previous state by both going to Africa and preaching to African slaves in the Americas.

The use of the term "Ethiopia" to signify all of Africa, or even, as Sandoval uses it, all people with dark skin around the world, suggests that the European vision of Africa in the 1500s and 1600s privileged Ethiopia, in the narrower sense of roughly the modern country, as an idealized Christian kingdom.[34] Ethiopia was an important target for the Jesuits, because it had retained its own special form of Christianity for centuries. In the early 1600s, not long before Sandoval began working on *De instauranda,* a handful of Jesuits went to Ethiopia. In 1622 they managed to convert the Ethiopian king to Roman Catholicism. Sandoval interpreted the king's conversion as an immense victory for the Company and Christianity. He could not have known that soon after, the Jesuits would alienate Ethiopians and cause outright rebellion with their desire to impose the strictest possible Roman Catholic rules on ancient Ethiopian Christian traditions. Their rigidity ended the Jesuit presence in Ethiopia, and the kingdom isolated itself from outsiders for centuries.[35]

In *De instauranda* Sandoval hopes to recruit other Jesuits to join in working with him in Cartagena, preaching to and baptizing African slaves. His most

34. See map of what Sandoval considers Ethiopia in Olsen, *Slavery and Salvation,* 81.

35. Adrian Hastings, *The Church in Africa, 1450–1950* (Oxford: Clarendon Press, 1994), 130–59.

successful disciple was Pedro Claver. Although he is never mentioned by name in Sandoval's book, Sandoval does occasionally mention a dedicated companion, probably Claver. Pedro Claver was born in 1581 to a family of poor but respectable farmers in Verdu, Catalonia. After many years of Jesuit training in Europe and Bogotá, in 1616 Claver went to work with Sandoval in Cartagena, after Sandoval had made numerous requests for helpers. Legend says that Claver converted three hundred thousand Africans in his nearly half century of labor, although probably only a fraction of that number actually passed through or lived in Cartagena from 1580 to 1640.[36] Like Sandoval, Claver did not promote abolition, and many of his actions show he adhered to the standard colonial social and racial hierarchies. At the same time, in a typically Baroque style, his saintliness was derived from the way in which he inverted those hierarchies. Reports collected a few years after Claver's death emphasize how he carried out his motto throughout his life: *semper aethiopum servus,* "slave to Ethiopians forever," or as it is commonly stated, "slave of the slaves."[37] Claver's hagiography stresses his humility in serving the slaves; he brought them gifts, helped them when they were sick, and patiently catechized and baptized them. Claver was one of the few Jesuits who carried out all of Sandoval's instructions; no evidence suggests that the Cartagena Jesuits continued to invest a great deal of their time and manpower in catechizing African slaves.

In the mid- to late 1600s the Cartagena Jesuits promoted their Company and their mission to African slaves by making a case for Claver's canonization, although he did not become an official Catholic saint until 1888. The decline of interest in working with African slaves after Claver's death illustrates that Claver and Sandoval's enthusiasm was the driving force behind this project. By the mid-1650s, with both Sandoval and Claver dead, the Jesuits lost most of their enthusiasm for the Cartagena mission to African slaves. Other institutions in the city also weakened dramatically after most of the population fled in the wake of the 1697 French invasion. The Jesuits in Cartagena decreased significantly in numbers and influence in the 1700s. Their focus became maintaining profitable businesses, especially a brick-making plant with a predominantly enslaved labor force. Occasionally, the Jesuits made another push for Claver's canonization, but little progress was made until an Austrian priest working in

36. German Colmenares, *Historia económica y social de Colombia, 1537–1719,* vol. 2 (Cali, Colombia: Universidad del Valle, División de Humanidades, 1973), 42.

37. Several of the witnesses whose observations were noted down in the canonization documents were African slaves from a wide variety of regions. These men and women were the interpreters Sandoval mentions often in *De instauranda.* The Jesuits used a total of eighteen permanent interpreters from the 1620s to the 1650s. One or more of the interpreters spoke the Angola, Congo, Wolof, and Fula languages.

the midwestern United States in the nineteenth century observed several miraculous cures done with a relic of Claver's body.[38]

It is easy to interpret Sandoval's work as an apology for Jesuit slave ownership, especially because the Jesuits eventually became major slave owners in the Americas. In Sandoval's time enslaved African interpreters worked for the Cartagena Jesuit college. Although early leaders such as Xavier did not oppose buying slaves to serve Jesuits, even in the sixteenth century, members of the Company of Jesus debated the use of slaves in their enterprises. Like Sandoval, António Vieira, a Jesuit working in Brazil, told slaves that they would be rewarded for their suffering on earth with an afterlife spent in heaven.[39] Sandoval published his books at the tail end of the debate about the Jesuit use of slaves; by his era and soon after, "most members came to regard their Order's reliance upon black slaves as a necessity."[40]

RACE AND ETHNICITY IN *DE INSTAURANDA*

For several decades scholars have studied the development of racial ideologies as a historical process, no longer viewing race as a biological or physical fact. Racial ideologies did not precede but emerged simultaneously with the rise of the nation-state, European imperialism, and Atlantic slavery. Sandoval lived on the very cusp of an era when the European perception of smaller divisions and distinctions between different polities permanently hardened into the three colors of white, black, and brown, which, in relation to each other, "are abridged, abstracted versions of colonizer, slave and colonized."[41] As soon as color labels became the definitive way to categorize the peoples of the world, these distinctions seemed immutable, "natural," and timeless.[42] This led to a conception of race as biological difference between human beings, and along with difference came perceptions of inferiority and superiority. Walter Johnson observes that "reducing slaves to a spectrum of color . . . produced abstractions . . . suggestive

---

38. This was also an era when the Catholic Church, threatened by the spread of Protestantism all over the world, sought new members, especially among Africans and newly freed African Americans. Pedro Claver still has a very strong legacy in the United States as the patron of many charitable institutions and parishes. The Knights of Peter Claver are an African American fraternal organization founded in the early twentieth century, claiming symbolic descent from Claver's interpreters and African assistants.

39. Alden, *Making of an Enterprise*, 507–11.

40. Ibid., 527.

41. Irene Silverblatt, *Modern Inquisitions: Peru and the Colonial Origins of the Civilized World* (Durham, NC: Duke University Press, 2004), 115.

42. Ibid., 220–21.

of subjects with no history beyond natural history."[43] Although Sandoval does use the word *negro* (black) to refer to Africans, he also refers to a dizzying array of African castes and nations, recognizing that their histories and experiences begin in Africa.

Defining difference by skin color emerged from medieval conflicts based around religious difference, especially the *Reconquista* in Spain. As Islamic principalities in Iberia weakened after the 1200s, Christians gained a stronger sense of a conquering destiny and identity based around their religion. Edward Baptist and Stephanie Camp observe that, even in the early 1600s, "religion and forms of government" had a greater influence than color did on "the process of ordering people and explaining differences in their status."[44] Historians tie the rise of a belief in race as an immutable, inherited characteristic in the Hispanic world to decreasing tolerance of non-Christians and less faith in the authenticity of conversion to Christianity. In the early modern Iberian world, the concept of *limpieza de sangre* (purity of blood) had far more importance than race in the modern sense of the word.

Laws governing *limpieza* and access to government positions, universities, and certain occupations emerged in the fourteenth century out of a changing perception of the validity of conversion from Judaism to Christianity.[45] Until medieval Iberians developed a concern over *limpieza,* in theory conversion erased an individual's Jewish heritage, at least in terms of access to social privilege. Many Spanish Jews converted to Christianity in the wake of late fourteenth-century persecution and pogroms. As the Castilian monarchs solidified their rule in the 1400s, the populace began to distrust these more recent converts from Judaism, labeling them "New Christians." They became scapegoats for frustration over unpopular royal policies, and their conversions were seen as suspect. One of the institutions that helped strengthen Castile and Aragon in this era was the newly formed Castilian and Aragonese inquisition tribunals, which harshly persecuted the New Christians, especially in the late 1400s. To the early modern Spanish, New Christians inherited the morals and characters of their Jewish ancestors, and thus their blood was "unclean." Jews did not have a different skin color, but according to the beliefs of this time, they could not be

---

43. Walter Johnson, "Introduction," in *The Chattel Principle: Internal Slave Trades in the Americas,* ed. Johnson (New Haven, CT: Yale University Press, 2004), 11.

44. Edward E. Baptist and Stephanie M. H. Camp, "Race, Slavery, and History," in *New Studies in the History of American Slavery,* ed. Baptist and Camp (Athens: University of Georgia Press, 2006), 8–9.

45. María Elena Martínez, "Interrogating Blood Lines: 'Purity of Blood,' the Inquisition, and *Casta* Categories," in *Religion in New Spain,* ed. Stafford Poole and Susan Schroeder (Albuquerque: University of New Mexico Press, 2007), 196–217.

true Spaniards, due to their non-Christian heritage. Examinations of ancestry preceded entry into universities, as well as some professions and religious orders. Through an increasing interest in *limpieza,* including in the Americas, religious intolerance developed into an early form of racism and a stronger sense of what it meant to be Spanish.[46]

With the growth of the Spanish empire in the 1500s, interactions with non-Christians further strengthened the relationship between Spain, Christianity, imperialism, and race. Acosta's work demonstrates how the Jesuits' experience in the Americas helped formulate an idea of race in terms of inheritance. Although the Jesuits had first accepted the half-Spanish sons of Andean women into the Company and felt positive about converting Andeans, by the 1580s they no longer allowed mestizos to become Jesuits. In *De procuranda* Acosta expressed severe distrust of Andean novice Christians, whom he felt were tainted by the customs of their ancestors, which saturated every moment of their day and every interaction they had with nature. The problem was culture, not race, but Acosta believed mestizos inherited these non-Christian customs from their mothers' milk.[47]

Unlike Acosta, Sandoval makes no negative judgments regarding the inheritance of non-Christian character traits among his African novice Christians. While he often uses the terms "Ethiopian" or "black" to refer to Africans, he also frequently specifies more precise African ethnicities, especially in Book 1. Of course, Sandoval does not use the word "ethnicities" but calls these groups *naciones* (nations) or *castas* (castes), two words used frequently in colonial Spanish America. Spanish Americans usually used the term *nación* to refer to an individual's place of origin, a very important concept for Europeans in the New World, who often distinguished each other by their home region in Spain. *Nación* in the early modern era does not refer to a large nation-state typical of the modern era. Spain itself was hardly a modern nation at the time. As stated by Tamar Herzog, "Spain emerged from the Middle Ages as a highly complex and fragmented political entity."[48] To describe someone as an *español* or *española* (Spaniard) in the Americas was very simplistic, although it generally equated to high socioeconomic status, in contrast to labels such as *negro, indio,* or *mulato.*[49] In *De instauranda* Sandoval uses *casta* and *nación* interchangeably, without giving *casta* a racial significance. On the other hand, often Spanish

46. Silverblatt, *Modern Inquisitions,* 18–19, 25.

47. Hyland, *The Jesuit and the Incas,* 65–69.

48. Tamar Herzog, *Defining Nations: Immigrants and Citizens in Early Modern Spain and Spanish America* (New Haven, CT: Yale University Press, 2003), 64.

49. Silverblatt, *Modern Inquisitions,* 137–39.

American elites labeled people *castas* to indicate that they belonged to the undifferentiated, nonwhite, or mixed race lower classes.

Sandoval emphasizes the linguistic differences between different African ethnicities, most notably in Book 1 of *De instauranda*. Although Sandoval relates appearance, religion, and culture to ethnicity, language is his greatest concern. In contrast, historians such as Paul Lovejoy define ethnicity,

> following Fredrik Barth[,] . . . as a characteristic of groups of people, in which groups sharing common ethnicity are usually perceived to be largely biographically self-perpetuating, to share fundamental cultural values, to comprise a common field of communication and interaction, and to identify themselves and be identified by others as constituting a recognizable group.[50]

Scholars have debated the value of ethnic distinctions that Europeans applied to Africans in the Americas. Some scholars negate their value entirely, arguing that African cultural distinctions could not survive the Middle Passage.[51] It is also possible that ethnic labels simply came from the port of embarkation in Africa, not from identity before enslavement. However, the research of scholars such as Paul Lovejoy, John Thornton, Michael Gomez, and Gwendolyn Midlo Hall underscores the importance of the study of African ethnicities.[52] According to Lovejoy and David Trotman:

> The use of ethnicity can be an important tool in the reconstruction of the history of the diaspora and the mechanisms by which the social and cultural life of enslaved Africans and their descendants, sometimes slave and sometimes free, were reflected in ethnic classification and identification. Deconstruction of ethnic terminology becomes a method in the reconstruction of the history of trans-Atlantic slavery and society.[53]

Gomez argues that African ethnic identities, influenced by politics, trade, religious beliefs, language, and culture, did exist before the slave trade, even if the trade itself solidified ethnic distinctions that were otherwise less important in Africa.[54]

---

50. Paul Lovejoy, "Ethnic Designations of the Slave Trade and the Reconstruction of the History of Trans-Atlantic Slavery," in *Transatlantic Dimensions of Ethnicity in the African Diaspora*, ed. Paul Lovejoy and David Trotman (London: Verso, 2004), 10.

51. Sidney Mintz and Richard Price, *The Birth of African-American Cultures* (Boston: Beacon Press, 1992).

52. John Thornton, *Africa and Africans in the Making of the Atlantic World, 1400–1680* (Cambridge: Cambridge University Press, 1992); Michael Gomez, *Exchanging Our Country Marks: The Transformation of African Identities in the Colonial and Antebellum South* (Chapel Hill: University of North Carolina Press, 1998); Hall, *Slavery and African Ethnicities.*

53. Lovejoy and Trotman, "Introduction," *Transatlantic Dimensions of Ethnicity*, 5.

54. Gomez, *Exchanging Our Country Marks*, 7.

Lovejoy proves the importance of ethnic distinctions in Africa through the work of the great Timbuktu scholar Ahmad Bābā (1556–1627), Sandoval's near contemporary.[55] After being enslaved himself by raiding Muslims from Marrakech, Ahmad Bābā wrote a treatise addressing "issues relating to the significance of racial and ethnic categories as factors in the justification of enslavement."[56] Ahmad Bābā subscribed to the idea that religion, not race, determined eligibility for enslavement. Muslim slaves could not be sold, especially to Christians. Ahmad Bābā listed Africans considered pagan or non-Muslim, including several ethnic designators (Bambara, Mandinke or Mandingo, Fulbe or Fula) that Sandoval also uses. The transference of these terms across the Atlantic strengthens the link between African and American cultures, especially in terms of customs relating to slavery.

Spanish reports describing seventeenth-century *palenques* testify to the importance of African ethnicity in the Cartagena region. The 250 residents of the Matudere *palenque* in the 1600s included Creoles as well as Africans of the Mina, Arará, Congo, Loango, Angola, Popo, Yolofe, Caravali, Bran, Biafra, and Goyo ethnicities.[57] The rebels appointed Manuel Arará, a slave of the Jesuits, as their leader. African military leaders controlled groups of men divided along the lines of ethnicity. The *palenqueros* practiced Catholicism alongside African religions.

Readers might find the dozens of African ethnicities listed in *De instauranda* confusing and overwhelming. To clarify, historians divide early modern Africa into larger geographic regions. Gomez makes seven groupings, which can be mapped onto Sandoval's smaller ethnic divisions: Senegambia, from the mouth of the Senegal River to the Casamance; Sierra Leone; the Gold Coast, or today's Ghana; the Bight of Benin (Togo, Benin, southwestern Nigeria); the Bight of Biafra (southeastern Nigeria, Cameroon, and Gabon); West Central Africa (Congo and Angola); and lastly, southeastern Africa, today's Mozambique, Tanzania, and Madagascar.[58] Sandoval rarely mentions southeastern Africa, although this region did supply some Latin American slaves. Within these seven regions, there could be a huge number of languages, as in Senegambia, or one dominant language, as Bantu was in Central Africa.

---

55. Lovejoy, "The Context of Enslavement in West Africa: Ahmad Bābā and the Ethics of Slavery," in *Slaves, Subjects, and Subversives: Blacks in Colonial Latin America*, ed. Jane Landers and Barry Robinson (Albuquerque: University of New Mexico Press, 2006), 9–38.

56. Lovejoy, "The Context," 10, 20–21.

57. Jane Landers, "*Cimarrón* Ethnicity in the Caribbean," in *Identity in the Shadow of Slavery*, ed. Paul Lovejoy (London: Verso, 2000), 38–41.

58. Gomez, *Exchanging Our Country Marks*.

In Sandoval's era, the variety in political structures throughout all of the regions—from large kingdoms to rule at the local level—challenged the growing understanding and bias toward nation-states. Sandoval offers many comments and judgments about African rulers. The disparaging tone reflects the belief that some African polities deserved neither recognition as states nor the diplomatic treatment accorded to European monarchs and their subjects. Religion, enslaved status, language, appearance, and government—Sandoval's understanding of all of these aspects of African heritage helped formulate his vision of Africans as part of the "Ethiopian" race.

DIFFERENT EDITIONS OF SANDOVAL'S PUBLICATIONS

This book was originally published in Seville in 1627 in Spanish under the Spanish-language title of *Naturaleza, policia sagrada i profana, costumbres i ritos, disciplina i catechismo evangélico de todos etíopes,* or *De instauranda Aethiopum salute.* A handful of libraries in the United States, Europe, and Latin America have copies of the original 1627 edition of this book.[59] In 1647 Sandoval published a book in Madrid with the Latin title *De instauranda Aethiopum salute.* Despite the title and the frequent use of the language among Jesuits, neither of these books was published in Latin. In the second edition, Sandoval focused on correcting and extending Book 1 of the 1627 work. He also added extensive indices of place names and sources. It is very difficult to find a copy of the 1647 edition. Two copies of this edition are in the United States, another is in the British Museum, and a fourth copy can be found in the National Library of Chile. The 1647 edition is also available on microfilm.

This translation is based on the 1956 Bogotá edition, edited by Angel Valtierra, who claims he "faithfully copied" the 1627 version from the library of Dr. Jorge Luis Arango. Valtierra gave his edition the title *De instauranda Aethiopum salute.* Only about one thousand copies of this edition were published, although scholars who seek a more complete exposure to Sandoval in the original language can find this book in large research libraries in the United States. A fourth version, edited by Enriqueta Vila Vilar, was published in Madrid in 1987, with the title *Un tratado sobre la esclavitud.* The 1987 edition lacks the seventeenth-century marginal citations supplied in Valtierra's version, meaning the scholar cannot further verify or explore Sandoval's references, a very serious shortcoming. Some scholars seem to incorrectly believe that Vila Vilar's edition is based on the 1647 *De instauranda.* As explained above, the two seventeenth-century books are different from each other: the 1647 book is an expansion of

59. Including the New York Public Library and the library at the Colegio de México.

1627's Book 1. All twentieth-century editions come from Sandoval's original 1627 work, and currently no modern version of Sandoval's 1647 book is available in print.

TRANSLATOR'S NOTE

The purpose of this abridged edition of the work of Alonso de Sandoval is to introduce English-speaking readers to a Spanish-language work that has been unfairly neglected. The translation attempts to make Sandoval's Baroque style more accessible to the general reader, while still preserving spelling inconsistencies and other unique nuances of the original work for the sake of authenticity. The questions and discussions preceding each chapter provide guidance for classroom use and even help suggest topics for written assignments. The footnotes within the text explain straightforward issues with vocabulary and other historic references. Brackets indicate text added by the editor, while parentheses indicate parenthetical asides in Sandoval's text.

Sandoval's work is in the "often cited, rarely read" category, and unfortunately even historians who read Spanish fluently have been tempted to make erroneous generalizations about the book without reading it. This version might tempt historians to take a closer look at the book before they make reference to it, although they should consult any Spanish edition to grasp its rhetorical and literary aspects.

Because this edition is meant to be readable for a more general audience, I have left out Sandoval's long quotes in Latin, his more in-depth theological and philosophical discussions, and his extensive marginal notations on sources he consulted. As he writes in the introductory matter included here, he generally repeats these quotes in Spanish throughout the text. In choosing what chapters and themes to include in this edition, I have focused on four themes: descriptions of life in Africa and the Americas in the 1600s, Sandoval's opinions on slavery and the slave trade, practical instructions provided for other Jesuits, and any information he includes from his own personal experiences teaching African slaves about Christianity. In some of the chapters dealing with these topics, Sandoval's style is more straightforward and direct, so it is possible to translate on a word-by-word basis. This work deserves an unabridged translation, including all of Sandoval's scholarly references and quotations, but such a project would result in a much longer, much more expensive book, suitable only for large libraries or collections.

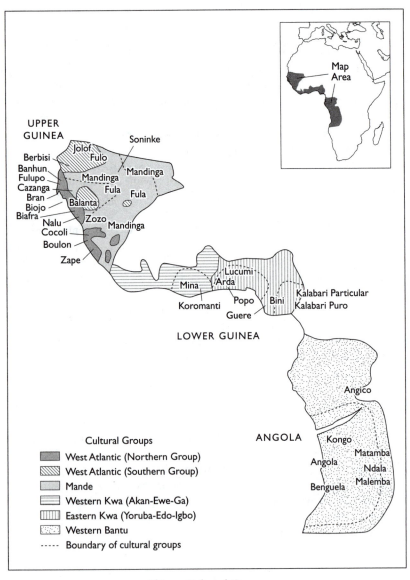

UPPER
GUINEA

Soninke

Berbisi
Banhun
Fulupo
Cazanga
Bran
Biojo
Biafra
Nalu
Cocoli
Boulon

Zape

Jolof
Fulo

Mandinga

Mandinga

Fula

Balanta

Zozo

Mandinga

Fula

Map
Area

Mina

Koromanti

Lucumi
Arda

Popo

Guere

Bini

Kalabari Particular
Kalabari Puro

LOWER GUINEA

Angico

ANGOLA

Kongo

Angola

Benguela

Matamba

Ndala

Malemba

Cultural Groups

West Atlantic (Northern Group)

West Atlantic (Southern Group)

Mande

Western Kwa (Akan-Ewe-Ga)

Eastern Kwa (Yoruba-Edo-Igbo)

Western Bantu

----- Boundary of cultural groups

African Cultural Groups

English Translation

of

DE INSTAURANDA AETHIOPUM SALUTE

BY

ALONSO DE SANDOVAL, S.J.

Originally published in Seville in 1627
First modern edition published in Bogotá in 1956

Edited by
ANGEL VALTIERRA, S.J.

Translator
NICOLE VON GERMETEN

OFFICIAL PERMISSIONS AND LICENSES TO PUBLISH THIS BOOK FROM LEADERS OF THE JESUIT ORDER

By the mid-sixteenth century, the Spanish Inquisition, the Vatican, and universities had compiled lists of banned books. All books had to have the approval of an official representative of the Catholic Church before they could be printed.[1] Sandoval sent his book out to several different leaders in the Society of Jesus in order to receive official letters of approval for his work. Sandoval also had another concern: other works that criticized slavery had been put on the list of books banned by the Spanish Inquisition. By having all of these authorities support him in writing, Sandoval protected his own work from future criticism. One of the letters even came from a calificador (examiner) from the Inquisition high court in Cartagena, an expert in Catholic theology and doctrine who determined what books would be censored. The other permissions here range from the general of the Jesuits, the highest office in the society, to the rectors or head administrators of Jesuit colleges in Panama, Bogotá, and Lima. Sandoval reached out to these leaders as a way to promote his book and the plan of action it contains. Jesuit readers would know that the Company of Jesus wanted to move forward with Sandoval's missions to African slaves. Throughout the book, Sandoval tries to prove that working with black slaves is a fundamental part of the Jesuit mission, and the letters of approval here are the first pieces of evidence he uses to support his argument.

License of the Provincial Father

I, Florian de Ayerbe,[2] provincial of the Company of Jesus, in the province of the New Kingdom of Granada, by special commission, received this book from our very Reverend Father Mutio Vitelleschi, general of the Company of Jesus.[3] I give license to print the tract entitled *De instauranda Aethiopum salute* or "How to restore the salvation of the blacks," written by Father Alonso de Sandoval, rector of the College of the Company of Jesus, in the city of Cartagena de Indias. My signature below certifies that learned Jesuit fathers approve this book.

Sealed with the seal of my office, in Santa Fe de Bogotá, April 1, 1624.

Florian de Ayerbe

---

1. See Daniel T. Reff, "Critical Introduction" to Pérez de Ribas, *History of the Triumphs of Our Holy Faith,* 27–28.

2. Florian de Ayerbe lived from 1569 to approximately 1638. From 1633 to 1637 he was the Jesuit provincial, or the head of a region called a province, of New Spain.

3. Vitelleschi was an Italian who served as the general from 1615 to 1645.

Approval of Father Balthasar Mas, Rector of the College of the Company of Jesus, Santa Fe de Bogotá

By order of our Reverend Father Florian de Ayerbe, provincial of the province of the New Kingdom of Granada, I have read the majority of the book written by Father Alonso de Sandoval entitled *De instauranda Aethiopum salute* or "How to restore the salvation of the Ethiopians." Respected, learned fathers in our college of Santa Fe de Bogotá, where I am rector, have read the entire work and believe it to be very worthy of printing and publication, because of the great spiritual benefit it will bring to the neglected souls of the blacks who have been captured and brought to foreign territories. It also provides very clear directions for carrying out this apostolic ministry. I am certain that this thought-provoking, erudite work will be read with great pleasure.

Signed in the College of the Company of Jesus, New Kingdom of Granada, West Indies, on December 10, 1623.

Balthasar Mas

Approval of Father Juan Antonio de Santander, Rector of the College of the Company of Jesus, Panama

By commission of Father Florian de Ayerbe, I have seen the book entitled *De instauranda Aethiopum salute,* composed by Father Alonso de Sandoval. I certify that readers will find many interesting and useful things in this book. Its publication will bring much glory to the Lord, and much good to many souls.

I sign my name to certify this in Cartagena de Indias, February 25, 1624.

Juan Antonio de Santander

Approval of Father Francisco Guerrero, Reader in Theology

I, Francisco Guerrero of the Company of Jesus, reader in sacred theology in this college of the Company of Jesus in Santa Fe de Bogotá, New Kingdom of Granada, have read most of Father Alonso de Sandoval's book, *De instauranda Aethiopum salute,* or "How to restore the salvation of the Ethiopians." Learned and wise fathers in this province have read the entire book and we believe it to be very worthy of printing, because it is very pious, inquisitive, erudite, and wise. This book is useful in helping those who wish to employ themselves in the salvation of souls, a glorious enterprise in great need of enthusiastic apostolic workers.[4] The

---

4. Guerrero connects Sandoval's book to the original goals of the Company of Jesus: missions traveling around the world teaching non-Christians about Christianity in imitation of the apostles.

entire book shows its author's apostolic zeal for the glory of God and the Company of Jesus.

This statement was given in the College of the Company of Jesus, of the New Kingdom of Granada of the West Indies, December 30, 1623.

Francisco Guerrero

Approval of Father Antonio Agustín, Rector of the College of Cartagena

I, Antonio Agustín, priest of the Company of Jesus, reader in theology, as well as *calificador* for the Holy Office of the Inquisition in the Indies, and rector of our college in this city, read this book by Father Alonso de Sandoval. Its purpose is to aid in the salvation of the blacks coming from Ethiopia.[5] I did not find anything in this book contrary to the doctrine of our holy faith or good customs. On the contrary, this book contains interesting information regarding the lands of the blacks and their customs and ceremonies. It is all very thought-provoking and necessary for their salvation. The information comes from rare and excellent books that describe these lands, as well as reports from captains and other important people who have lived and dealt with the blacks. Father Sandoval has almost twenty years of experience helping the blacks achieve salvation and administering the holy sacrament of penance when they are near death. He baptizes thousands of blacks that come to this port every year. He encourages parish priests to administer the other holy sacraments at the appropriate times, even to the *bozales*,[6] when they are capable of receiving them, because they are in great need of salvation.

Despite the fact that we refer to their slavery as "rescuing [*rescatar*]" the slaves, they are not baptized properly in their own lands or when they are sold as captives in miserable servitude. They are in great need of instruction, which must be done well and without committing serious sins. Their baptism, the moment when they enter into the Church, is done very badly in many parts of

---

5. This word is used in several different ways in this book. Very rarely, it refers to the geographic region in northeastern Africa, which includes the modern country of Ethiopia. Most frequently, Ethiopia refers to all of Africa, and Sandoval also uses "Ethiopian" to refer to any dark-skinned non-Christian. In this case, Agustín refers to all of Africa.

6. The Spanish commonly used this term to refer to slaves who had just arrived from Africa. The word literally means "rough" or "crude" and especially refers to Africans who spoke no Spanish. Because there is no exact word for this in English, I leave the word *bozal* in Spanish throughout this book.

Guinea.[7] Priests who perform the holy sacrament of baptism and other sacraments commit sacrilege in these cases. The captains of the slaving fleets do not care about their salvation but are only concerned with earthly wealth. The priests in the slaves' homelands or in the Ethiopian ports also do not care for their salvation. They do not understand the slaves' numerous languages. The slaves come and go like sheep, not pilgrims or passengers. When they arrive in the Americas, it is assumed that they are already baptized Christians. It is very difficult to communicate with them because they come from so many different countries with different languages.

This book addresses all of these concerns. I have personal experience with the book's subject, because I lived and worked at the mission in Cartagena for several years. I testify that this book is very thought-provoking, useful, and necessary for everyone who lives in the lands of the blacks, or in the lands where the black slaves go to work, and for all those obligated to help them achieve salvation. Thus this book merits publication so that it can be easily read and discussed all over the Old and New Worlds, and my signature attests to this.

Cartagena, October 1, 1623.

Antonio Agustín

Approval of Father Vicente Imperial, *Predicador* [Preacher] of the Company of Jesus

This next letter is written by a well-known Jesuit preacher and thus takes a more poetic tone than the others. Father Vicente Imperial incorporates some common European conceptions of Africa from his era and later: he repeatedly uses the color white to symbolize purity and goodness, while black represents sin, ugliness, and the devil. However, Imperial believes blackness can change to whiteness, as African souls become Christian. Although black and white are contrasted, these ideas do not represent modern racism, although they do move toward it. Imperial shows a lack of toleration instead for non-Christians, who in this case happen to be Africans. Their lack of Christianity is not an immutable inherited racial characteristic but something that can change, leading to symbolic whitening. Imperial introduces a theme seen throughout the book: the devil and God play an active role in the Jesuit vision of their world and history at this time, and Europeans must "save" Africans from the influence of the devil. Under paternalistic Jesuit tutelage, Africans can weaken the influence of the devil and return to Christianity.

---

7. The word "Guinea" is used throughout the book to refer to all of Africa. A more narrow region called Guinea includes the coast of Africa south of the Niger River, including the modern countries of Ivory Coast, Ghana, Togo, Benin, and Nigeria (Adrian Room, *African Place Names* [London, 1994], 80).

The devil, the enemy of the human race, uses his craftiness and schemes to impede the conversion of men; so Our Lord Christ, through his ministries, with divine wisdom and sovereign providence, must seek the salvation of souls in a thousand ways. This book's purpose is to defeat the devil and carry out the plans of our merciful God. Who would have thought that this clear and resplendent light would illuminate the road to heaven now in such darkness? Who knew such effective methods existed to help these destitute people, when helping them was previously thought impossible? This book hopes to transform them—if not their skin color, it will at least make their souls white with grace. Father Alonso de Sandoval wrote this book in order to whiten so many souls and free them from the ugly blackness of sin. By order of the very Reverend Father Florian de Ayerbe, I have read every page of this book. I say it is very worthy of printing, because it is the first book that deals with this issue. For those who are curious, it includes many stories and mentions many saintly places. It ponders the holy scripture as well as subtle moral points. To say it in a word, it is like a garden full of a thousand species of plants. The viewpoints in this book include that of a preacher in his pulpit, a reader in his study, and a confessor in his confessionary. This entire book conforms to proper beliefs and should be printed and spread throughout the Catholic Church, especially in the lands where these forgotten blacks live. In conclusion, all serious men should set their minds to instructing these people, who so lack the spiritual succor enjoyed by other Catholics.

Santa Fe de Bogotá, June 1, 1624.

Vicente Imperial

To Our Very Reverend Father in Christ Mutio Vitelleschi, General of the Company of Jesus: The Father Alonso de Sandoval, of the Same Company, Wishes You Happiness in the Lord

Sandoval writes this letter to introduce the head of the Society of Jesus to his work and to seek his approval and patronage. He also associates whiteness with goodness, purity, and Christianity here. Sandoval refers to the blood of Jesus Christ, shed during his crucifixion, as something that can cleanse Christian souls, thus symbolically changing blackness (an evil association with the devil) to whiteness (Christian purity).

I place this book, *De instauranda Aethiopum salute,* at your feet, to display my labor to you and to ask that you grant me your favor. The book's purpose is to help people who are poor and abandoned. Although they are black, they can be washed clean by the purity and whiteness of Christ's blood. Pass your eyes over this book and you will see how many souls can be taken from the fires of hell to heaven. Under your leadership, many sons of the Company will carry out the goals of the founders of our order, to help the Ethiopians. As your humble son, I beg your pardon for daring to present this work to you, but I believe it necessary and my obligation to encourage the sons of the Company to help these neglected and lonely people. Your leadership can ignite flames in the hearts of all members of this Company, so they will not feel discouraged by hard work and challenges but will continue in their labor to bring souls to heaven. May the Lord preserve you for the sake of the Company of Jesus.

From this College of Cartagena de Indias, April 1, 1624.

Your humble son, Alonso de Sandoval

To the Christian Reader:
The Purpose of This Book

Christian reader, many learned books have been written to help people spiritually. We should also try to help the Ethiopians, who, because of their color, are commonly called blacks. This book's goal is to encourage the desire to help the Ethiopians, a nation[8] with a small role on the world stage but a designated place in God's plan. Some will say that, in Christ's robes, the black and white threads are intertwined, and the souls of blacks are as important as those of the whites.[9] And thus my work is unnecessary, because all souls are the same. I respond that the blacks' fate is so sad and dark, and slavery is so unbearable, that I must describe both of these conditions here in order to inspire compassion, in hopes of helping overcome these difficulties and improving their fate. The souls of the blacks are no less precious than those of whites, nor did they cost less of the blood of the Lamb of God shed for all.

    The title *De instauranda Aethiopum salute* means "How to restore the salvation of the blacks," because its primary and fundamental goal is not to motivate people to go to their lands to convert them (although this is a secondary goal) but instead to go to the ports where the slaves disembark. These slaves are

---

8. Here he uses the word "nation" in the sense of "race," as in "African race."

9. Reff, citing Bakhtin, calls this rhetorical structure the "hidden polemic, "constantly replying to but never quoting critics of the missionary vocation" [Reff, "Critical Introduction," 12]. In this case, Sandoval is responding to his colleagues or superiors who must have criticized him for working with Africans. In fact, the entire book might be viewed as a response to criticism from within and even outside the Company of Jesus that said Sandoval spent too much time or resources working with Africans.

incorrectly judged to be Christians,[10] so we must ask them if they have been baptized. If they have not, we must instruct them. Once they have been well instructed, we can baptize them and restore their spiritual health, which has been lost.[11]

This tract is divided into four books. The first describes the extended empire of the Ethiopians, in the West as well as the East, and its many nations and diverse customs. I present this description to inspire those who work in spiritual labor to join in this glorious task. The second book describes the unsurpassed misery and unhappiness endured by Ethiopian slaves and the great need for this ministry. The third book explains how to teach them. The first book will delight, the second inspire, and the third teach. Because I especially want to motivate the sons of the Company of Jesus, my fathers and sons, to join this holy ministry, I added a fourth book, in which I discuss the great esteem that the Company itself has always had for this ministry.

I quote some of my sources in Latin, because their words are more effective and forceful in the original, especially in the case of the words of sacred scripture. So that this will not be an impediment for those who do not understand Latin, I will also translate them to the vernacular.[12]

I pray to the Divine Majesty that this work will inflame the hearts of the ministers of the Church so that they will reach out to the forgotten, miserable slaves. They deserve charity; let this charitable fire burn brightly. Farewell.

---

10. By their masters and priests, who assume Africans are baptized before they leave Africa and who might encounter them when they attend church or participate in Catholic rituals.

11. Throughout *De instauranda* Sandoval uses biblical references and accounts taken from other ancient and medieval sources to argue that the apostles went to parts of Africa and preached Christianity. Since that time, he believes, the devil (and, closely linked, Islam) has influenced Africans to lose their Christianity and their "spiritual health." He hopes his work will return this health to them.

12. Sandoval's original work was in Spanish with some lines in Latin. This translation has left only a few select lines in Latin, with English translations provided.

BOOK 1

In Book 1 Sandoval, from his desk in the Jesuit college in Cartagena, South America, tries to elucidate African geography, language, culture, religion, and even scarification and hairstyles for his readers. He gathers a great deal of information scattered throughout many ancient, medieval, and early modern books and letters. This ends up as an accumulation of centuries of information, misinformation, and even fantastic tales and exaggerations. Sandoval's greatest concern is to identify the wide variety of languages African slaves speak in order for Jesuits who might be interested in working with slaves in Cartagena to be able to communicate with them.

Chapter 1. Description of the four parts of the world, with an emphasis on the most important Ethiopian kingdoms, located all over the world

Because this is such a unique and difficult subject, the reader must understand the author's motives for telling this story and will thus more easily understand the author's purpose. For this section of the book, I consulted scholarly books on Ethiopia and other black kingdoms and empires. I also studied the writings of the Jesuit fathers who went to Ethiopia as missionaries.[1] Additionally, I have communicated personally with some Portuguese sea captains who spent many years in Africa, eyewitnesses to what happens there. Although different authorities have different perspectives on the subject, that does not worry me. It is best to bring together many opinions, because some people will see things others ignore. This should not make us suspect that one or the other is dishonest. To gain a good understanding, I depend on many Catholic authorities, both ancient and modern, for my information.

Europe

Sandoval starts his description of the world with Europe and immediately reveals his bias. Living at a time of expanding European empires, Sandoval justifies imperialism through his belief in European superiority over other world civilizations and his confidence in Christianity as the one true religion.

The European land is the smallest of the four parts of the world, but it is the most noble, virtuous, magnificent, and civilized part of the world. Long ago, Europe ruled over all of Asia and Africa under the Greek and Roman empires.

---

1. Here Sandoval uses the word "Ethiopia" to refer to all of Africa.

Now the authority of the Holy Apostolic See [the papacy] leads the entire Christian world from Rome. Europe's great power extends over many provinces and kingdoms, from the East to the West Indies.

Africa: Western or Interior

Following a north-to-south trajectory, this section sums up Sandoval's understanding of many of the language groups, cultural divisions, settlements, kingdoms, smaller polities, and ethnicities from Cape Verde and southern Senegal to the Cape of Good Hope. The footnotes provide further information on the different peoples Sandoval lists, if it is possible to find out more about them. The ethnic labels Sandoval uses fit a conception of Africa specific to his era and cannot be applied to the usage of these words in different centuries. For example, in nineteenth-century Brazil, the label "Mina" was applied to a very broad region of coastal Africa. All of the complex groups of people listed here were subject to the Portuguese slave trade in the 1500s. How does Sandoval give a negative characterization to some of these ethnicities or polities?

There are many kingdoms in western Africa, especially along the Guinean rivers. Many nations, including Spain, bring people from this region to the Indies. There are so many different kingdoms that if we described them all here, it would be necessary to start another much longer book, a book very different from the one we are writing.[2] I am only going to discuss those on the seacoast and highlight others in general. I will emphasize the essential points necessary for understanding their customs, their nature and their values, and the barrenness of their false religion and gentile[3] ceremonies. The color black symbolizes multitudes and abundance—there are so many black nations that their number is incomprehensible.[4]

To begin: in Cape Verde, the leaders are called Iolofos [Wolofs or Jolofs]. The Berbesi[5] Wolofs live fifty leagues from Cape Verde toward the mouth of the

2. In fact, Sandoval did do this, in an expanded version of this book published in Madrid in 1647.

3. By "gentile," Sandoval means non-Christian or pagan.

4. Sandoval observes here that black as a color did not always have negative symbolism in Europe. The scholars Linda Van Norden (in *The Black Feet of the Peacock: The Color Concept "Black" from the Greeks Through the Renaissance* [Lanham, MD.: University Press of America, 1985]) and Gwendolyn Midlo Hall (in *Slavery and African Ethnicities*) describe other positive associations with the color black. Van Norden observed that the popular, folk association of black with evil and the devil did not appear very frequently in the Renaissance sources she collected.

5. The word Berbesi in Spanish is Burba Siin in the Wolof language. Siin was a small polity in Western Senegal speaking the West Atlantic language Serer.

Gambia River.[6] Inland from them is the empire of the Great Wolof, comprising Moors and Fulos.[7] The Fulopo blacks live in the southern band of the mouth of the Gambia River. Above the river live a band of people vulgarly called Mandingas.[8] At the mouth of the Ladigola River, Biafras can be found.[9] At the mouth of the Gambia River, to the south, is the Santa Maria Cape, extending along the coast until it meets the Casamance River. The Bootes caste, commonly called Fulopo or Banunes Bootes, are a very cruel people who live here.[10] Going up the Casamance River, one passes regions controlled by the Bootes as well as the Soniquies [Soninkes][11] or Mandingas, who live in a cool climate in fertile verge between the Gambia and Casamance rivers. The other southern band is called the Banhuns. At the head of this river is the court of the king of Casamansa, emperor of all the Banhuns, Cazangas, and some Mandingas.[12] He is a great friend of white people but an even better friend of his money. He does not do anything that does not bring him profit. He does not allow any harm done to a Christian in his kingdom. There are Boote villages all along the southern bank of the Casamance River. The main port for all of Guinea is three leagues from the mouth of the Cacheu River and goes by the name Cacheu [Guinea-Bissau]. Here live the Bran caste of blacks and to the north, the Banhuns and Cazangas. Brans and Bootes populate a plain south of the Cacheu River.[13] Inland is the

---

6. The Berbers have lived in North Africa for thousands of years. They converted to Islam in its early centuries. Sandoval is probably referring to Islamic Wolofs here.

7. The words "Fulo" and "Fulopo" refer to the Fulbe, who eventually built a large empire in the 1700s in Senegal and Mali (Willie F. Page and R. Hunt Davis, eds., *Encyclopedia of African History and Culture*, vol. 3 [New York: Facts on File, 2005], 87). These people are called the *Peul* in French.

8. A West African civilization, also called Mande. Some Mandes, called Mandinka or Manding, founded the great Mali empire of the 1200s to the 1400s (ibid., vol. 2, 151–52).

9. Biafra was a very common ethnic designation for Senegambians sent to the Americas as slaves in the 1500s.

10. Banunes are Banhuns, a small group of peoples still living in Senegambia and Guinea-Bissau (Richard Lobban and Peter Karibe Mendy, *Historical Dictionary of the Republic of Guinea-Bissau* [Lanham, MD: Scarecrow Press, 1997], 82–83). I am unable to find any modern reference to the Bootes.

11. The Soninkes are a Mande-speaking people.

12. The Casangas lived on the Casamance River. Their king in the 1500s, Mansa Tamba, was heavily involved in the slave trade in Cacheu (Lobban and Mendy, *Guinea-Bissau*, 123).

13. A group of people now called the Brames lived in this region (B. A. Ogot, *UNESCO General History of Africa from the Sixteenth to the Eighteenth Century*. Abridged Edition. Vol. 5. University of California Press: Berkeley, 1999, 205). The ethnic label "Bran" was common in sixteenth-century Latin America.

Biafara kingdom called Guoli.[14] Another nearby nation is the Nalus, who do not trade with the Spanish.[15] Twenty leagues from the Nalus live the Bagas, one of the innumerable castes of Zapes.[16] The Portuguese have a great deal of trade with various Zape groups, who also live in the kingdoms of Magarabomba, Logos, Limbas, Birgas, Zumbas, and so on.[17]

Numerous barbaric nations live in the region of Sierra Leone. Many Mina towns are in this area.[18] Another large kingdom is called Arda.[19] Inland from the Ardas are the Lucumis, an important and numerous people.[20] After this comes the Vini kingdom [Benin]. Nearby is the Guere [Warri] kingdom, whose king and subjects are said to be Catholic. Under the supervision of priests who come from Sâo Tomé, they supposedly commit no errors against our faith.[21] Another kingdom in the region is called Zarabu, populated by cannibals.[22] Another caste in this area is called the Caravalis [Kalabaris].[23] In this region, there are also another forty or fifty towns made up of many different castes and

---

14. The correct spelling is the Guinala kingdom of the Beafadas in what is now Guinea-Bissau. This was an important kingdom in the 1500s and 1600s and a source of many slaves (Lobban and Mendy, *Guinea-Bissau*, 187–90).

15. The Nalus lived in the area called Guinea-Conkery in southern Guinea-Bissau (ibid., 244–45).

16. The Bagas were found in southwestern Guinea-Bissau (ibid., 79). Spaniards commonly used the word *Zape* or *Sape* (from the Portuguese spelling *Çape*) to refer to people from coastal Sierra Leone in the 1500s and 1600s who were often slaves in Spain. Today, these people are referred to as Temne (Kenneth Wylie, *The Political Kingdoms of the Temne* [New York: Africana Publishing Company, 1977], 4).

17. When he says "Logos," Sandoval probably refers to the Lokos, who lived on the coast of Sierra Leone and spoke Mande. The Limba are another group in coastal Sierra Leone. In the 1400s the Portuguese perceived that there was a Zape kingdom that was actually a confederacy of several coastal peoples, presumably including the ones Sandoval mentions here and in other chapters in Book I (Ogot, *Africa*, 196–97).

18. Mina refers to a Gbe-speaking people, now called Popos, who live in Ghana, Togo, and Benin (Diagram Group, *Encyclopedia of African Peoples* [New York: Facts on File, 2000], 151).

19. Arda equals Allada, an important kingdom in Lower Guinea, an area that includes southern Ghana, Benin, Togo, and Nigeria, also known as the "slave coast" (Thornton, *Africa and Africans*, 75).

20. A Yoruba-speaking people from the region of modern-day Benin (ibid., 83, 112).

21. See Introduction for more information on where Catholic priests were based in the 1500s and 1600s.

22. No other information on this kingdom is available.

23. This name comes from the coastal city called Elem Calabar, Nigeria. Slaves called Caravali in Sandoval's era came from the Igbo-speaking people from the Bight of Biafra.

black nations that are called Caravalis, although they really are not Caravalis. Because they are captured to be sold as slaves with the Caravalis, we incorrectly label them Caravali. These Caravalis do not have a king, so the idea that they are captured as prisoners in a just war is very doubtful.[24] It is certain that they capture each other and even sell their women and children, and they all eat human flesh. They also sell their neighbors. Many boats are lost in this region, but these people are so very charitable and have such compassionate hearts that instead of harming the castaways, they give them gifts and feed them until they can go on to Sâo Tomé. Five leagues inland from this is another separate nation called Banta.[25] In this region is an island called Principe. All the captives from the various nations of Sierra Leone are sold on this island.

Not far from the Cape of Lope Gonzales is a very large kingdom called Loango.[26] This kingdom has an infinitely large population of a different caste and language than their Congo and Angola neighbors. Passing Cabinda and the Popotano River, we are in the land of the Congo kingdom, eighty leagues inland. The river runs north–south to Angola, whose king rules over extended provinces of many people, including Angicos, Malembas, Mongiolos, Jaggas, and others.[27] From Angola we go to the Black Cape and from there to the Cape of Good Hope, which is what we have been aiming for since we left Cape Verde.

Eastern or Upper Ethiopia

In this section, Sandoval refers to parts of Africa that were not heavily involved in the Atlantic slave trade.

Eastern Ethiopia, beginning at the Cape of Good Hope, runs along the Ethiopian Sea, from the north in the Levant to the Bermejo Sea. There are countless eastern kingdoms. Motivated by my desire for greater glory for the Lord, I will only refer to the ones that relate to the goals of this book. The first kingdom is Sofala [now part of Mozambique]. North of Sofala and its subordinate kingdoms is the great Manomotapa empire.[28] The island of Mozambique and the

---

24. This is the first time Sandoval mentions one of the ways in which slavery was justified in his time. He goes into much greater detail on this topic in Book I, Chapter 17.

25. Though the reference here is unclear, 'Banta' might refer to Bantu, the major language and cultural group of Angola, Congo, and other regions of Central Africa.

26. In what is now Angola.

27. Bantu-speaking polities or ethnicities in the interior of Angola. Jaggas were also called Imbangala.

28. Also spelled Monomotapa. The Portuguese saw the Bantu-speaking peoples who lived along the Zambesi River in what is now Zimbabwe as an empire. The word probably derives from a local Kalanga word for "chief."

mainland country of the same name are populated by Cafres[29] called Macuas, barbarous blacks with curly hair. Other maritime kingdoms include Melinde [Malindi, Kenya]. Inland is the large Cafre [Kaffir] nation of Moseguejos. Further inland is the Mongallo kingdom [in Central Africa]. To the north is the great Munimugi kingdom, surrounded by the Mauxuca and Embeoe lands. Leaving the coast, we go south to the Abyssinian lands, whose emperor we vulgarly call Prester John. The ancients called this land Upper Egypt. The eastern Ethiopian desert is so sterile that it does not have a single green leaf, fountain, or stream, only great dunes and barren land. Many ostriches live there. Near the island of Socotra [an island off the coast of Somalia] are other small islands populated by people of a light color, more barbarous than almost any other nation in the world. Finally, Ethiopia ends in the beaches of the Red Sea. The Red Sea was given this name for the coral that grows in its depths.

Chapter 2. The nature of Ethiopians, commonly called "blacks."

In this chapter Sandoval explains the origins of the word "Ethiopian," depending on biblical and classical sources. He usually uses this word in a much broader sense than in reference to the modern northeastern African country. How are his explanations of how skin color is inherited different from explanations based on genetic inheritance? Why does Sandoval have to explain the origins of black skin in the world but not white skin? Sandoval contrasts black and white as skin colors in this chapter: does he view one color as normal and the other as an aberration? As is the case throughout the book, Sandoval combines personal observation and his own experience with trust in ancient sources and divine intervention in human life throughout history. Sometimes the ancient sources cannot explain the early modern experience, so Sandoval has to provide new explanations based on contemporary observations.

In an era where later ideas regarding race were in their infancy, how does Sandoval formulate his standards of beauty and ugliness in this chapter? Very specific standards for ideal beauty were formulated in Renaissance Europe. One's outward beauty was also thought to represent one's value—the image of a truly beautiful person conveyed moral purity and incorruptibility. For example, Europeans painted and sculpted thousands of images of the Virgin Mary based on female models judged as possessing the characteristics of ideal beauty. When he discusses and rates physical appearance, Sandoval generally

---

29. Sandoval often uses the term "Cafre" throughout the book. This equates to the word "Kaffir," a derogatory word commonly used in twentieth-century South Africa, where it is now illegal to use this word. The word "Kaffir" derives from an Arabic word that Muslims used to refer to African natives who were not Islamic. These people were often sold as slaves to the Portuguese, who began to use the term as Sandoval does, as a kind of ethnic description.

only refers to women. As slaves, African women's designated function in the Americas was to work, while European women represented purity and virtue, their beauty formulated around their wealth, honor, seclusion, luxurious clothes, status, and leisure. If an African woman was thought of as beautiful on these terms, she would also be considered virtuous, pure, worthy of a man's protection, and of high social status, and thus not a suitable slave. Along the same lines of argument, characteristics associated with hard work, such as large feet or bestial strength and endurance, gradually became stereotypical attributes of African women. A beautiful woman, according to Renaissance conceptions of beauty, would not be physically capable of arduous labor. The marvelous births described here contradict and confuse this ranking of physical beauty, so Sandoval relates them as wondrous events. In the last paragraph of this chapter, how does Sandoval equate ugliness with careless and disorderly women?

Since this entire book will deal with Ethiopians, or blacks, we should first of all explain the meaning of their name. The great thinkers of the early church called Ethiopia *Ethera,* meaning "sphere, heaven, or the element of fire." Other authorities say that the sacred scripture in the original Hebrew called Abyssinia *Chusia* and the Abyssinian natives *Chuseos,* derived from the name Chus, son of Ham, who populated this land.[30] Pliny gives the origin of the name as Ethiope, son of Vulcan, who presided over these regions.[31] Others say the word means "to burn," and thus Ethiopians are men with burned faces.[32] It is convenient to call all black nations Ethiopians, although each has their specific name. These nations include Guineans, Caravalis, Ardas, Lucumis, Congos, Angolans, Cafres [Kaffirs], Macuas, and many others.

Aristotle said that because rational beings have imaginations, children are sometimes born with an appearance very different from that of their parents. Experience proves this: it is very common to see ugly children born from beautiful parents, and the contrary, beautiful children to ugly parents. Brown or even very black children have been born to white parents, and very white, blond, blue-eyed, or red-haired children have been born to black parents.[33] Such is the force of the parents' imagination during the conception of their

---

30. Ham is the name given to one of the sons of Noah who went to Egypt, called the "Land of Ham" in the Psalms. His son was called Cush or Kush, spelled Chus here. In the Bible, Kush was the name given to a large region of northeastern Africa.

31. Roman god of fire and volcanoes. Sandoval refers to Pliny the Elder, who lived from 23 to 79 C.E. and wrote an encyclopedic work that collected most of the knowledge of his time. Sandoval often cites Pliny for his information on Africa.

32. This is the most accepted modern etymology of the word. The Greeks called the people in the region *aithiops,* meaning "burnt appearance."

33. Probably Sandoval is referring to albinism here.

children that they imprint on them what they see and what they are contemplating. I will prove this theory with a few eye-opening examples.

A noble Roman matron once gave birth to a baby girl black as an Ethiopian. The mother was accused of adultery. At the last moment before she was about to be punished for her atrocious crime, the judges decided to investigate if there was a portrait of an Ethiopian child in the bedroom where she had conceived her daughter. They found just such a picture in the room, and this picture was thought to have caused her to conceive a black child, so the judges freed her from blame.

On the other hand, in the land of Sofala, in the kingdom of Mocaranga in eastern Ethiopia, some Cafre Ethiopians have given birth to very white children. These children are as white as the Flemish, although their parents are black. In 1600 the captain of a fleet of ships took one of these little Cafres, white to the eyelashes, in his boat, and she was given as a gift to the viceroy of India, Don Francisco de Gama. She was the daughter of two black Cafres who died at sea.

An Ethiopian queen once conceived a very white daughter because, at the time of conception, she fixed her eyes and her imagination on an image of the beautiful Andromeda[34] that she had in front of her.

I have heard that in the kingdom of Beni[n], many black women with black husbands also give birth to white children who are nearsighted and have silver hair. The children of these white individuals give birth to blacks, but some are effeminate and useless, and are witches. They are never sold into slavery, although they could bring a large price. A noble and trustworthy Portuguese captain said he would give one thousand *cruzados* [Portuguese currency] for one of these individuals, if the person had attractive features (because usually they are ugly like the other blacks). The captain hoped to give the unusual slave to the king of Portugal, with authentic testimony that he was born of black parents, but the Beni[n] would not sell these people.

Many Portuguese say that in the kingdom of the great Fulo, there are numerous Fulos, men and women, who are paler and blonder than the Germans. They have long, straight, golden hair like women have in Europe. These people are never captured or taken to Spanish lands. Black Fulos, as well as Fulos who are mixed or mulattos, *pardo* [brown], *zambo,* of light color, chestnut, or bronze, live here in the Indies.[35] The people of this nation have a wide variety of skin colors, the same as all the other black nations we have mentioned. With my

---

34. A woman mentioned in Greek mythology.

35. The terms *pardo* and *zambo* were common labels in colonial Latin America used to describe the offspring of Africans and Europeans or indigenous Americans. See also note 67.

own eyes I have seen a boy called Francisco in Cartagena de Indias. He was seven years of age, with Angolan parents, but he was born in the town of Quilombo.[36] His parents were dark black, but he was white beyond compare. He was extremely pale and blond, with very Spanish features. His appearance shocked and stunned the entire city, so he was taken around as a marvel. His eyes were brown and very nearsighted. The only sign of his black heritage was his roman nose and his hair, which was gold but very crinkly. Juan Correa de Sosa, governor of Angola, knight of the Order of Christ, bought him to give to the king as something wondrous.

I saw another marvel of this kind in Mompox, a town located in the same province as Cartagena. Four of the most trustworthy Jesuit priests in the province of New Granada were shocked and amazed at the appearance of three little girls. They were the legitimate daughters of Martín, a black Angolan, and his wife Maria, also Angolan and black. The parents were slaves of Martín de Istayza and Ana Gómez his wife, residents of Mompox. The first daughter was named Juana. She was nine years old, with a very graceful appearance and Spanish features, but she had black skin like her parents. The second daughter was six years old and called Ventura. She was hideous, flat-nosed, and big-footed like a black woman, but more pale, blond, and blue-eyed than a German. She was excessively white. I have never seen such a pure whiteness, although she had crinkly hair like a black woman. Her hair was a combination of golden and silver in color. The third daughter was called Teodora. She was two years old, white, blond, and blue-eyed and also nearsighted like the second, but uglier. When the first of these two monsters was born, we heard that jealousy and suspicion raged in her house, and people accused the mother of infidelity. To put out the fires of suspicion, the husband and father certified that she was his daughter, because in Angola he had a son with another black woman. This daughter was as white as his newborn daughter. He also had sisters, daughters of his mother, born either white or black. The second birth calmed people and stopped the suspicions. A few days after meeting this family, while traveling on the Magdalena River,[37] everyone saw the black parents (rowing in one of thirty canoes with the flotilla) of two brothers, born in this same town, one dark black and the other a unique, burning orange color. The unusual color of these children was caused by the

---

36. *Quilombo* [kilombo] is a Central African term meaning Imbangala defensive camps and warrior bands. It was used in the Americas for rebel slave communities. See Joseph C. Miller, *Kings and Kinsmen: Early Mbundu States in Angola* (Oxford: Oxford University Press, 1976), 162, 176–223. In Spanish America, usually the term *palenque* was used to refer to rebel slave communities.

37. An important river in Colombia often used as a transit route between the coast and Bogotá in the colonial era.

vivid imagination of their parents. At conception, the idea of an imagined thing is imprinted on their minds and on the child that comes out of this fixed idea. Thus we can attribute the Ethiopians' color to their imaginations.

Throughout the world, color seems to depend on the climate of the land where a given person lives. This theory is supported by what we know of the East and West Indies, the coast of Africa, and even China, where people in Canton are black like those in Fez [Morocco]. People who live in the inland provinces of China are white because they live in a cold land. The same applies to Spain, where some are dark and others are blond or red-haired like the Germans. Scholars say that Ethiopians are black because the extraordinary heat of the sun in their hot lands burns off the first layer of their skin. They also say that the land is full of serpents, basilisks, dragons, unicorns, and other beasts. The black inhabitants curse the sun for burning them so harshly.

I believe these opinions have some basis in fact, but if climate causes skin color, Spaniards who live in Africa and are married to Spanish women will engender black children. And, vice versa, blacks living in Europe will give birth to white children. However, obviously experience belies this supposition. One could infer, not without some basis, that the black skin of the Ethiopians not only comes from the curse Noah put on his son Ham but also is an innate or intrinsic part of how God created them, so that in this extreme heat, the sons engendered were left this color, as a sign that they descend from a man who mocked his father, to punish his daring. Thus the Ethiopians descend from Ham, the first servant and slave that there ever was in the world, whose punishment darkened the skin of his sons and descendants.[38]

Others have a very different theory, one I agree with, even if what I have just finished saying seems a sound philosophy. This last theory says that Adam cursed his son Cain for the shamelessness he showed in treating Adam with so little reverence, that Cain lost his nobility and even his personal freedom and became a slave, along with all of his children.[39] This was the first servitude in

---

38. The book of Genesis says that Noah's son Ham saw him when he was drunk and told his brothers about it. The brothers covered their father and did not look at him, but Ham was cursed for rudely looking at his drunken father. Noah said that Ham's descendants would be servants, and they then populated Africa. Europeans often used this story as a justification for African slavery. A physical characteristic becomes a permanent mark of shameful lineage, which brings Sandoval closer to modern ideas of race.

39. Genesis also tells of how Cain displeased his father Adam and was forced to wander for the rest of his life. He was not a slave, but Sandoval interprets his punishment as a loss of freedom. Some early Christians viewed the "mark of Cain," a mark made on him by Adam to stop people from killing Cain, as a stain or blackening on his skin. This is another biblical passage that has been used to justify slavery.

world history. Although Cain was of light-skinned lineage, he was born dark. Thus blacks are also born as slaves, because God paints the sons of bad parents with a dark brush.

Scholars say that Ethiopian hair is crinkly and curly because of the heat. Animals' skin also crinkles up and twists when it is burnt. Galen said hair becomes crinkly because it has difficulty pushing through the pores of the skin. He also says that the fineness of their pores and the hardness of their skin occasionally cause the Ethiopians to have thin hair. Avicenna says their hair is so black because of the excessive heat of where they were born.[40] However, contradicting this theory, people called Majacatos, who have straight hair and very slender facial features, live inland from Mozambique.

The extraordinary whiteness of the Ethiopians' teeth is caused by the heat of the sun, which dries them out. Sometimes people wonder: if they have such white teeth, why aren't their fingernails also white? The reason is that the skin where the fingernails grow from is black and the nails carry the same color and are burned by the sun. Some say that the large feet of many blacks are also caused by the excessive heat. Others do not agree with this theory, saying that their rough features are due to godmothers and midwives who, because they are so crude and disorderly, do not shape babies' faces or other parts of their bodies after they are born, as the Spanish do. When people carelessly shape newborn bodies, we see the same defects, ugliness, and deformities, even among whites.

Chapter 3. Why extraordinary monsters and other marvelous things are found in Africa, especially in Ethiopia.

To Sandoval and his contemporaries, Africa and everything connected to Africa needed explanation, due to the European perception of the extreme difference of this continent. Sandoval expresses wonderment and confusion, typical European reactions in reconciling new information with the classical and biblical authorities they depended on for centuries. Sandoval generally uses Greek and Roman philosophers to provide explanations, but he mixes their theories with anecdotes from the Americas, places that were unknown to the classical authorities. Here Sandoval tries to show that, although they may seem shocking at first, a place in the natural and divinely ordered world can be found for new peoples and creatures, and that Africa's inhabitants and fate are certainly part of a divine plan. Why does Sandoval discuss monstrous infants? How does he explain them? How does this connect to Chapter 2's discussion of Africans who had light-skinned children?

---

40. Galen was a Greek doctor in the second century C.E. who had a great influence on medieval and early modern medicine in Europe. Avicenna, or Ibn Sina, was a tenth-century Persian doctor and scientist.

Some readers will struggle to believe the many strange things that this book describes. This chapter seeks to explain why extraordinary monsters are said to inhabit all the black kingdoms. A person might also find it difficult to believe that it is possible to have skin the color of Ethiopians' skin: how can we believe this before we see them? But what new discovery does not appear miraculous the first time that it comes to our attention? How many things previously thought impossible eventually come to pass? If we only look at small parts of nature, we will never believe in the force and majesty of her universal power and grandeur. Nature's works show us her unseen power. Who believes in dwarves or hermaphrodites until they see one? Aristotle tells us of androgynes, who sometimes have male sex organs and other times female sex organs, with a right breast like a man's breast and the left one like a woman's. The beardless [American] Indians shocked people who saw them in Spain. People would also be shocked to see women with beards on their breasts, but these women are said to live near the Bermejo Sea in Ethiopia. Although we see it every day, who could believe that there are so many ways for a face to be beautiful, if beauty supposedly only means good proportions and symmetry? Even if we find nature's secrets marvelous when we read or hear about them, we should not consider them impossible, because if we ponder these marvels at length, we will find that many seemingly impossible things are in fact true.

Before we can understand the diversity found among Ethiopians and in other black kingdoms, we must clarify why monsters are born. Aristotle says this happens when nature fails to achieve the perfect goal of each being engendering another creature like itself. When this happens, a monster is born. However, it is more reasonable to say that a monster is nothing else but a sin of nature that happens when nature does not achieve perfection through lack or excess of any part of a creature. For example, these sins could be when an animal is born without a limb, with three arms or six fingers in each hand, or two heads, four arms, or four feet. This happens most commonly in the most fecund birds, and in animals that give birth to several offspring at once, because the matter of more than one infant is confused and mixed. This confusion occurs in the litters of a little animal about the size of a rat, called a *sopel* by the natives of Sinaloa, México. This animal has thirty-three children, all connected to its body, so that only their eyes can be seen. Sometimes creatures are born with body parts not in their natural place, such as the goat Aristotle describes with a horn on her leg. Some are deformed from birth: it is said that in 1591 a woman gave birth to a serpent with two wings in place of arms. Aristotle relates having seen a boy born with the head of a sheep or a bull and animals born with limbs resembling those of other animals. He says that nature, due to defective material or natural heat, is sometimes not able to engender a perfect animal according to its species, so she tries to engender what she can and thus introduces the most accommodating form for that material.

[Here Sandoval describes the monstrous child that will be born if a woman has sex with the devil and then relates stories of various men who have had relationships with other devilish beings.]

Returning to the point: many monsters are engendered by intercourse between two animals of different species, and the result is neither one nor the other but a third species with aspects of both. Many scholars attribute Ethiopian monsters to this kind of mixing because Africa, and particularly Libya, is so dry and sterile that animals will travel great distances to find water. At watering holes, they mix amongst themselves and later give birth to various monstrosities, composed of more than one species of animal. Pliny says this leads to the vulgar Greek saying, "something new always comes out of Africa." Monsters can also be born from the great force of the father's imagination. His imagination transfers what is in his soul to his son when he is conceived in his mother's womb.

In the next few chapters, Sandoval stretches the labels "black," or "Ethiopian," to describe the inhabitants of many areas of the non-European world. Many of these people were also targeted for Jesuit missions (and Iberian imperial expansion), especially those led by Francis Xavier, so Sandoval wants to show that the Jesuits have always sought to Christianize people who can be very loosely described as "blacks," as a way to validate his own mission to Africans in Cartagena and include it as part of the primary goals of the Jesuit order. For example, Sandoval quotes from a letter written by Xavier describing the natives of Cape Comorin, in the southernmost tip of India, as "black." Sandoval also includes the residents of the region that now comprises Indonesia, Papua New Guinea, and the Philippines in his category of black or Ethiopian.

Chapter 11. Ethiopians in Guinea and their land, rivers, and ports.

Sandoval focuses on Sierra Leone in this chapter because two Jesuits had entered the area in 1604, attempting to found churches and preach Catholicism. The 1606 Jesuit report on the Sierra Leone coast is probably the source for the information related here, including Sandoval's brief mention of "sorcerers." One of the priests died in 1617 and, due to pressures from other European trading nations Sandoval mentions in this chapter, the mission disappeared.[41] Despite the Jesuits' failures, how does Sandoval present Sierra Leone in a positive way at the beginning of the chapter?

Sandoval must not have realized the mission's failure was permanent when he wrote this chapter in the 1620s; he blames the Jesuit problems on local rulers or barbaric local customs, not the ultimate impossibility of a few priests having a strong influence on the

---

41. Adrian Hastings, *The Church in Africa*. (Oxford: Clarendon Press, 1994), 119.

beliefs and traditions of an entire region. In Sandoval's era, Europeans commonly envisioned African political systems and governments as illegitimate, immoral, or even nonexistent, with people living in a disorganized, uncivilized state of nature. This meant that Europeans did not have to recognize and interact with African rulers with the same diplomacy, ceremony, and formality as they afforded the heads of other European governments. How does Sandoval characterize the civilization and government of the Zapes, Branes, Bisaos, and Bijogoes?

Sandoval also believed that some of the polities of Africa, which he viewed as corrupt or barbaric, were more vulnerable to the influence of the devil and Islam, a religion that was successfully expanding into sub-Saharan Africa at this time. Although Muslim rulers had been ejected from Spain in 1492, European Catholics in the late 1500s and early 1600s greatly feared continuing Islamic expansion, especially in the region of the Mediterranean. In response to the growing Ottoman empire, the Spanish monarchs supported military and naval expeditions and programs of social control, including seeking out and persecuting Islamic converts in Spain [moriscos] who might be aiding Muslim pirates. Sandoval correctly observes that Islam spread throughout Africa via prosperous trading routes. He saw his work Christianizing African slaves in Cartagena as one line of defense against Islamic expansion. He mentions isolated Christian churches and missions in Africa to demonstrate that Christianity, thanks especially to Jesuit efforts, has made some inroads in Africa, despite the powerful Islamic states mentioned here. What opinion of Islam does Sandoval voice in this chapter?

The land of Guinea (whose name comes from its most important city, called Genna or Genni [Jenne], on the banks of the Senegal River), is huge and very hot, although it is located well beneath the torrid zone. But this does not mean, as many believe, that it is uninhabitable. In the past, it was heavily populated with great kingdoms, large provinces, and many great cities, villages, and towns, although all were barbarous and rough. The buildings were made of mud and straw, but they were comfortable because cool, fresh breezes blew through them. Many of the kingdoms are very temperate, according to the Jesuit fathers who preach there, especially the kingdoms in Sierra Leone. The best European climate does not surpass Sierra Leone's climate, because it is neither excessively cold nor hot. It is also rare for people there to die of the ordinary illnesses so common in Europe. Instead, people die of old age, poisoning, or evils caused by sins of the flesh. Great rivers, lakes, estuaries, and inland seas make it easy to travel by boat in these kingdoms. The inland roads, due to constant floods, are very bad, and one must cross lagoons, steep mountain ranges, impenetrable swamps, and dense spiny brush dangerous enough to wound one's feet. There are also large savannahs, lowlands, and plains, and fertile land for breeding livestock to produce meat, milk, butter, and cheese. People usually travel by elephants that walk twenty leagues in a day and from whose teeth they make great quantities of ivory.

All the Ethiopian Guineans are shipped from ports on the Guinean rivers. The Gambia River is the deepest, most powerful, and most turgid of all of the rivers. The other river is the Senegal River, which is virtually impassable. Both rivers breed many fish and animals, including crocodiles, sea horses, and serpents with wings.

The Senegal River's north bank crosses the great Wolof kingdom, dividing it from the Moors with whom they trade. Other adjacent kingdoms include Cambaya, Ioala, Brasolo, and other kingdoms. Gambia is on the south side of the river. Fifty leagues inland is the great kingdom of the Berber Wolofs. On the borders of this kingdom are Moors and the Fulo kingdom. The empire of the Great Fulo is nearby. Next are the numerous Mandingas, who energetically interact with all the Guinean kingdoms with the goal of infecting them with the cursed Mohammedan sect [Islam]. They travel inland five hundred leagues, trading salt from the Gambia River for gold. The Portuguese live in two ports on this coast. Other nations, especially the English, Dutch, and French, enter these ports to trade. The largest port is Ale [Saly Portudal, Senegal] and the other is called Ioala. These black nations also trade with the Berber Moors, who come in caravans from the Libyan deserts bringing horses, camels, donkeys, and other goods to trade for Berber and Wolof children under seven years old, in order to make them join their cursed and deadly sect.

Between the Senegal and the Gambia rivers is the kingdom of the Grand Fulo, a powerful king who rules over many subjects. The Fulopos also live along the Gambia River from the Santa Maria Cape to the port of Cacheu [Guinea-Bissau]. North of the river live Soninkes, vulgarly called Mandingas. Inland six or seven leagues from the mouth of the Gambia River, where it opens into the Casamance River, live Banhuns, Bootes, or Boyochos. Some understand Fulopos because these groups interact. The Casamance River, passing through the Boote territory, goes into Soninke territory. Casanges and Banhuns live to the south. Their languages are very similar.[42]

Cacheu has a trading post, market, and church, which has a priest appointed by the king. This is the most important port in all of Guinea. Ships from Seville, Portugal, the island of Santiago, and many other places come here to trade in black slaves and many other things. Many people have been successfully baptized here, but these black Christians have little knowledge of Christianity and interact with gentiles. This means they easily return to rites that are not part of our faith. This applies especially to those who before being baptized were called *gabazones,* or sorcerers, who perform prophesies and cures using remedies and spells they learned from Satan. Brans also live at this port; one of their kings has

---

42. Sandoval relates information about languages to help Jesuits in Cartagena communicate with African slaves in the port. See Book I, Chapter I for more information.

four hundred wives. Nearby live the Bisaos [Bissaus], a cruel people without a king, who live under the rule of the strongest. They are often sold into slavery as punishment for their crimes and as prisoners in their wars with the Branes and Biafaras. I could mention many other kingdoms in this region, but I will move on at this stage so that I do not become tiresome by repeating seventy unpronounceable names. The Bijogoes live on small islands. They are very warlike, great pirates who venerate and invoke their heroes while they are dying, as we would invoke saints. They are constantly at war, and they win due to their great valor. Because of this they are said to be false, shameless, and arrogant.[43]

From these islands we go to the mainland and the kingdom of the Nalus, who are traded by Biafaras. The Zapes called Bagas live at the mouth of the Nuno River. The Bagas are very weak, but they raise many chickens, which they take to the Spanish port of Cagandi, twenty miles upriver, and trade for their needs. In this port the Portuguese also trade with the Farinlandama and Cocoli people, who sell many slaves, and with Mandingas called Zozos [Sosos], who live twenty leagues inland. Another group of Zapes called Boulones also live along this coast. The Zape Manes live in Sierra Leone, where the Portuguese, English, and Flemish trade. Most important, the Jesuit priests have a church here called San Salvador. There is another Zape kingdom here called Magarabomba.[44] Further along this river is an island called Caracore, where the Jesuits founded their first church in these kingdoms. Our third church is in a port called Tumba. The fourth is at the end of the river, where the Portuguese do much trading and where there are also many Jesuit fathers. The fifth and last church founded by the Jesuits in these kingdoms is called San Juan Evangelista. In the Zape kingdoms, two groups of Zapes are constantly at war.

Our Jesuit brothers suffer greatly in these ports due to the rulers' tyranny and greed. Whenever a king needs money (or pretends that he needs it), he sends an envoy to the Portuguese. The envoy takes a large entourage, entering people's houses as if the residents were slaves who should not dare to deny them anything they want. The king will confiscate any ship in the port, along with its contents, and get away with it. One gets a sense of their customs from a conversation that took place between a Muslim trader and a priest. The priest, in response to a comment by the merchant, who wanted to know why whites are free and blacks are slaves, said that God first created whites and then blacks. Because the blacks came second, they must serve their older brothers.

---

43. Here Sandoval refers to the peoples of the Bissagos Islands, off the coast of Guinea-Bissau.

44. See Thornton, *Africa and Africans*, xvi, for a map of these cultural groups, and Chapter I for more information about them. All of the groups of people mentioned in this paragraph live in the region of modern Sierra Leone.

Chapter 12. The nature, morals, and customs of the Guinean Ethiopians.

Sandoval modeled this book on the writings of José de Acosta, who argued that indigenous Americans would never become good Christians due to their strong cultural traditions and the constant interaction between their spiritual beliefs, the natural world, and their day-to-day life. By describing West Africans as eager to imitate Europeans, even when they are still in Africa, Sandoval suggests that it is easier for Africans to give up their traditional customs and become Christians. Sandoval tries to provide evidence for his argument that Africans can become good Christians throughout De instauranda. *What other characteristics does Sandoval give to the Africans considered to be the "best slaves"? Why might these qualities make West Africans "good slaves"?*

The ethnographic details described in this chapter relate to Sandoval's purpose of promoting his Cartagena mission. Coming from Jesuit reports on their African experiences, slave traders' stories, and possibly what Sandoval heard from Africans in Cartagena, many of these observations reflect actual African beliefs and customs. However, the way in which Sandoval presents the ethnographic evidence reveals more about his values than about African life. Most of the customs described here strike at the heart of Spanish patriarchal values, especially the ways in which Africans interact with their rulers, pass on leadership, connect dress to status, and punish adulterers. In his opinion, some of these practices show that Africans are not inherently evil, even if they have succumbed to the influence of the devil. Other habits, such as everyone eating from the same platter, to Sandoval demonstrate a nonsensical lack of order and hierarchy. By describing some good customs (modesty in dress in front of Europeans, respect for a ruler), or explaining how others have at least some degree of misguided logic (killing servants when the king dies to discourage assassins), Sandoval portrays Africans as within the realm of redemption. For example, how does he say that cannibalistic Africans can improve upon their lifestyle?

In the traditions associated with the dead, Sandoval also demonstrates that Africans do possess a sense of what is right by Baroque Christian standards: they honor the dead and surround the passage to the next world in communal ceremonies. Preparing Christians for a "good death" through Catholic ritual was a fundamental aim of the Society of Jesus, and Sandoval would have appreciated the fact that Africans also placed importance on funerals. But how, why, and under what influence do African funerals diverge from what Sandoval considered appropriate rituals?

We will now discuss the Guineans, black slaves who have the most value to the Spanish. These people work the hardest; they cost the most and have the best dispositions. They are attractive with a keen wit, glad hearts, and a joyful spirit. They never pass up the chance to drum, sing, and dance, even while they are doing the most difficult work imaginable. They are very noisy when they come together in this way. Their music combines the sounds of sonorous instruments and many voices, and they celebrate without sleeping, day or night. The energy that they put into shouting and dancing is amazing. Some play guitars similar to our Spanish-style guitars, although they are made of rough sheepskin. Many of them are fine musicians. These Guineans serve the Spanish best and adopt our customs readily, because even as gentiles in Ethiopia they learn our language and dress up for fiestas in the Spanish style, wearing clothes they receive as gifts. They praise and exalt our holy faith and detest their own. They want to have more Spaniards in their land and more clothes and European things in their houses. Even in the inland regions, they permit many Christians of different nations to live among them. Due to this interaction and the presence of the Spaniards in the ports, the blacks learn many mechanical arts, especially blacksmithing. They do this in the manner of Spanish gypsies, making many weapons and whatever else they want.

When they are alone and the Spanish are not watching them, these people go about naked. When they have dealings with the Spanish, both men and women cover themselves, wearing clothes suited to their rank and what they can afford. They usually have very little money for clothing and are hardly able to dress themselves decently. The maidens wrap thick blue strings around their waists. They hang a piece of cloth or linen from these belts. This cloth denotes virginity. Once, when a Jesuit priest went to Sierra Leone, the king ordered all the women to go inside their houses for the duration of his stay. They were not allowed in his presence unless they were dressed decently.

Leaving aside their clothing, some Wolofs and Berbers have incredibly nimble and elegant feet. They run and leap as gracefully as swift steeds. Many Berbers, in imitation of the Spaniards, wear lavish gold and pearl earrings. On their wrists and ankles they wear elaborate gold bracelets. Women wear skirts like Spanish women, but they do not wear just one skirt but instead five or six, dyed blue. From the waist up, they wear only one layer of clothing, but it is bright and elegant.

Whenever the Berber king wants, he can call up five or six thousand mounted men, because there are many noble warriors in his kingdom. They usually fight wars amongst themselves. When the common people encounter the king, they kneel down on the floor and extend their arms and hands and throw dirt on their heads three times. If a noble person encounters the king, they squat down but do not throw dirt on their heads. The women and all others do the same kind of bow, according to their rank. When people speak to the king, they do so through interpreters, even if the king understands their language.

Everyone, even the king, eats sitting on the ground, like the Moors do, or reclined on mats on the floor. They eat well if they can afford to, although most people usually subsist on very little food. Their plates are made of wood, and cups are fashioned from calabashes. The kings have silver cups that they use ostentatiously when the Spanish are present. When they eat, they make no distinctions among themselves, with everyone eating from the same plate. When one person grabs all the food, they leave everyone else to eat scraps like dogs. They make their wine not from grapes but from palm trees. They have no shortage of drinks to use in celebrating their binges. During their fiestas, they sip their wine and marvel at how much one of us drinks in one gulp. They love drunkenness so much that a person who is a heavy drinker is highly respected. One of their drinks is called *po*. It is made of millet and a fruit they call *salmiron*, similar to a Castilian apricot. They also drink palm wine. Some sleep on elevated mats covered with colored drapery. They raise dogs and cats, which accompany them and clean the houses.

Some of these nations practice cannibalism to this day, although it is in decline, especially among those converted to our faith. When they convert, they burn their idols, sending up a poisonous smoke, and throw the instruments and vessels of this abomination out of their houses. How can we believe that barbarians who put human flesh in their mouths are devout Christians, sons of the Church, soldiers in Christ's militia, fighting with God's flesh in their mouths? The Congo kingdom was destroyed in the time of King Bernardo, who conquered all the coastal lands to Sierra Leone, after a war of ten years. When the region became calm again, they stopped eating human flesh regularly except for eating people they killed in war or executed for their crimes.

They marry as many women as they can as a sign of wealth and nobility. One king of the Logos [the Lokos from Sierra Leone] had 63 sons and 52 daughters, and currently his descendants number three thousand people. Usually the kings do not keep all their women and children with them but instead leave it to the mothers to raise the children. Mothers take care of their children until they come of age and start to work doing farm labor and trading like everyone else. When they are mature, if they seem able to govern, their fathers give them land and villages so that they can rule as lords over their property. If the king's sons please him and do his will, he promises to give them his treasures when he dies, as a sign of his love.

Some nations punish adultery and others do not. In the Bran kingdom, adulterers are decapitated. Plebeians and nobles are not killed for adultery, but they are imprisoned and sold into slavery. Women are not punished. The Biafaras have the same punishments, even for their kings. They capture and sell adulterers but show honor and respect to the women who give themselves up to this cursed misery.

They usually bury the dead on a high platform, covered in very fine cloths and a mound of sand. They enclose all this in a straw hut. When someone dies, the death is announced in all the villages where the deceased has relatives. They usually have a large number of relatives because they have so many wives who live in different villages. Everyone brings all of their friends to the funeral, and it is celebrated with much mourning. They bring whatever wealth they have in their possession: some bring gold and clothing, others bring Portuguese trade goods. When they enter the village of the deceased, they cry loudly and the cry grows as more people arrive. The gifts are divided in three parts: some gifts are buried with the deceased, some are for the king, and some are for the deceased person's closest relative, to go toward the expenses of the funeral. Kings are given secret night burials, in the presence of only a few close relatives, because the kings are buried with a great deal of gold treasure, which they accumulated over their lifetimes. They do not want anyone to know where the treasure is buried. They bury the kings near a river or creek channel so that later on the water will run over their tombs. The kings are also buried accompanied by male and female servants. A few years ago, when a Bran king died, thirty-three of the most beautiful black men and women were killed. When another king died, sixty-five people were killed, including some Christians. It was said that the Christians were killed because they would be better servants to the king in the next world. They also kill three or four more people every thirty days for the first year after a king's death. This is done for political reasons. The fact that so many people, including criminals, will die when the king dies means no one wants to assassinate the king.

Others are buried in their villages, with many of their own possessions and the possessions of their friends and relatives. This custom actually motivates them to acquire more possessions, because the devil has persuaded them that they will take what they bury with them into the next world. If the deceased is noble, they erect a house over the sepulcher until the body is putrefied. This shrine is decorated. Relatives come to these houses to speak to the dead and tell them of their troubles so that the dead will ask God to help them. Soon after the burial, they celebrate the funeral with much eating, drinking, and dancing, loudly drumming and singing night and day. To praise the dead, they prepare more food than anyone could possibly eat, and they have enough wine to make everyone go crazy. When a king has a celebration, it is also considered a wake for his ancestors and past kings, and they sacrifice some cows for those who died long ago. A girl, dressed in fine clothes and adornments, is also sacrificed during the ceremonies they learned from the devil. These lands are full of tall ceiba trees called *poilones,* which serve as memorials to all of their actions because they plant a *poilon* in honor of a funeral, upon the marriage of a daughter, when a parent dies, and at the death or succession of a king. This is always done with sacrifices and superstitious rites. They revere the *poilones* planted for their dead kings as if the trees truly were the kings.

Chapter 13. The false religion, rites, and gentile ceremonies of the Ethiopians who live on the rivers of Guinea.

Before race prejudices were formulated as based on inheritance and skin color, Europeans divided and distanced themselves from others by religion. Those who were non-Christian, not those with a perceived racial difference, were possible slaves. In this

chapter, Sandoval exoticizes African beliefs and practices, despising them for their dif-
ference from Christianity. No particular race in the modern sense is conceived of here,
but Sandoval contributes to a process of formulating a generalized, racist view of Afri-
can barbarity, due to religious difference. Because Christianity defines and encompasses
his entire worldview, to Sandoval, religions outside Christianity are not organized belief
systems but simply errors encouraged by the devil. He sees African supernatural forces
as demons, not as another way to explain and organize the natural world. He views
African priests as sorcerers. The descriptions of religion in this chapter are meant to fur-
ther prove Sandoval's belief that Africans are under the devil's influence and desperately
need Christianity to save them from eternal damnation.

By far the most threatening of all non-Christian beliefs to Sandoval is Islam.[45]
Opposing the growth of Islam was an inherent part of the early modern Spanish and
Catholic identity. By emphasizing the successful growth of Islam in Africa, its orga-
nized hierarchy, and its motivated adherents, Sandoval seeks to further inspire his read-
ers to join him in combating the spread of Islam by teaching Christianity to Africans. In
his mind, Jesuits should make at least as much effort as do Islamic preachers.

Although some Africans did not fully convert to Islam in the strictest sense, many
adhered to some aspects of the religion, as Sandoval observes in his description of cir-
cumcision rituals. To Catholics of the time, circumcision was the ultimate symbol of
rejecting Christianity, even a sign that Inquisition tribunals in Spain and the Americas
might look for in prosecuting those whom they believed were false Christian converts.
Although the rituals described here are not specifically Muslim, how does Sandoval
describe them in a way that emphasizes how they differ from Christian values and
European culture? In the final paragraphs of this chapter, how does Sandoval specifi-
cally connect Islam and the devil's influence?

These gentiles are so ignorant and blind to their fate after death that they think
everything in the afterlife is a physical object to be used like the things in this
world. They do not believe in hell, and they think everyone who dies goes to be
with their God, and that those who are more important in this life are worth
more to him in the afterlife. They make offerings to beg God to free them from
the power of demons. They fear these demons so greatly that some, in their last
wills and testaments, request to be buried with their weapons to defend themselves from the demons in the next world.[46] Each kingdom has a place where
they make solemn sacrifices to these demons. They also fear that they will be

---

45. Sandoval ends *De instauranda* with another description of successful Islamic proselytization. See Book 4, Chapter 15.

46. With this point, Sandoval seeks to emphasize that Africans did not perceive the
afterlife as a nonphysical domain where only the soul can go. He also wants to stress that
they must be taught the Christian beliefs in rewarding the good with an afterlife in heaven.

killed when they pass one of these shrines unless they make offerings of rice, oil, or whatever else is on hand.

Those who serve as the devil's priests use witchcraft and concoctions to kill people whenever they please. The people are convinced by the idea (until it drives them mad) that if they agree with any part of our faith or adore the cross, they will certainly die.

They adore and revere idols as their gods. These idols are statues of their ancestors, called *corofines,* made of wood or clay. They also worship superstitious images that the priests sell or give them, persuaded that these images will protect them from any harm, including casualties in battle.[47] Others bring animal skins into battle for good luck. The kings and nobles also bring decorated sheepskin hides with them when they go out on horseback. The idol they most fear and worship is called a *china.* This is a clay pyramid full of very destructive white ants, which I have seen eat a desk full of papers and a chest of clothes in a night. After buying a slave [in Africa], the first thing they [the African masters] do is take him to one of these *chinas,* asking the idol to make snakes, lizards, and leopards kill the slave if he flees. This makes the poor slave very frightened and he does not dare escape, no matter how badly his master treats him. Other nations do not believe in idols. I am told that the Brans worship only one god, whom they believe created the world. They pray to this god for help in sickness and drought. But they know nothing of Jesus Christ or his law.[48]

While it is true that not every Guinean nation has received the perverse Mohammedan sect [Islam], their infernal priests scar them all from infancy with the lethal brand of circumcision. We know that in the kingdoms of the Wolofs, Berbers, Ancollar, Cambaya, Ioala, and Brasola, at the age of fourteen boys must shave their heads, wear white shirts and pants like Moors, and be circumcised. For forty days they cannot enter populated areas, and they go wandering around the countryside. The women have their lower lips pierced, very slowly increasing the size of the hole until their lip is hanging down. The women are also obligated to wander like the men. In the year of circumcision, boys are not allowed to fight with their neighboring kings. In the Bran kingdom of Bacerral, boys are circumcised when a new king is elected. It is publicly decreed that all men must come together in the mountains and other places

---

47. Although Protestants perceived Catholics devotion to images of the saints as idol worship, early modern Catholics wanted to clarify their practice by contrasting it with the practice of those they viewed as savages. Instead of idols to be worshipped, Catholic statues and paintings were meant to inspire prayer for the intervention of the saints with an all-powerful, but more remote God.

48. With this kind of example, Sandoval hopes to prove that Africans can become good Christians.

where there are no women or even female animals. This abominable ceremony goes on for two months, because only one man does the circumcising. They heal slowly, aided by herbal remedies. When all are healed, they march in a procession, celebrating and drinking. They celebrate by spending eight days in every village of the kingdom. The men are esteemed and venerated after completing this initiation, because they cannot go to war until they are circumcised. Some fight as soon as possible, because this is thought to be the time when they are strongest and bravest. The man who is not circumcised also cannot marry. They say that circumcision is healthy, because it allows them to have many women without harm. Some Bran nations will not elect a king until he is circumcised. Some castes or nations use this time to change their way of speaking, to a kind of boys' slang, full of continuous cursing. This language sounds like the speech of demons in hell. Before they leave the mountain where the circumcision ceremony takes place, they have a drunken celebration, erecting a pile of stones where they sacrifice cows, goats, dogs, and other animals to the devil. They also sacrifice one of their own. The celebration continues until the new moon, when they finally regain their reason. Then they make a secret oath that only the participants understand.

In Guinea the main priests of this cursed sect are Mandingas, who live along the Gambia River and inland more than five hundred leagues. They not only drink the poison of Mohammed's sect themselves but also take it to other nations. They bring it with their trade goods to many kingdoms, and the devil gets a good bargain for their labor. They are great horsemen, and wherever they go they help kings in their wars, riding always in the vanguard. Kings have great esteem for them and give them privileges and land. These priests have mosques and a clerical hierarchy similar to our rankings of archbishops and bishops. They have schools where they teach the Arabic letters they use to write their scrolls. When the high-ranking clergy travel, they are received in different places as if they came from heaven. When they arrive in a new town, they announce the day when they will begin their sermons so that many people from all over the region will know to gather there at that time. They decorate a plaza and hang a few scrolls that seem to give their lies some authority. Then the priests stand and raise their hands and eyes to heaven. After awhile, they prostrate themselves before the infernal writings and bow to them. After getting up, they give thanks to Allah and to his great prophet Mohammed, sent to pardon their sins. Then they praise the doctrine written on the scrolls and ask everyone to pay attention. No one speaks, sleeps, or lets their eyes wander for two hours as they read and discuss the writings. Orators praise their kings and lords, puffing up their vanity, as the priests speak of their victories and those of their ancestors. They mix many lies into their stories, degrading our holy faith and praising Mohammed's cursed sect, eloquently persuading the kings and everyone else to reject Christianity.

Chapter 14. The customs, nature, morals, false religion, and gentile ceremonies of the Ethiopian kingdoms from Sierra Leone to the Cape of Lope González and the island of Sâo Tomé.

Ethnographic details about customs in the Bight of Benin clash with this chapter's denunciations of the devil's influence on the beliefs of the peoples of this region. Sandoval believed that educating his Jesuit readers about African beliefs and practices helped them defeat the devil's power over these peoples. The Jesuits needed information in order to challenge the misguided customs. For Sandoval, the Africans were victims of the devil, not co-conspirators. Sandoval appreciates the courteousness and orderliness of life in these kingdoms and their almost excessive respect for their king; he contrasts these parts of their culture with descriptions of human sacrifice, snake worship, and magic. How do Sandoval's descriptions show that the Popo kingdom is well governed and organized? What aspects of their daily routine does Sandoval find ridiculous? How does he show that people from this region might be good Christians? But what influences corrupt this essential goodness? What reaction might Sandoval be seeking from his readers when he discusses the worship of vultures and the sacrifices made to them? How does this description contrast with the final paragraph in the chapter?

Beyond Sierra Leone, there is no noteworthy slave trade until Las Palmas Cape, a distance of 150 leagues along the coast, which runs east to west. However, inland from this coast there are many nations of barbarous, gentile blacks.

The Popo kingdom covers fifty leagues of the coast and extends inland for sixty leagues.[49] They have a secure port ruled over by a tyrant who is cruel to all who arrive at his port. The Popos only know enough to worship idols and are also very superstitious with their dead. One of their superstitions is that when they are in mourning, they bring together all the cloth and silk they own and throw it in the caves used as sepulchers for their ancestors.[50]

South of the Popo kingdom live the Ardas or Axaraes,[51] and also located here is another principality called Fulao, where there is much slave trading. In ancient times the Fulao were ruled by the Popo king but revolted against him, cutting off his hand. Since then, they carry it during their fiestas, celebrating their victory and vengeance. The king has only women and eunuchs as servants, although they are not abused as is the case in many other countries. The reason the kings have an infinite number of wives is their custom of taking on all the living wives of dead kings, other than their own mothers; each king's mother

---

49. A Gbe-speaking people from the Bight of Benin, called "PauPau" in English.

50. Another observation made to highlight how Africans lack understanding of the Christian view of the afterlife.

51. See note 19.

carries the title of principal queen. All have private idols in their houses, where they revere and adore them. They also worship snakes. The king has his own temple full of idols, dressed as well as possible in the Spanish style. He asks these idols for help in his wars. On the inland border of the Ardas live the Lucumis, a very faithful people, both in their wars and in serving the masters that capture them.[52] In this region also live people with no trade whatsoever, and further south is the Vini kingdom [Benin?].

The main city of the Popo kingdom is enclosed by walls and moats two leagues in circumference. The city gates are guarded so that no people can leave without registering what they are carrying. Along the roads, at every league, stands a guardhouse, where all goods must again be registered, so that it seems impossible for anything to be hidden, lost, or stolen. The houses in the city are made of clay and roofed in straw. Every night, men patrol the streets to make sure none of the roofs catch on fire and burn down the city. The palace is a city of its own, because it houses all of the important people. Although it is not built of stone, it has many corridors, doorways, and well-built wooden pillars, decorated in brass figures of men, animals, and birds that are so well made that one of our silversmiths could not do it so well. The streets are very large and populated with people who usually walk around nude. One must have a license to wear clothes, which all the married women have. The men usually wear blankets around their loins, and some wear cotton cloths down to their knees. Over these they wear a lighter cloth, from their chests to the floor, made of very soft cotton.

When they wake up in the morning, the first thing they do is brush their teeth with a twig. Then they wash the floor and walls of their houses with water mixed with clay, so that all is colored orange. Then the women arrange their hair, dampening it with oil that makes the hair very black and smooth like the hair of a Spanish woman, although in this case their hair extends down to the insteps of their feet. After doing this, the people of all of these nations then eject the devil from their house, because they detest the devil. But the way they do it is laughable. When they wake up, they begin to cook a kind of mush, boiling many different bird feathers in it. They also throw in some of their idols. After performing some rituals and songs, they carry the mush out into the street and throw the food on the ground, where many birds come to eat it. Then everyone goes back into the house feeling very satisfied, saying that the devil has been ejected from the house. They do this every day.

They also perform a ritual before going about their business, trying to predict if that day will go well or badly. If their luck does not go the way they want, they gird themselves in short swords of iron that cut as well as steel. More than thirty

---

52. See note 20.

thousand men gather in the plaza in front of the palace, shouting to the king to send them out to fight. When the king does not acknowledge them or cannot make war at that time, they ask to go to other kingdoms that are in a state of war. But if the omens look favorable, they leave their houses happily, visiting each other and showing each other great courtesies. The most common gesture is to take their sword out and move it three times near the face of someone they want to honor. The closer they bring the sword, the more respect they are showing. Women and others who do not carry swords do the same thing by extending their arms with a clenched fist mimicking the sword. They also make this gesture to the Portuguese and say, in their language: "God protect you, son of God." When they enter a house, they fall on their knees and raise their arms, extending their hands, to show how honored they are to see the person they are visiting. Others share their good fortune by riding horses to other people's houses. They have many small horses, and they ride in a half-sitting position, with one foot raised onto the horse's neck and the other hanging. They protect themselves with mats from the sun and rain, and they travel along playing music.

This is how they pass the morning until it is time to eat. When they come back home to eat, they again clean their teeth for a half hour with a special stick called *cuaquo*. Sometimes they hold this stick in their mouths to make themselves spit. But the more respectable blacks, whom they consider to be gentlemen, do not spit on the floor but instead use spittoons carried by their servants. These people go out only once or twice a year, but when they do, it is with a lively entourage, music, and celebrating.

The kingdom is governed by a cabinet of wise men. Each shows his office by the color of his clothes. Some wear white, others yellow, others blue or green. The judges lead the cabinet, listening to various debates and conflicts. The king's servants are not natives of the country but foreign Lucumis. They serve him well and also can be punished, if necessary, without fearing the revenge of their relatives. When the king does a favor for someone, however small it might be, the recipient covers himself in lime and proclaims the favor he has received in the streets. The king sends gifts to the Portuguese or to members of his court. The gifts are usually a large number of goats, hens, or cows, sent without any formality. On the other hand, sometimes they only send a quarter goat, a half chicken, or a bit of fruit, but they do it very formally, by placing it inside a special container and then putting that container inside another, wrapping it all in a colorful mat. The gift is then carried on the head of a well-dressed young male servant, accompanied by three venerable old men dressed in white and wearing large hats. By their sides are two nude boys, wearing strange brass jewelry on their feet and arms. These boys carry sticks and shout out, *lefina, lefina,* which means "let us pass, let us pass." Everyone moves aside until the procession passes. They do this even though the present is inconsequential, because it still comes from the mouth, table, or plate of the king. They so revere and honor the king that even when they are bringing water or wood to use in his kitchen, they carry it in a procession of two hundred people dressed in costly livery, accompanied by six well-dressed old men and many serving boys. Crowds separate when they pass, and people fall on their knees, even those that are on horseback. The noblest people show the king the most respect, obedience, and reverence, because they believe him to be immortal. It is illegal to say anything about the king dying, because he is like a ruling deity, although every man must die, including every king in the world.[53] The king rarely leaves his house and is only seen occasionally in the market, where the people are allowed to look at him. The markets are marvelous, full of many unusual, costly items presented in a well-ordered way. In conclusion, the king is so respected and his subjects are so at the mercy of his will that every week they tell him everything that has happened in the kingdom, including the details of all births and deaths. No matter how difficult his commands seem to be, they always carry them out.

At certain times of the year, the king honors the dead with festivals that last for three days, when they sacrifice sixteen thousand souls, men and women. They sacrifice them by opening up their stomachs and hanging them from trees to be eaten by vultures. They also sacrifice another 150 virgin girls of fourteen or fifteen years of age. They bring the girls to the sacrifice nude, adorned with long strings of glass beads and lightly covered by a white cloth. When they arrive at the sacrificial grounds, they cut off their hands and feet and throw their bodies into a vault covered by a slab, where the girls moan and cry until death. All are very happy to do this in service of the king. When the sacrifice is over, a great procession is made all over the kingdom. Crippled people have their own procession, as do invalids, the blind, the mute, and the deaf. All the disabled and sick people come together, and the king feeds them well. Nobody other than those who are taking part in the procession can leave their houses at this time, and they are only allowed to eat and drink in their houses, without doing any other activities. I will leave this now, because there are many other things to describe for other nations, and I do not want to tire the reader by repeating descriptions similar to things I have already described.

All have idols in their houses, in the form of dogs', goats', or other animals' heads. The Popos also worship live goats. The idols have teeth made of ivory. The people give them food whenever they eat, and they grease the idols with palm oil. They also worship the fish that live in a large river that flows through their city; they would not eat or kill this fish even if they were dying of hunger. They also worship vultures as gods, giving them food as if they were children

---

53. Sandoval wants to prove that the kings are overly revered in Africa; the Spanish monarchs were closely connected with defending Catholicism, but never had a godlike reputation or status.

and showing them great respect and fear. They worship the devil and give him sacrifices, throwing part of everything they eat on the floor. When they are in pain or sick, they invoke the names of JESUS and MARY, a custom they have undoubtedly taken from the Spanish.[54] They often respect and adore the cross as if they were Christians. They imitate us by having crosses in their houses and near the bodies of the dead. Once a lazy Portuguese was killing time by doing some pointless drawings, including one of a cross. He erased it when a black man entered the room. When the man asked what it was, the Portuguese said it was nothing. The black man responded, "Wasn't it a cross?" and the Portuguese said it was. The appalled black man replied: "Then the cross is nothing?"[55]

The island of São Tomé, called this because it was discovered on Saint Thomas's feast day, is eighteen leagues in circumference. It is populated by the Portuguese and their governor and bishop. Many of the clergymen are black. It is well known that these clerics surpass the Spanish clergy in the care they take in carrying out the ecclesiastical ceremonies and in their learning, wanting to make up for their color. This ends my account of the regions south of Sierra Leone where slaves are sold.

Chapter 15. Ethiopians in the Congo and Angolan kingdoms.

In contrast to West Africa, late sixteenth- and early seventeenth-century Central Africa had larger kingdoms, less diversity in language, and, under Portuguese influence, widespread exposure to Christianity. Sandoval wants to prove that the Central African kingdoms of Congo and Angola are examples of how successful Catholicism can be in Africa. These two kingdoms contrast with other African polities mentioned in the preceding chapters and with Loango, described briefly at the beginning of this chapter. In the 1620s Jesuit missions did go to Loango, but they experienced no success. In line with missionary strategies that concentrated conversion efforts on important leaders, Sandoval mainly describes Christianity in Central Africa from the top down. He focuses on the rulers, the luxuries enjoyed by the elite, and the Catholic Church infrastructure in the cities. To Sandoval, Congo and Angola prove that Africans can be good Christians, especially through Jesuit efforts. The potential for Christianization or, from Sandoval's perspective, moving toward the correct religion and civilization justifies the Jesuit mission to African slaves in Cartagena. What are the most notable aspects of European culture in Central Africa? How does Sandoval show that the Central African kingdoms are Christian? How did Pedro II want to strengthen Catholicism in his kingdom?

---

54. Presumably from missionaries who passed through the region.

55. Perhaps this anecdote criticizes Portuguese traders in this region of Africa.

South of the Cape of Lope González is a port called Moyambe [Mayumba], where instead of slaves a valuable red wood is traded. In this land it is called *tucula;* we call it sandalwood. Further south is a great kingdom called Loango, with an immense population and countless subject principalities. These people, their language, and their gentile rites and ceremonies are very different from the neighboring Congo and Angola. They are idolatrous, worshiping many different idols made of wood. One is not allowed to spit in front of the idols; the people become very angered when a Portuguese does this. Portuguese and Dutch live together in this kingdom's port and trade in ivory, cloth, parrot feathers, and elephant bristles. The bristles are used by black men and women to gird their heads and waists, and they are priceless in Angola.[56] This nation buries its dead with a large part of all their wealth, believing that they need their goods with them to navigate the road more securely and to be received in the afterworld by their idols and god.

To the south is a port called Cabinda, a freshwater stop for Spanish ships passing from São Tomé and other places. Further south is the Congo River, called Zaire by the blacks. It flows down from the Nile River to the sea, and it is one of the most powerful rivers in Africa, although the ancients knew nothing about it. It is ten leagues wide and so rapid that its freshwater extends twenty leagues into the sea. Often its currents carry islands with trees that seem like dry land. The Bamba and the Barbela rivers also flow from the Nile. Other important rivers in this region are the Loanza, which runs on the border between the kingdoms of Congo and Angola, and the Lunda, where crocodiles and hippopotamuses live, as well as a huge fish that can weigh five hundred pounds. The port of this river is called Pinda and is subject to the Congo king. One of his dukes lives there, called Manisono.[57]

The kingdom of Congo begins at the Cabo de las Vacas [near the city of Benguela], 13.5 degrees from the South Pole, and ends at Cape Catalina, at 2.5 degrees. It is about six hundred miles wide and is divided into six provinces: Pomba [Mpemba Kasi]; the heart and center of the kingdom, Bata [Mbata]; Pango; Sunde [Nsundi], furthest to the south; Songo, beginning at the mouth of the Zaire River; and finally Bamba [Mbamba], the noblest and most important province.[58]

---

56. The regions of Central Africa traded extensively with each other, including in cloth, described in detail below.

57. *Mani* is a title given to leaders in this region, although Sandoval misspells it a few lines down, using the word "Magnicongo" instead of Mani Congo.

58. The kingdom of Congo arose out of the expansion of the fourteenth-century Mpemba Kasi polity, located near Matadi (John Thornton, *The Kingdom of Kongo: Civil War and Transition, 1641–1718* [Madison: University of Wisconsin Press, 1983]). The Mani

The province of Bamba lies below Congo, 150 miles inland. The royal palace and court of this province are in a city called São Salvador [Mbanza Kongo, renamed in the 1500s], on the peak of a mountain. There are many great and noble men in this city. The king is given the title of Magnicongo [Mani Congo]. He is Christian, and a large part of his kingdom has also received the faith in the last 150 years. He is a friend to the Christians and does them many favors. The current king is called Pedro II.[59] He was previously the duke of Bamba. Even outside his kingdom, the world knows he is a wise Christian and Catholic king. He ordered all his subjects to immediately convert and receive Jesus Christ's law and faith, but everyone does not obey him, because they prefer to retain their numerous wives. Some have between 50 and 150 wives! The king venerates and reveres the Church. He encourages its growth and attends Mass every day in the presence of the Holy Sacrament. Although kings in this country are forbidden to remove their golden silk cap, he takes his off and holds it in his hands before his Lord and God. This shocks and amazes his subjects and makes them realize the grandeur and majesty of that great Lord and King of Kings. Because he is so pious, he tries to find out if all the priests in the kingdom live well and guard their chastity. If he learns that they are careless, the king insults them publicly, saying that priests who hold the Holy Sacrament in their hands must live virtuously and chastely. Along with this concern for the priesthood, his good judgment and prudence make him want to encourage the young by having the Company of Jesus open a seminary college in his kingdom. The sons of the titled lords are nurtured with this healthy, saintly milk of the Catholic doctrine so that they will grow to govern for the benefit of the kingdom.

The monarchs of Portugal always show the Congo kings great love. They write them letters, which are read in public so that everyone knows of the honor and esteem bestowed upon them by the Portuguese. Some of the noblemen are allowed to join the Order of Christ.[60] This friendship continues due to the excellence, grandeur, and Christianity of the current king, Pedro. His Holiness the pope also esteems the king: just in the last year, His Holiness sent his ambassadors with a small but precious box full of relics and

---

Congos of the sixteenth century sought to expand their Christian kingdom with the help of the Portuguese, creating this larger kingdom of Congo.

59. In a time of internal unrest and Dutch invasion, Pedro II ruled only from 1622 to 1624.

60. A very important Portuguese military/religious order, founded in 1319. By extending membership to the Congo nobility, the Portuguese recognized the legitimacy of Congo ideas of nobility, and the Christianity of the Congo elite.

indulgences. This gift was received with great veneration, solemn processions, and great festivals.

The king and the nobility dress in the Spanish manner, but they wear large capes made of fine cloth from London, or made of black velvet. These two fabrics are the best merchandise to bring to this kingdom. From the waist down, they wear rich silk and gold cloth made in their own kingdom. When the Spanish came there, the king received them seated on an ivory throne, wearing an intricately woven palm leaf bonnet in the manner of a diadem. He was nude to his waist, with a silk cloth covering his legs. On his right arm he had a golden bracelet, but his main jewelry took the form of a horse tail hanging from his shoulder, which only kings can wear. However, this style of dress is no more, because they have received the faith and Christian customs, so now the king and queen dress luxuriously in the Spanish style. The king adorns the palace with rich curtains and gifts from the Spanish of silk, silver, and gold. No black woman in the court covers her head nor even has any hair. It is considered most stylish to keep the head very clean. The important women wear velvet slippers on their feet. These women also pride themselves on knowing how to read and going to Mass every day. Many Portuguese live in this city, mainly married to white women. There is a cathedral with a bishop and clerics, like all other churches. Among them are many black men who are great Christians. Much of the clergy is this color, and they pride themselves on knowing how to play the organ.

The freshwater river Bengo passes by the island of Luanda, where many ships full of slaves leave Angola every year. The Portuguese live nearby on the navigable waters of this region, and from here more than fifteen thousand blacks leave annually for the Indies, including Brazil and other places.

The houses in this area are good, even though only the royal palace is built of wood. The land of Luanda is enriched by religious orders and churches that sustain the faith of Our Lord. Among them is a college run by the fathers of our Company of Jesus. The Portuguese value this college and realize how necessary it is, so they have provided it with a liberal endowment.[61] The college is located in the middle of the central plaza, in the best, most sumptuous and pleasing building in the city. The Jesuit fathers who work there show their customary charity, laboring in the Lord's vineyard, admired by the world, and gladdening heaven through the souls they convert. Besides the religious houses and the main church, there are other churches. One is called La Misericordia, and it has a large hospital that charitably takes in the sick and buries the poor. Another church is called San Anton. A church located on the beach is called San Telmo.

---

61. The Jesuit college was founded in 1607 to create an African priesthood, but it ended up catering to Portuguese residents.

This church serves as a hospital for the people who live near the sea. There is also an illustrious convent of the Franciscan Third Order.[62]

All of the land in Angola and Luanda is very sterile, and thus the people of these lands must import maize and millet from inland areas. They also import beans. The land is so dry because it sometimes does not rain for five or six years. They have a more abundant supply of goats and cattle. This kingdom also has minerals, including silver and copper, as well as red and brown sandalwood, the best possible kind, said to have marvelous medicinal value.

The Angolans currently wear clothing in our style, made from linen brought from eastern India. Women wear skirts in this style, with a huge number of pleats so that each skirt requires more than fifty *varas* of cloth, in the Flemish manner. In the past, and sometimes even now, this style of dress was not possible in inland areas, and they only covered themselves with tree fronds. They eat the food we have already mentioned, eating off the floor, without any manners or cleanliness. They sleep on cane grills, without covering. Through their connections with the Spanish, they now have cats and dogs, which make them very happy. They have naturally happy hearts and play little guitars called *banzas,* played by placing the head of the guitar on the breast in a very delicate and graceful way.

The Angolan king is very powerful and has numerous subject kings, who have enough armies to put fifty thousand archers on the field.[63] These archers are so skilled that they can let fly twenty arrows, one after the other, before the first one hits the ground. All of these people are very docile. It seems that we could easily teach them to become Christian because they do not worship idols. They believe in a god in the sky called Zambiampungo.[64] All speak the same language, with some variation. The Mogiolos live in a land called Ocanga, north of Zaire. The Mogiolos are detested by everyone, but they are not as hated as the Iagas [Jaggas], a terribly cruel cannibalistic people, greatly feared as warriors.[65] Fifty Jaggas can fight like five hundred men from any other nation.

---

62. The city of Luanda had several churches and Catholic charitable hospitals, not unlike other capital cities throughout the Iberian empires of the time. The ruins of some of these buildings can be found in Luanda today.

63. The Congo and Angola kingdoms were militarizing at this time, leading to a long period of conflict in Central Africa.

64. Or Nzambi a Mpungu, "the high god and creator of the universe." See John Thornton, "Religious and Ceremonial Life in the Kongo and Mbundu Areas," in *Central Africans and Cultural Transformations in the American Diaspora,* ed. Linda M. Heywood (Cambridge: Cambridge University Press, 2002), 75–76. Sandoval would view the belief in an otherworldly creator god as a very good sign that Africans could become good Christians.

65. Jaggas, or Imbangalas, were Kimbundu-speaking raiders from slightly inland who greatly disrupted life in Central Africa, resulting in more slaves brought to the Americas

They have very few women, because they kill anyone who cannot fight in war. They have no king and no laws but fight amongst themselves in a territory of three hundred square leagues. South of Angola is Cape Negro, near a rugged, barren chain of mountains. From here, one navigates in search of the Cape of Good Hope.

Chapter 16. A description of the black castes and nations from the Cape Verde Islands to Angola; the most common slaves in the Americas, and how to recognize them.

While much of Book 1 discusses African cultures in Africa, this chapter relates more directly to Sandoval's mission to African slaves in Cartagena. When they arrived in Cartagena, African slaves did not lose their connection to complex social, cultural, and linguistic networks; many carried permanent bodily markings that reaffirmed their African identity.[66] African cicatrization denotes an individual's membership in a very specific ethnic group or lineage. Bodily markings might also be made in initiation rituals and denote membership in military or religious societies in Africa. Sandoval observes that even if slaves in Cartagena do not know each other, they form bonds based on similar bodily markings.

Sandoval recognizes and clearly illustrates the dizzying diversity of African cultures and societies, but his goal in this chapter is to promote the Christianization of Africans. He seems caught up in appraising their value as slaves here. Sandoval describes body tattoos and scarification because he wants to help other Jesuits in Cartagena teach African slaves about Christianity. Sandoval recommends that they use these visual clues to determine which languages the slaves understand and then seek out interpreters who speak the same languages. What opinions does he express about the cicatrices? How does the description of skin, hair, teeth, and bodily markings further promote dehumanizing Africans and thinking of them as purely physical commodities?

There are four principal ports of origin for the black slaves who come to the port of Cartagena de Indias, which is the primary destination for slaves in the entire world. Slaves come here from the Guinean rivers and ports of the mainland, the island of Cape Verde, São Tomé Island, and the port of Luanda or Angola as well as from some other unknown lands in both western and eastern

---

from this region (Joseph C. Miller, "Central Africa During the Era of the Slave Trade, c. 1490s–1850s," in Heywood, *Central Africans*, 46–47). Other European observers also mentioned cannibalism among the Imbangalas (Thornton, "Religious and Ceremonial Life," 82).

66. In the eighteenth-century United States, Africans were still identified by their "country marks" in advertisements for runaway slaves. See Gomez, *Exchanging Our Country Marks*.

Ethiopia. From the latter region, I have seen many who are as dark as Guineans but with less kinky hair. We call all the people who come from these nations black, but not all are dark; instead there is great variation among them. Some are darker, others are lighter. It is said that some are the color of a cooked quince. Others are *zambos* or *loros* of light coloring, half mulatto with tan skin.[67]

Rivers of Guinea

As we have already observed, the blacks from Guinean rivers and ports are judged to be excellent slaves. They are much more faithful than the others. They are intelligent and talented, and they have a more attractive appearance. They are healthy and work hard, so they are valued more than any other slaves. To describe all the different groups that live on the coast would be an unending task, but I must mention those that are very pertinent to our goals. These are the Wolofs, Berbers, Mandingas, and Fulos. Other groups are Fulopos, Banhuns, Bootes, Cazangas, Brans, Balantas, Biafaras, Nalus, Zapes, Cocolis, and Zozos.[68]

The Wolofs, Berbers, Mandingas, and Fulos usually are able to understand each other because they have frequent communication, although they have distinct languages and castes. All these nations belong to the cursed sect of Mohammed [Islam]. This must cause great confusion among the Christians. For this reason, we often have difficulty converting them, so we catechize them using only the most articulate translators. We question them very carefully and listen attentively to their replies. Among these four groups, the Mandingas are the most numerous. They are spread out among many kingdoms and know many different languages. The best way to recognize them is by their unpierced ears. They are prouder than the Angolans and Congos, who also do not pierce their ears. Fulos are distinguished by their light skin coloring, although many are very dark-skinned.

It would seem from their names that many of these nations are related to each other. However, this is deceptive and wastes time when we are trying to catechize them, because they are in fact very different. For example: Banhun is a very different caste from Banhun Boote or Boyocho, but when asked their caste, both will say Banhun. If we try to catechize the Banhun with the Banhun Boote, one of the two will not understand what is being said, unless we find a

---

67. *Zambo* is a word used to describe a person of African descent in Latin America, usually with possible indigenous or European heritage, depending on the region where the word is being used. The word *loro* means parrot, but Sandoval uses the term here to describe people of diverse racial heritage.

68. See Chapter I for more information on the ethnicities mentioned here.

Boote interpreter. Bootes call themselves Banhun, and their kingdom is in between the those of the Fulopos and Banhuns, so they understand the Fulopos and sometimes the Banhuns. The Banhuns can understand the Cazangas, because the Cazangas rule over the Banhuns. They also speak Bran and Mandinga. To pick out Banhuns, look for two or three lines of tattoos the thickness of a small, pointed garbanzo bean. These tattoos run symmetrically down their entire face, circling under their temples with a certain grace and beauty. Others have rows of six round markings on both sides of their temples, perfectly symmetrical and graceful. Others have the same tattoos all over their bodies, beautifully and laboriously symmetrical.

Branes

When we ask the Brans their caste, they specify one of the following: Cacheu, Baserral, Bojola, Papel, or Pesis. All of these are Bran. Each language is somewhat different but not as different as the names might seem to indicate, so we can catechize all of them together. Brans understand many languages, including Banhun, Fulopo, Balanta, Mandinga, and Biafara. Many Brans have markings similar to those of the Banhuns, while others differ in that their tattoos are closer together, smaller, and darker.

Balantas

Many castes fit under the name "Balantas." Some do not understand each other's speech, because they come from distant lands and do not communicate amongst themselves. Many others understand different languages well enough to understand the catechism. Sometimes Balantas speak Bran and Mandinga. Most Balantas have three markings, one on each of their temples and another above the nose, between the eyebrows. Others have only two markings. Some have a pattern of half moons all over their chests, while others have no markings at all.

Biafaras

All the Biafaras usually speak one fairly elegant language, although their kingdom is very large and diverse. They are divided into Ubisgues, Gulubalies, Guolies, Guinalas, and Bugubas. Commonly, Nalus and Biafaras understand each other. Because we see them nude, like all the other slaves, we have noted that some have a tattoo of a circle around their navels.

Nalus

Nalus have two deep lines above their noses running across the entire face, similar to a marking seen on Zapes Cocolies. These Nalus can understand Biafaras.

Biojoes or Bijogoes

Although the Biojoes or Bigogoes [Bijogoes] come from many different lands, they speak only two distinct languages. One caste is just called Biojoes, and the other is called Biojoes Vizcainos. They are very dark and slender, and they have good features. After they cut their hair, they style it very attractively.

Zape

The Zape caste includes a large number of languages and nations. In order to catechize them, one must distinguish between pure Zape, Zape Cocoli, Zape Yalonga or Zozo, Zape Baga, and an infinite number of other castes all called Zape. They do not generally understand each other's languages, so you must look for interpreters to help them understand baptism and confession. The Zapes have many colorful and attractive markings. For example, I saw a man with two blues lines along the length of his face. From his temples to his cheeks, he had five long lines covering most of his face. Under his eyes, on his cheeks, he had three more thin blue lines. On his throat he had three broad lines, like a necklace, that ended on each side in four heavy lines. On his right side he had four lines extending down his entire torso. On his chest he had two castles painted in blue. His thighs and the rest of his body were covered in various other signs.

Zapes and all the other castes we have discussed shape their teeth. They do it for beauty and not for cleanliness, although it prevents food from sticking between their teeth. When they are sold amongst themselves, they value slaves less if their teeth are not carved. They will not go out in public or interact with people without decorated teeth.

Cape Verde Islands

All the castes that we have already discussed, especially those who originate in the Guinean rivers, come to Cartagena in great numbers every year. They are not born in Cape Verde, but many are sold on this island. From Cape Verde they go to Cartagena, and from Cartagena they are sold in Peru. Three kinds of slaves come to Cape Verde: one, *bozales* like those brought from Cacheu; two, *ladinos* who speak Portuguese and are called *criollos,* not because they were born in Cape Verde but because they were raised there from infancy and were originally *bozales* from the Guinean rivers. These two types of slaves must be thoroughly examined to see if they have been baptized. The third group are called *naturales* [natives], because they were born and raised on the Cape Verde Islands. They were baptized as children, similar to those blacks we call *criollos*[69] here in Cartagena

---

69. The word *criollo* comes from the verb *criar,* "to nurse or breed," and here means born in the Americas.

because they were born and raised in our country. In both cases, they were baptized as infants so we do not need to examine them.

Some ships laden with slaves leave directly from São Tomé Island's port. We say these slaves come *from* São Tomé, although they are really from mainland ports and kingdoms where the Spanish go to capture slaves. The São Tomé slaves are of lower quality and are worth less than those who come from the Guinean rivers. They are more valued than Angolans and Congos because they work harder, resist disease better, are brave, and are less likely to run away.[70] The castes usually brought from these parts are Minas, Popos, Fulos, Ardas, Axaraes, Offoons, Mosaicos, Agares, Gueres, Zarabas, Iabus, and Caravalis. This last group is very large and divides further into groups (Ambo Caravali, Abalomo, Bila, Cubai, Coco, Cola, Dembe, Done, Evo, Ibo, Ido, Mana, Moco, Oquema, Ormapri, Quereca, Tebo, Teguo) who do not understand each other's languages. Their languages sound as different as their names. The *criollos,* or natives, of São Tomé have developed a kind of lingua franca in order to communicate with people from barbarous nations who pass through São Tomé. Almost everyone speaks a corrupt and complicated version of Portuguese called the language of São Tomé. This is similar to the corrupt form of Spanish we use to communicate with the blacks that come here from so many different nations. Sometimes pure Caravalis, Ardas, and Lucumis understand each other, even though sometimes there is no understanding among the Lucumis themselves because they come from different Lucumi lands.

We can recognize people from these different nations by the markings on their faces and bodies. The Popos have a bow and arrow on both sides of their temples, with the arrows extending from their eyes toward their ears. The Ardas have a variety of markings. Most are marked with a different color on both temples than on the rest of the face. They also have similar marks between their eyebrows, and the entire face is covered in lines of no set pattern. Others are strangely beautiful, with three or four deep lines on their faces and a few lines under their eyes. Some have some long, broad, deep lines encircling their entire face on both sides: three, four, and five on each side, coming together at the mouth. These markings look brutal and shocking when one is not used to them. Many people do not want to buy black slaves with these markings because they are frightening, and this means they are sold at a lower price. Besides these lines encircling their faces, they have two more on their foreheads.

---

70. Linda A. Newson and Susie Minchin argue that port of embarkation and general conditions in Africa, including nutrition prior to enslavement, have a strong correlation with slave mortality onboard the slave ships and upon disembarkation. See "Slave Mortality and African Origins: A View from Cartagena, Colombia, in the Early Seventeenth Century," *Slavery and Abolition* 25, no. 3 (December 2004): 18–43.

On each cheek they have a round blue mark. Others have six raised scars in the middle of their foreheads, made with graceful symmetry. They have another twelve marks in a line from their eyes to their ears. These people also have markings on half their shoulders and arms: from a distance, it looks like they are wearing a doublet. Their bodies are also painted down to their waist. Others have six lines from their neck to their waist, drawn in perfect symmetry and proportion. Other tattoos look like ancient or Chinese writing. This nation also paints their bodies with tattoos and lines that are very similar to those used by the Zapes and Zozos, but I cannot describe all of them because I do not know how to organize or group them in any kind of order. Some have no lines or markings on their faces but instead mark their bodies or style their hair in a thousand different interesting hairdos. These markings are beautiful, but they have more meaning than just vanity: they must be loyal to others with the same markings. The Lucumis' markings are very similar to those of the Ardas. Some have three long deep lines: one encircling the length of the forehead to the nose and two on the temples. Some have another six lines on each side of the face, three that meet at the mouth and another three that arc from the brows to the nose. Lucumis Barbas have no markings but pierce their left nostril. Lucumis Chabas paint their entire bodies, and in the middle of their foreheads they paint an oval with two squares on either side of it. From the corner of their mouths, two lines extend to their ears. On each side of their heads are six lines, three that cross their neck to their ears and three more crossing their cheeks to each temple. The Caravalis also have very distinct markings, but I cannot describe all of them here because there are so many different Caravali nations, languages, and castes.

Often some blacks from the kingdoms and nations of eastern Ethiopia, such as Mozambique and Malindi, travel in the boats that leave from São Tomé. Slaves also come from India, including from Ceylon and Parava. The Mozambicans have three markings like spines on their temples and foreheads. Others have one on the forehead and three on each temple.

Luanda and Angola

Angolas, Congos, and Monicogos often come to Cartagena. Occasionally we encounter a few Angicos, Monxiolos, and Malembas from Luanda. All of these people generally understand Angolan. These blacks are valued less because they are useless and good for almost nothing. They are most vulnerable and least resistant to diseases. They have cowardly hearts and die very easily. It is easy to recognize these nations because the men have a very different hairstyle from all the other slaves; they grow their hair on the backs of their heads like a wreath. The women also style their hair distinctly. All have pierced ears, which they do in a unique way. If they only pierce one ear, it is usually the left ear. All are marked from childhood with scars on their temples, although they do not have as many as the Ardas. The Angicos have a raised painted sign between their brows. Others have five colorful lines on their temples and brows that make their faces appear very gentle. All have sharpened and separated teeth. The Malembas have two teeth missing in the back, and the front ones are slanted. They paint their cheeks in order to beautify their faces.

This ends my summary of the different markings for each caste and nation. Some nations are distinguished by the fact that they have no markings. One must understand their markings in order to be able to determine what groups they come from, because there is no other way to divide them into language groups for baptism or confession. When I first began my work, I did not use this method. I worked with them in a large, confused group because I could not figure out what nation they came from. This meant that the sick were in danger of dying without the benefit of the holy sacraments. Knowing their markings makes it easier to find suitable interpreters in order to teach and help them.

Chapter 17. General points relating to slavery among the Guinean blacks and at other ports.

This chapter begins one of the most debated sections of De instauranda. *Sandoval voices his opinions on the institution of slavery, discussing it in a complicated and self-contradictory fashion. Here, Sandoval's main concern is how Africans become slaves, because the Catholic Church and Spanish law set down rules for legitimate enslavement—most commonly, that it was legal to enslave prisoners of war, who could later buy their freedom. This kind of slavery was common on both sides in the medieval Iberian wars between Christians and Muslims. Paying a ransom to free a prisoner of war was viewed as a charitable act and guaranteed that medieval slavery was at least theoretically only a temporary condition.*

However, if individuals have been enslaved illegally, Europeans should not worry about it, according to Sandoval. It has nothing to do with their acts or consciences. Instead, he argues that African leaders are to blame when their subjects are unfairly, according to Christian law, enslaved. Sandoval and his sources agree that slavery is "justified" if slaves become Christians, and it is better to be a Christian slave in a Christian country than to be subject to the whims and superstitions of an African king. Therefore, Sandoval shows a Eurocentric disdain for African leaders: he does not view them as legitimate, so their subjects do not have to be treated with the same care given to Europeans. On the other hand, Sandoval does refer to laws and customs in Africa that might have different regulations for enslavement, implicitly recognizing that different types of legal slavery did exist in Africa.

Sandoval is also concerned with explaining why slave traders, Jesuits, and anyone else involved in slavery should not feel guilty about participating in it, nor should they feel that they are committing sins by harming other human beings and ignoring basic Christian concepts of charity and love. How does Father Brandão's letter help Sandoval's readers not feel guilty about slavery? What different conditions lead to enslavement in Africa, according to Sandoval? What kinds of discussions does Sandoval have with slave traders?

In order to get his book published and not have it banned by the Spanish Inquisition, Sandoval does not reject the institution of slavery or call for abolition. By focusing on the slave trade, he draws attention away from the use of slaves in the Americas and the institution as a whole. Instead, he takes a paternalistic, reforming approach. To Sandoval, slavery is allowable if slave traders and masters abide by certain rules. The crucial rule is that slaves must become good Christians, and everyone who deals with slaves in any way, from traders to masters to parish priests, must take responsibility for this.

The debate among scholars on how to justify the arduous and difficult business of slavery has perplexed me for a long time. I could have given up on explaining it and just ignored it in this book. However, I am determined to discuss it, although I will leave the final justification of slavery to legal and ecclesiastical authorities, especially the Jesuit Luis de Molina.[71] I will only mention here what I have learned after many years of working in this ministry. The readers can formulate their own ideas on the justice of this issue.

We have just said that black slaves usually come here from the ports of Cacheu, Guinea, the Cape Verde Islands, São Tomé Island, and Luanda in Angola. In reference to the slaves that come from Cape Verde Island, we should not worry about enslaving these blacks, because this island is not an Ethiopian land. Cape Verde is the main slave-trading port where slaves come from other parts of Africa. When the slaves arrive here, they have already been bought and sold three or four times. We should also not worry about the justice of buying and selling these slaves in our ports. In order to further discuss the issue of the morality of slavery, we will now discuss the port of São Tomé.

A short story helps me explain how to morally justify black slavery. I was once consulted by a captain who owned slave ships that had made many voyages to these places. He had enriched himself through the slave trade, and his conscience was burdened with concern over how these slaves had fallen into his hands. His concern is not surprising, because he also told me that one of their kings imprisoned anyone who angered the king in order to sell them as slaves to the Spaniards. So in this region, people are enslaved if they anger the king.[72]

---

71. Luis de Molina (1535–1600), an influential Jesuit theologian, argued that all human beings had free will and could be enslaved in war.

72. In other words, the slaves were not enslaved in a war, meaning that their enslavement was not done according to Christian law and that the African leaders were tyrants.

With regard to the blacks that come from Angola and so on, I have more information. These slaves might also be enslaved unjustly. I received a letter dated August 21, 1611, from Father Luis Brandão, rector of the college of our Company founded in San Pablo de Luanda. The letter says:

> I received a letter from Your Reverence dated March 12, 1610. I felt great consolation in learning about the work Your Reverence does to help these souls go to heaven. Your Reverence does a great service to God. You will be rewarded for working so hard and taking so much trouble with the black people. I speak from experience, because here in this college we also work a great deal with *ladino* blacks, although Christ deserves much more effort than we give to this cause. Your Reverence wrote to me to find out if the blacks who come through Luanda to go on to Cartagena are justly enslaved. I do not believe that Your Reverence should worry about this. In Lisbon, wise men of good conscience do not find slavery reprehensible.[73] The bishops in São Tomé, in Cape Verde, and here in Luanda, wise and virtuous men, never argue against slavery. Jesuit fathers have been here for forty years, and there have always been learned Jesuit fathers in Brazil. None of us has ever considered this trade illicit. We and the Brazilian fathers buy slaves to serve us without feeling any guilt.[74] When someone in Cartagena buys slaves, he buys them from a merchant in good faith, so he should feel no concern whatsoever. Here we should worry more, because we buy blacks from other blacks and from people who might have stolen them. But the merchants who take them from here do not know this, so they can buy them here and sell them there in good conscience. However, I know from experience that no black slave ever says that he deserved to be enslaved. Thus Your Reverence should not ask them how they were taken into captivity, because they will always say they were stolen or taken illegally, hoping that this will help them get their freedom. I would also argue that in some of the slave markets, some of the slaves for sale were stolen or their leaders commanded them to be sold for trivial reasons, so they do not deserve to be in captivity. But there are not many of these cases. Among the ten or twelve thousand blacks that leave from this port every year, it is impossible to find more than a few who were unjustly enslaved. Because so many souls are saved through enslavement, we serve God better if we save all those who were captured legitimately instead of not saving any of them for the sake of a few that were enslaved unjustly. The blacks are enslaved for many different reasons that abide by their laws and customs. Most of these reasons sufficiently justify their captivity. I cannot tell Your Reverence any more than this, because this is a very broad issue.

---

73. The writer might be referring to jurists, philosophers, and religious and secular leaders.

74. During Sandoval's lifetime Jesuits were increasing their use of slaves on sugar estates in Brazil. Especially in the 1700s, Jesuits ran large plantations worked by hundreds of slaves. However, it is not correct to argue, as have some scholars, that the purpose of *De instauranda* was to explain why it was morally correct for Jesuits to own numerous slaves.

Nor can I tell you about their rites and customs, because I do not have the time or health to do it.

Once, the captains of two slave ships coming from Angola consulted me on this issue, wanting me to help them understand if the slave trade was moral. They disagreed and wanted me to reassure them, so I listened and tried to help. One said: "Father, I go to Angola to buy blacks. This is a dangerous and expensive voyage. When I leave, after having spent a great deal on the slaves, I feel guilty. I ask myself, am I satisfied with how slavery is justified? The journey is very dangerous and costs a great deal in terms of time and labor. What if I bring them to live the rest of their lives in Christian lands, but they never become Christian?" I said to him, "Your trade is not immoral, and you will not be punished, because you say you bring the blacks here in good faith and for a good reason."

On another occasion a captain of a slave ship came to me very distressed because his fleet, carrying black slaves from Angola, was shipwrecked in a bay called Negrillos, not far from Cartagena. Only thirty out of nine hundred slaves survived. This story caused me great pain. The number of enslaved Angolans in the ships shocked me. I was also shocked by the reasons for why there were so many slaves in these ships. The rector Father Luis Brandão (whose letter we just quoted) had preached a sermon saying that some of the slaves were unjustly captured, so many of them had been set free. The captain of the ship explained why they had been captured, and his reasons were different from what the father preached. The captain said that two powerful kings were at war with each other. One sent his ambassador to us to enlist our help in bringing a great number of blacks as a gift. Although the gift of slaves included many good soldiers, the other king did not hide but took advantage of the gift. Then they both began a cruel war. The king who won was the one who had many slaves, as well as many captives from the losing side. All of these people were sold into slavery, which led to the huge number of slaves that came to Cartagena at this time.

There is a more standard way in which slaves are traded and later shipped in fleets of ships to the Indies. Near Luanda are some black merchants called *pumberos* [*pombeiros*] worth a thousand pesos.[75] They travel inland eighty leagues, bringing porters with them who carry trade goods. They meet in great markets where merchants called *genses* gather together to sell slaves. The *genses* travel two or three hundred leagues to sell blacks from many different kingdoms to various merchants or *pumberos*. The *pumberos* buy the slaves and transport

---

75. Joseph Miller describes *pombeiros* as "itinerant peddlers ... [who] took modest quantities of [European] goods on consignment and hawked those goods on a cash basis in surrounding villages and local markets (or *pumbos*) for whatever slaves they might buy" (*Way of Death: Merchant Capitalism and the Angolan Slave Trade, 1730–1830* [Madison: University of Wisconsin Press, 1988], 189).

them to the coast. They must report to their masters how many died on the road. They do this by bringing back the hands of the dead, a stinking, horrific sight.

It is likely that many of the slaves that come from the Guinean rivers, especially Cacheu, a major slave-trading port, are enslaved illegally. When a merchant or ship owner comes to this port, they sell merchants their goods, normally printed cloth from India used for cloaks. They also sell wine, iron, and garlic to the Portuguese who live there, who are called *tangomaos;* in exchange for blacks. They also have agents, called carriers, whose job is to go inland with these goods to find blacks to exchange for the goods. This is how black slaves end up in Cacheu. In the Berber and Wolof ports, they sell prisoners of war or criminals. They fight wars over rumors and theft. The criminals who are sold into slavery have usually committed adultery, homicide, and theft. When someone commits these crimes, they bring together all the old men of the republic in the middle of the plaza. The criminal appears there, and they vote on the punishment, which could be death or, more commonly, captivity. The slaves remain at home working for the king or end up being sold on the coasts.

Many blacks are sold in the Bijogoes' port. The Bijogoes perform a ritual where they sacrifice animals, especially cows and sheep. After a bloody sacrifice, their military captains must fight with and capture whomever he encounters, even his relatives, friends, neighbors, and acquaintances. They transport these slaves, along with their captain and navigator, all rowing furiously, on huge canoes that can carry up to fifty blacks, who are forced into being warriors. In this way they quickly pass through the inland rivers and streams until they find blacks to ambush. Sometimes they hear Biafaras dancing and ambush them. This has led to the destruction of Biafara kingdoms. They approach the festivities at night and wait until just before dawn, when the revelers are sleeping, tired from dancing. Then they capture them, tie them up, and take them to their lands. Usually they sell the captives to Portuguese boats, after making a sacrifice to their gods of some of the hair from the captives' beards or heads. The weapons these pirates use in their pillaging are spears with iron tips, iron javelins, and swords in the shape of a sickle. They carry the weapons with a shield on their left arms. They also carry thick rope, used to tie up five of the slaves they capture but still leave their right hand free to fight. Because the men want to be efficient warriors and not waste time doing anything else, they make their women build their houses, cultivate their lands, and plant and harvest their rice and millet.

I have spent a great deal of time discussing this subject because slaves are captured in many different ways, and this disturbs the slave traders' consciences. One slave trader freely told me that he felt guilty about how the slaves he had bought in Guinea had come to be enslaved. Another slave trader, who had bought three hundred slaves on foot, expressed the same concerns, adding that half the wars fought between blacks would not take place if the Spanish did not go there to buy slaves. Another time a slave trader asked me to meet with him because he was ill and needed to clear his conscience. I asked him what he felt about how slaves were captured and put into slavery in Guinea. Before he responded, he thanked God that he had only dealt in a few slaves, and he understood that these had been enslaved fairly. But he did feel bad about what he had seen on some other ships. He had seen some ships take away free people as captives. Other times he saw a captain buy blacks cheaply and secretly at midnight. Another slave trader came to me showing great pride in himself. He asked me if I would like to hear how he gathered together three hundred slaves in Guinea for his slave ship. I told him I would gladly hear this. He said that the king was told when he arrived in Guinea. The king decided how many male and female pieces[76] he needed. The king then told the slaver to return in so many moons and he would be provided with all the slaves he wanted. The slaver left and came back with the predetermined payment at the assigned time, and the king gave him the slaves. This slave trader also said that the king customarily has many women and commits adultery with whomever he captures. The king also allows women to have as many men as they want for a specific period of time. Afterward, he investigates which men have been with the women. Then the king collects on all these men's debts and their relatives' debts. After this, he punishes and captures the men, and this is how these men are sold into slavery. I was very surprised at this story and even more surprised at how proud the slave trader was to tell the story.

A clergyman once went to Guinea in a fleet of slave ships. He went to investigate what he had heard about unjust wars in Guinea, the kings' power there, and black captivity. After he did his research, he said that there are no free blacks in Guinea, because all are slaves of the king. Here in the Americas a lord might own cattle and pigs in order to earn money on his farm. In Guinea the kings make a profit off of black slaves. With absolute power and dominion over them, they sell the slaves to anyone who wants to buy them. Thus there are no free blacks in Guinea—all are slaves.

I laughed heartily at this fantastic story, and I believed it deserved my laughter. But afterward, a document came into my hands that I will describe briefly, because it proves our point. This notarized document came from a court case here in Cartagena against a black man who came from Guinea and was trying to prove he was legally free. Although it could be proved that he was legally a slave, he could not prove his freedom. The case included a document that said that the king of Casamansa, as absolute lord of the Banhuns, commanded that this black man be sold into slavery as punishment for committing certain

---

76. *Pieza de indias* was a term meaning one healthy male slave or more than one weaker, older man or woman.

crimes. All Guinean kingdoms have the custom that when a black man commits a crime in his kingdom or another kingdom, even if he is a free man or a nobleman, the king can condemn him to perpetual servitude and slavery. All his relatives can also be punished by enslavement. This is not justice but absolute power. The king has the inviolable right to capture, buy, and sell as many slaves as he wants, even if the captured individuals are noblemen. Because the king commands it, all the slaves sold in his lands are legally enslaved and they remain slaves to those who buy them. They may never demand their liberty because no black are free if they are subjects of the king. Although this is completely unjust, this is what the witnesses said in this case. This evidence, along with the moral justifications argued by scholars, is the best we can do to carefully address this irredeemable situation and the very difficult business of the slave trade.

Chapter 18. The slave ships.

This chapter is well known by historians for its descriptions of the terrible conditions on the slave ships, where significant percentages of African slaves died in the horrific Middle Passage. What is the source for Sandoval's information about the slave ships? Perhaps worse than the description of the ship is Sandoval's description of life upon arrival, where the slaves are often very sick but are still neglected and left to die miserable deaths.[77] He takes this opportunity to promote his own work with the slaves, when they are confined on land, waiting to be sold and transported south. The Jesuits especially valued the charitable act of providing a person with a good burial; here, Sandoval provides harsh details of the horrible neglect that their bodies suffer after dying because their masters do not pay to bury their slaves. How does Sandoval use his understanding of Christian doctrine to introduce his descriptions of the worst aspects of the slave trade? How does he intertwine arguments for his mission with descriptions of the terrible conditions of the slave ships and barracks in Cartagena?

We all know that when He created the world, God Our Lord did not populate the earth with masters and slaves, although clearly the Guinean kings mentioned above do not believe this. We also know that it was not until time passed and people became malicious that they began to tyrannize over the liberty of others. Solomon said that the poor man and the king, the monarch and the shepherd, were born with the same fate and under the same laws. In nature's forge, the prince and the plebian are crafted in the same way, and gentlemen are

---

77. According to Newsom and Minchin's data from 1626 to 1633, slaves waiting to be sold in Cartagena died at a rate of up to 0.71 per 1000 individuals per day. For illegal slaves, captured as contraband by the Spanish authorities, slaves died at an average rate of 4.2 per 1000 per day. See "Slave Morality and African Origins," 32–33. Sandoval does not specify if he is speaking of legal or illegal slaves.

not born with more elegant clothes than peasants. Nobles do not have more eyes, feet, or arms than commoners. All of us live under the sky, the sun shines on us all, and we breathe the same air and endure the same elements. Both the king and the slave strive for liberty.

The Gospels of Mark and of Matthew say: Go all over the world, preach the Gospel to everyone regardless of lineage or condition, and make no distinctions among men. The Company of Jesus values a noble soul more than a noble body. We care more for a man's soul than for his status and fortune. God does not distinguish men in this way, nor should we so judge and measure them. True liberty comes from avoiding sin, and the greatest wealth comes from being virtuous. The redemption and blood of Christ, who bled for all of us, also equalizes us. A man's low condition and status do not prevent him from having value, nor does a grand lineage make him especially praiseworthy. Only faith matters, because slave and freeman are the same to Christ, and each one will receive a good or evil reward depending on what they have done in life. Servitude does not take this away, and liberty does not guarantee it, because both have the same importance to the Lord. There is no difference between the merits of a slave who serves well and those of a freedman who enjoys his liberty, because everyone should serve Christ. Servitude can be glorious, because God bought all of us equally with the blood of his holy son. All faithful workers, black or white, free or enslaved, have the same value. In order to complete the important discussion of the justification of black slavery, we must describe how the poor black people are brought here to be sold. The rest of this chapter will discuss this issue, because understanding their miserable bodily captivity will inspire us to work with all our strength for their spiritual liberty.

Only God knows if these blacks are enslaved justly, but after they have been captured, they are put in brutal prisons. They remain in chains until they arrive at the port of Cartagena or another port. The slave ships have shelves built into their holds in order to transport three, four, five, and even six hundred or more slaves or however many it takes to fill the ship. Normally twelve to fourteen ships with this many black slaves in each ship enter this port [Cartagena] alone every year. Small loads of slaves are called lots. They are transported together in lots from the port on the island of Luanda in Angola so that none can escape. Others come from the Guinean rivers, imprisoned in very long chains called *corrientes* or with other cruel inventions designed to keep them from escaping on land or sea. They are taken to various places on the coast. Shackled in chains, they endure misery and misfortune for two months. They receive only the most disgusting food and drink and thus become very sad and melancholy, believing they will be rendered into fat and eaten. One third [of the slaves] die during the voyage. I know individuals who have endured this journey. They say they are extremely cramped, nauseous, and mistreated. They are shackled at the neck along a chain of six-by-six slaves, or two-by-two, fettered at the ankle.

They are imprisoned in the ships, lying with one person's head at another person's feet. They are locked in the hold and closed off from the outside so that they cannot see the sun or moon. No Spaniard dares to put his head through the trapdoor to the hold without becoming ill. Even staying down there for an hour runs the risk of serious illness, so powerful is the stench, the cramped space, and the misery of it. The slaves look forward to eating once every twenty-four hours, although they get no more than a half cup of corn or crude millet and a small cup of water. Other than that, they get nothing else besides beating, whipping, and cursing. Many people I know have experienced this, although I once believed that some of the slavers treated them more gently and kindly these days.[78]

After all this fine treatment, they arrive here looking like skeletons. They are taken to land naked and sore and put into a large patio or corral. Countless people go there to see them, some because they are greedy, others to satisfy their curiosity. Some want to show the slaves some compassion. The fathers of the Company of Jesus make up the last group. They go to catechize, indoctrinate, baptize, and confess those slaves who are actually dying. They prepare them for extreme unction, and they find a way to bring them communion. Although they try to do their work as quickly and carefully as possible, they always find some slaves that have already died without receiving the holy sacraments. Others barely survive long enough to receive them. The Jesuits bring clothes in order to cover the slaves decently, because their nakedness is a very evil sight for chaste eyes. They also bring them some sweets or a gift in order to put our religion in a positive light.[79] For those who manage to stay healthy in this place, they do get some relief, because during this time they are fattened up in order to be sold at a higher price. Even though these poor people have already endured so much, they may become even sicker when they arrive here, but after their time on the ships, any kind of treatment seems pleasant to them. Because they are fed so little for so long, they quickly become ill, and these illnesses can spread to the entire ship as quickly as the plague. Their masters become impatient with this, because even the poorest master usually tries to cure the slaves' illnesses. Rich masters, who are very busy and occupied with their own affairs, usually leave their slaves in the care of cruel and ungodly caretakers who put the sick ones in the hospital. This means they will soon populate the cemetery of the dead. Some die from the cruel chafing their bodies endure on the ship.

---

78. Apparently, Sandoval did not understand conditions on slave ships until he had spoken to African slaves in Cartagena.

79. Daniel Reff argues that this kind of basic care might have actually helped improve the health of some of the targets of Jesuit proselytization, making the Jesuit message more appealing to them. See Reff, *Plagues, Priests, and Demons,* 75, 118.

Some die from severe fevers, others from smallpox, typhus, and measles. Others die of a disease called "incurable Luanda sickness," which makes their entire body swell up, putrefies their gums, and leads to sudden death.[80] They supposedly get this disease due to bad treatment on the island of Luanda.

One feels great pity and compassion for them, because they are so sick, so needy, and so neglected by their masters. Their masters usually leave them lying on the floor, naked and without a blanket or any other shelter or covering. They remain there to perish, with no one caring for their bodies or their souls. It is no surprise that one wonders if they die from their diseases or from being abandoned. I see this all the time, and it drives me to tears. In some cases, the slavers furnish large rooms with planks for beds. They divide the men from the women and enclose them in there to sleep for the night. The people who live in these rooms live there without hope. They are thrown in the room, where they cry out in their misery and misfortune until finally, eaten by flies, stacked on shelves one below the other, they die. I remember one occasion, among many similar occasions, when I saw two slaves already dead, naked on the floor, as if they were beasts, facing upward with their mouths open and full of flies. Their arms were crossed, which to me signified the cross of eternal damnation that their souls experienced because they died without the holy sacrament of baptism, because no one was called to administer it. I was shocked to see the dead treated so inhumanely, and even more shocked to see their burial shrouds. Normally, someone finds a worn-out mat and rolls the dead person up in it and then throws them in a corner. This treatment is slightly better than just leaving them to lie naked on the patios or in the corrals and corners. They are ignored and never moved again as soon as their illnesses become serious. I once found a corpse repulsively shoved behind the door of a house, and another thrown naked in the middle of a street, waiting to be buried. This shocked and scandalized everyone who happened to walk past. I could go on and on describing these incidents, but I only want to mention one more thing that I found truly shocking. A few days after I helped one of these poor people learn about the faith of the Lord, I went to help him die in this faith. When I arrived, I discovered that he had died in the middle of a patio where many people were living. He was naked, face down with his mouth open to the floor, covered in flies that seemed to want to eat him. There he was left as if he were less important than a dog. I begged and pleaded for someone to cover his body with proper Christian decency. This was done, but only by taking clothes from another poor person who was dying nearby. Leaving this sick

---

80. Weak gums are a sign of scurvy, a common disease suffered by those who did not get enough vitamin C on long sea journeys.

man uncovered, the dead one was covered with a small mat that happened to be on hand.

Here I end my description of the slave ships and how these poor blacks suffer. I hope this humble book will help them. I pray to God, full of good intentions and a desire to do well, that my words will interest readers, inspiring and motivating them to help these people, who are otherwise abandoned, to endure their suffering. When I am no longer able to work for their salvation, this book will live on. If it does not serve to continue to help them, I am the only one to blame.

[Chapters 19 through 30 go back to descriptions of African cultures and religions and discuss how Christianity has a presence in Africa, especially in the eastern regions of the continent. Sandoval's sources are ancient scholars, Marco Polo, and priests and friars writing closer to his era of history. He repeats the legend of Prester John and discusses how Christianity is practiced in Abyssinia (Ethiopia) and how it differs from Roman Catholicism. Sandoval also discusses the island of Malabar, in line with previous discussions that categorize people from all over the world as blacks.]

Chapter 31. Unique and miraculous things found in the Ethiopian kingdoms.

After the seriousness of Chapters 17 and 18, Sandoval sees Chapter 32 as a diversion, a catalogue of some of the unusual human beings, animals, and other strange natural phenomena thought to be found in Africa. These stories show that, for Europeans, Africa was essentially confusing, bizarre, and foreign. Jesuits in the Americas could also expect to be shocked by the strange people they encountered there. The chapter mainly uses information from Pliny's Natural History, *written in the first century C.E., as well as Jesuit reports. It is hard to say if Sandoval believed in the monsters he describes; he might just want to imitate a popular literary style to entertain his readers. The continuing interest in these legendary beasts shows how little was known about Africa and how tempting it was to populate a foreign land with fantastical creatures. Often the "monstrosity" of these creatures comes from their confusion in their gender roles or traits. How do the African men resemble women? Which of the animals described in this chapter resemble actual animals we know of today?*

We learn about history for two reasons: to discover the truth and because we enjoy it. All history must be told truthfully, but we can also be entertained by it, and I hope most of this book manages to achieve both of these elements. However, I believe this chapter is the most entertaining one in the book, because it is full of strange stories about unusual natural occurrences in Ethiopia. Every land has its unique qualities, but Ethiopia is perhaps the most unusual of all, because of not only the color of the men who live there but also the strange animals, birds, fish, monsters, plants, trees, and minerals found there. A Cistercian monk even said that some Ethiopians only have one eye, in the center of their forehead.

Men

This same Cistercian monk also described headless Ethiopians, who do have eyes and a mouth; however, these are located on their chests. Some Ethiopians have heads but without eyes—because their eyes are on their shoulders. Others have flat faces without noses and a huge lower lip that they pull over their faces when they sleep, to protect themselves from the harsh rays of the sun. Some only have one enormous foot that they hold over themselves as a sunshade when they are sleeping. They move very rapidly on their one foot. Other Ethiopians do not have a special foot to block out the sun, so they constantly curse the sun for beating down on them and burning them. Some hate the heat so much that they never light a fire. The people who have eyes on their shoulders also have a mouth on their chests, but it is such a tiny mouth that they have to use toothpicks to put their food in their mouth, and they have no tongue. They cannot speak, so they communicate through signs.

Near the Brisón River, south of Ethiopia and Egypt, some Ethiopians, more like beasts in human form, have thighs that are twelve feet long. Just as marvelous, or perhaps I should say, just as monstrous, are people that are sixteen feet tall and seven feet wide, with white bodies, large heads, and huge ears that almost seem like wings. Some Ethiopians have the horns and feet of goats. These people are called gorgons. None of this should shock anyone. We should also not be surprised that the black residents of the Maluku Islands have spurs on their ankles similar to those of fighting cocks, and that the natives of Batampina Island have tails. The men who live in Malabar have monstrously large feet and legs. Many authors tell other strange stories. For example, when the wife of a Cafre [Kaffir] called Pedro died, he fed their daughter at his breasts for a year until they dried up. Another Cafre who lived near the Buenas Senales or Quilimane River had breasts as large as a breast-feeding woman, although they had no milk. He claimed that this was normal for him and that his mother's father also had the same trait. This does not surprise me, because here in Cartagena de Indias, I have seen a black man of the Arda caste with large breasts, a monstrous thing. No one in this town had ever seen anything like this. So many people crowded to see him that he almost had to stop accepting visitors. Even stranger is something reported by the Jesuits who work in the Brazilian province. They say that some peculiar people live there. Among these people, the men, not the women, have large breasts full of milk that they use to suckle the infants. Women have very small breasts, and some have none at all.

Women

Aristotle talks of the Carthaginian captain Hanon, who landed on some islands near Ethiopia inhabited by women whose bodies were covered with fleece like sheep. They had very long hair and were cruel, valiant, and agile. In northern Ethiopia, near the Bermejo Sea, there are some frightening women, with beards down to their chests, who dress in animal skins. They ride horses and hunt tigers and leopards. Some women who live in the mountains have teeth like wild boars and hair down to their feet. They bind their loins with bull tails, are seven feet tall, and have bodies as hairy as camels. In Spain there is a woman from Peñaranda who speaks in a deep voice and has a thick beard down to her chest. The women who live near the kingdom of Damute are very manly and courageous. They always carry weapons to hunt wild forest animals. They are braver than warlike men, to say nothing of weak women. They burn their right breasts when they are young so that it dries out and does not grow, in order to use their right arms for shooting their bows and arrows. Their husbands are very weak and effeminate; we do not know if this is their nature or if it comes from a tradition of acting like women. It is said that these Amazon women live without men for most of the year. When they give birth to a boy, they nurse him for a while, and then send him to his father for his upbringing. Miraculously, their queen has never known a man, but everyone worships her like a goddess.

Animals

Pliny says that Ethiopia nurtures many monsters, like horses with wings and horns, called Pegasus.[81] Another animal is half-dog, half-wolf and can break off anything with its teeth and digest it in its gullet. *Cercofitecos* have black heads and donkey's pelts and make a very strange noise. Bulls there can have one leg or three. A wild, cruel animal, the *leocrocuta,* looks like a small mule but has deer's legs, a lion's mane and tail, a badger's head, long claws, a mouth that opens as far as its ears, and a large, solid bone instead of teeth. Its cries sound very human. There is also an animal called an *eael,* black and red in color and the size of a sea horse but with an elephant's tail, cheeks like a wild boar, and a long, flexible horn. They use these horns to play with one another, moving them backward and forward. This land also has savage, cruel bulls that run very fast and have red skin, dark green eyes, huge mouths open to their ears, and movable horns. The hide around their shoulders is as hard as flint. Another animal called a *maticora* has the face and ears of a man and blue eyes, but with

---

81. Sandoval uses the term "Pegasus" as if it referred to a species of animal, rather than to one mythical creature.

three rows of teeth all lined up in its mouth, red skin, a lion's body, and a sharp tail like a scorpion. Its voice sounds like a combination of a flute and a trumpet. It is very agile and loves to eat human flesh.

Pliny also tells of a beast called a *catotoblepa* that lives at a spring called Nigris, at the head of the Nile River. It is a small, lazy animal with a large, heavy head, so it is always looking down. But any human who looks it in the eyes dies instantly. It is like a ferocious bull with long ears, blood-red eyes, and a mane like a horse. The mane covers its face, making it look very fierce. It eats poisonous plants so that when it opens its mouth, it lets out a horrible, putrid breath that makes other animals and birds lose their voices and fall to the ground without moving. It also said that in Ethiopia some dragons have rubies and topazes inside their heads.

Fish

In the lands of the great Manomotapa empire, the Cafres fish on the beach for a ferocious animal that gives out such a loud bellow when it is decapitated that it can be heard in villages half a league inland. It is covered in hair that is gray on its back and white on its belly, like the pelt of a bull but much rougher. It has the head and mouth of a tiger, with huge teeth and long, thick white moustaches. Its tail is a foot thick. Its nails are like a dog's, but its arms seem human, without any down on them. It has large flippers on its tail. Next to its tail, it has two small feet, similar to a monkey's feet. It has no legs, and its toes are webbed like a duck. Its fingernails are large and sharp like a tiger's claws. Its innards are like a pig's. Another fish looks like a woman in its upper body, with very good and healthful flesh. It nurses its children at its breasts and has a large tail and fins like a shark. Its belly is soft and white, but its back is as rough as a shark's. It has arms but no hands, only flippers. It has a deformed head, nothing like a human head, with a large mouth and nostrils, thick lips, and teeth like dogs' teeth. When it is killed, it screams like a human and dies slowly in the water. Many of these fish live on the Boecias Islands, fifteen leagues from Sofalo, on the southern coast. In the freshwater rivers of the Sofalo coast, there is a fish that the Portuguese call *tremedor* and the Cafres call *tinta*. No one can touch it while it is alive, because this causes pain that extends from the hand all the way up the arm. When this fish dies, it is very tasty and good to eat. The natives of the area say the skin of this fish can be used to cast spells. They also toast it, grind it up, and mix it into wine, using it as a medicine for colic. There is another fish in these rivers that is like a lamprey, colored like a snake. This fish is able to survive when the lakes dry up by putting its tail in its mouth and sustaining itself that way for three months, until the rains come back and it grows larger again.

Chapter 32. Illustrious people and saints
of the Catholic Church from Ethiopia.

The "illustrious Ethiopians" and African Catholic saints described here include the African queens Saba (Sheba) and Candace (and her unnamed eunuch), Princess Ephigenia (see Book 2, Chapter 6), Moses's wife Sephora, the black magi, Saint Elosboam, Saint Moses the Ethiopian, Saint Serapion, and the early modern Italo-African saints Antonio and Benedict of Palermo. For Sandoval, these individuals represent Africa's historical connection to Christianity and the potential of every African to become an exemplary Christian. He uses the Bible and medieval sources for information about the lives of most of these people, demonstrating his learnedness to his readers.

END OF THE FIRST BOOK.

BOOK 2

THIS EXCELLENT MINISTRY IS VERY NECESSARY BECAUSE IT HELPS EASE THE BLACKS' SUFFERING

In Book 2 Sandoval describes the suffering he sees in slaves' lives: to him, the worst part of their lives is their ignorance of and nonparticipation in the Catholic Church. He blames the slaves' questionable Catholicism on their masters and on negligent priests. He also tries to prove the value of his mission to Christianize slaves arriving in the port of Cartagena, and to encourage his readers (mainly Jesuit priests) to involve themselves in the work. Sandoval gently criticizes the tendency for Jesuits in the 1600s to focus on urban schools targeting the sons of the elite or on other work that shies away from the Company's purpose of apostolic missions. Sandoval most likely struggled to attract Jesuits to his mission; here he begins his attempts to interest them in working with African slaves. The most compelling motivation he can provide is that priests' charitable efforts and virtuous behavior in taking on this task will result in an afterlife spent in heaven.

These beliefs derive from the Catholic idea of merit. Merit is achieved by doing good deeds or charitable acts and leads to God's reward of heaven. This idea is part of the Catholic tradition going back to the Bible, specifically 1 Timothy 6:18–19. Augustine, Thomas Aquinas [1225?–1274], and several other Church authorities also support and elaborate on the concept of charity, good works, and merit in their writings. In Book 3 Sandoval shows he is especially influenced by Aquinas's Summa Theologica, *Part 2, Question 65. The belief in merit and good works leading to an eventual reward was confirmed by the Council of Trent, the church council that met from 1545 to 1563 to codify Catholic doctrine, beliefs, and practices as a reaction to the Protestant Reformation. The selections chosen from Book 2 focus on issues related to slavery and practical discussions of what the mission to the slaves involves, with less emphasis on Sandoval's explications of the spiritual goals and benefits of the ministry.*

Argument of Book Two

Christian reader, any kind person who sees the terrible misery that black slaves endure will not be able to ignore it and will try to help. At the beginning of Book 2, I describe the slaves' suffering and how we can help them spiritually. Once you know what they endure, you will pity them and feel compelled to help them. The rest of the book will show how this ministry does many good deeds by working with black slaves. Our most important and spiritual task is to bring more souls to the Lord. I provide an honest assessment of how important this task is. God sent his Son to live as a man in order to tell us about his Eternal Father. His example shows us that the best thing you can do in life is teach another person about spiritual things. I also describe the special benefits priests will receive when they take part in this ministry. I explain what participants must expect from this work and how it serves the author of our faith, Jesus Christ.

Chapter 1. The blacks suffer more misery than any other men.

On a whole this chapter gives a rather depressing view of life, in line with a common worldview of the time, that life was a vale of tears to be endured in hopes of a better afterlife. What are some of the reasons for suffering that Sandoval explains here, and what is the worst cause of human pain? How do non-Christians seem different from others, according to Sandoval? Why would Sandoval argue that being a slave makes a person feel less pain? Sandoval appears to believe that slaves are more suitable for pain and suffering because their physical being dominates over their mental and spiritual side—he believes Africans are physically stronger and mentally less civilized than other peoples of the world. Their bodies rule over their minds. This is part of the standard justification of African slavery in Latin America: Africans can work more because they are stronger than Indians and less civilized than Europeans. As slavery increased in the later 1600s and especially the 1700s, the dehumanization of Africans also increased. How far has Sandoval gone in the process of objectifying African slaves? How are masters obligated to make slavery tolerable?

Although spiritual deficiencies are the worst, Aristotle highlights the many worldly problems humans face. We are the victims of many things that we cannot control, including sickness, accidents, disaster, pain, death, and sadness. We have memories of the pain we endured in the past, we are afflicted in the present, and we will probably suffer in the future. We also experience bad fortune, such as being poor and friendless. Even worse is when we try to help others and instead of appreciating it, they reject our help. In this case we are punished, not rewarded, for trying to do a good deed. But all of these evil things seem unimportant when we compare them to a soul in need or a person who is immoral through ignorance.

Many things make men miserable and unhappy. Who has not felt overburdened or in pain or, worst of all, who has not experienced death? Who does not feel ashamed when poor or friendless? Who has not, in looking for friends, found enemies instead? Everyone knows that when you help these so-called friends, they turn on you.

Again, all of these bad things mean nothing when compared to spiritual problems, because physical problems do not affect the center of our being, our soul. A person whose heart lacks faith is so blind that he appears more brutish than human and does not seem to be made in God's image. When a person's will is misdirected, he lives in an abyss burning with the flames of a thousand evil desires. His body provides shelter for the devil, who is lustful, whimsical, and full of rage. The pinnacle of all evil is to be disinherited from God's glory and destined for hell.

Job said that human life is an unending struggle. Some ancient wise men said that they did not know if nature is our mother or stepmother, because our lives are inflicted with such misery. Others have said that it would be best to have never been born, or to die at birth. Some also say that if they had the choice, knowing what life was like and having experienced it, they would choose to reject life.

Enduring pain is part of being human, but life is far worse for the blacks because they are slaves. Homer[1] said that God takes away half of a slave's comprehension of the world. Homer did not say this because he believed that slaves were less intelligent than free people, but because being enslaved prevents their souls from understanding what goes on around them and increases their physical appetites. I hope that slaves actually lose more than half of their minds, because it is so awful to be a slave on a ship under the control of slave traders. In order for slaves to survive, it would be best for them to lose their minds entirely as their misery grows. It is sometimes said that it is very fortunate for slaves that divine will wants them to be oblivious to their suffering and lacking in delicate feelings and temperament. We could also say that the slaves' diminished understanding increases the owners' obligations to help them physically and spiritually. Slave owners usually do not comprehend that they need to take more care as masters over slaves who understand so little. People who rule over others must make up for their subjects' faults. A slave owner has to look into the slaves' eyes and see their needs and try to understand their language in order to speak kindly to them. The next chapters will go into greater detail about all the misfortune slaves endure.

Chapter 2. The evils of nature and fortune endured by the blacks.

To Sandoval, the existence of slavery does not mean that masters can ignore the princi-pals of Christian charity for the poor. This chapter sums up the contradiction inherent in Sandoval's work: slavery is allowable in a Christian empire, but only if it abides by cer-tain standards. Sandoval judges the practice of slavery in his time as un-Christian; what other civilizations and religions does he mention to highlight this point? How might Sandoval have heard the truth about the woman who murdered her slaves? What further examples of the dehumanization of slaves does Sandoval present here? In line

---

1. The Greek poet who lived around 700 B.C.E.

with the Spanish crown's policy toward Indians, who were granted the status of legal minors and theoretically offered judicial protection from abuse in charitable courts, Sandoval argues for a more paternalistic form of slavery, especially considering his observation that the protection of Indians has failed by the early 1600s. From his point of view, the Church can help the slaves, in its role as a mediator between subjects and secular rulers. But if the Catholic Church or slaves' masters do not help them, the slaves have to help themselves: Sandoval observes that slaves form charitable brotherhoods in order to make collections to pay for burials of slaves who share their ethnic or language group. Despite all of the sadistic abuse described here, how and why does Sandoval portray slaves as capable and tolerant of hard work?

We now describe the terrible things that happen to slaves—men and women condemned to a life more suited to beasts. Their masters beat them until their skin falls off and they die from the cruel blows and horrible torture. Masters will do this for any trivial infraction. Or they terrorize them until they die, rotten and full of worms. Every day the courts[2] hear cases with accounts of this kind of abuse. Many times I have seen things with my own eyes that make my heart cry out with shame. No one could see a poor black man covered in terrible wounds from beatings done for no reason whatsoever without feeling moved to pity. If slaves do not show up for work one day, their masters will shackle yokes with four cruel spikes in them to their heads. Anyone would be enraged by the fact that just a few days ago a noble and important lady killed her black slave woman, and then she killed another two slaves, for a total of three murders. The woman killed the first slave to punish her, but after she did it, she put the slave on a pole in her house, saying that the slave had hung herself. Then she tied two stones to the slave and commanded a black man to throw her in the sea so that no one would see the wounds and figure out that this was a murder. Moving on from these endless beatings, I can hardly describe the cruel way that slaves are imprisoned in chains, fetters, handcuffs, shackles, balls and chains, collars, and other horrible inventions designed to imprison and punish them. A person I know, not the kind to exaggerate these things, was imprisoned for three years in Argel.[3] He observed that Christians punish their slaves more in a week than the Moors [Muslims] do in a year. We might be able to ignore the physical treatment, if their masters spoke to them more kindly, because verbal insults are more hurtful; however, slaves are con-

---

2. Spanish colonial courts, with civil, criminal, or ecclesiastical judges, might hear cases of excessive abuse. Slaves found ways to bring their masters to court in other parts of Latin America, especially when their master violated an accepted Catholic principle, such as forbidding their slaves to marry. Sandoval does not provide any more specifics, and most local records for Cartagena have been lost.

3. A North African Muslim town, controlled by the Spanish from 1510 to 1529.

stantly insulted by being called dogs, *bozales,*[4] horses, and many other rude names. When a slave is good, he deserves rest, but the bad slave risks terrible punishment.

If masters applied the principle of disciplining slaves with both carrot and stick, we might forgive them. But this is not the case. The slaves arrive here naked and pay for their clothes with their own sweat. They are given hardly enough food to survive, and they are fed only on workdays, unless they are forced to work on holidays, oppressed by their masters' need for more income. Usually they are not allowed to celebrate holidays or rest on the days God designates that we should do so. On these days, they work for their masters to buy their own food, which their masters do not provide.[5] This is very common: if they do not work, they are not fed, as if they only exist to work and only receive food so they can work. Thus their masters' carelessness leads them to sin and offend God, because it is their masters' fault that they are in need.

Without food or clothing, after beatings and insults, they fall asleep at the end of the day. It may seem like they sleep half of their lives away in order to endure the other half, but this is not the case. If a black slave is a miner, he works sunrise to sunset and often during the night. From the time they wake up in the morning, slaves spend the entire day in the sun or rain, working in the mines. At night they try to rest, but only if the mosquitoes leave them alone. They wake up at three in the morning to endure the same thing all over again.

Slaves who work on farms also suffer. After spending the entire day swinging a machete in the sun and rain, exposed to mosquitoes, horseflies, and ticks, the slave has time for only a snack or a quick drink. At night, until ten or even later, the slaves shred yucca to use in cassava bread. This work is difficult, but they try to make it more enjoyable by entertaining themselves with the beat of a tambourine, working in a rhythm, like silkworms. Many slaves have to stay up all night to help their *hacienda* [their master's estate or farm] prosper. They endure this patiently and in good spirits.

Although the slaves in the Sierra [of Colombia] endure terrible work and misery, words cannot describe the suffering of those who risk their lives to dive and fish for pearls in the Hacha River and in other rivers, or the lives of those who row in the great Magdalena River.[6] I will briefly mention those who might

---

4. A Spanish word for crude and rough. The full definition of this term is given in note 6 on p. 5, and in the glossary.

5. Slaves in Latin America were often allowed access to a plot of land to raise their own food. This lessened the masters' burden to feed the slaves, but it also sometimes meant that slaves were able to earn money selling their produce.

6. The Magdalena River was a major transit route used on part of the journey from Cartagena to the capital at Bogotá. The Hacha River flows into the Caribbean Sea.

seem to have easier lives because they serve masters in the house. After doing a thousand chores all day long, they get up at midnight to hull the corn they are forced to eat. The gentiles considered this job so unendurable that they made martyrs do it.[7] But the masters are not satisfied with this. They take away all the slaves' possessions. They prevent them from talking to their relatives. They do not allow them to rest, nor do they help the sick. Once I heard about a black woman who was dying of lockjaw. Her master's blows "cured" her without his spending any money on a doctor. Did she die of lockjaw or of the beating? The cruelty of slaves' lives in some houses reminds me that Emperor Octavian said that in Herod's house it was better to be a pig than a son.[8]

I am sure that some masters care more for their animals than for their fellow men. All we have to do to prove this is compare the horses' stables with the black slaves' dormitories. The horses, animals with no understanding, have beds to sleep on. When the horses wake up in the morning, a miserable slave must clean, curry, comb, and wash them. The horses receive gifts, care in illness, and blankets covering them from head to toe.

I must remind the reader of something else that makes these evil deeds seem even worse. Everyone knows that the Spaniards abused the Indians so that in many provinces there are very few Indians left. In other places they have disappeared entirely. The blacks came here to replace these Indians. Huge numbers of slaves come here to work on Spanish land and to mine gold to make the Spanish rich. The slaves sustain the Spanish through their hard work, sweat, and industry. But instead of sheltering them, curing their illnesses, and defending them, because slaves bring them wealth and honor, the Spanish abandon them. They will not waste four *reales*[9] to help a sick slave but instead leave them carelessly to die, rotting in their own excrement. Our black translators do not dare to look at this foul, ugly, evil, and disgusting sight. Because the masters do nothing, priests are even more obligated to spend the time necessary to help the slaves spiritually, as an act of true Christian charity.

Masters, in order to save money, set their slaves free when they are sick, and assign them the job of getting well. Once they are well, they must return to service. If slaves die, their masters should bury them, but they do not. I am not talking about those who die on the slave ships. After arriving here, slaves will not be buried unless their relatives provide money to pay for their burial. People from their own caste [ethnolinguistic group] will collect donations and bring

---

7. Possibly a reference to Roman torture of early Christians.

8. A reference to the Roman emperor Augustus Caesar (27 B.C.E. to 14 C.E.), who was probably referring to Herod the Great, a Roman king of Judea born in 74 B.C.E.

9. A *real* was a small unit of money in colonial Spanish America worth one eighth of a peso.

the money together over the dead body. They also depend on their brother-hoods to bury them, even if they are very *ladino*[10] and have lived many years in the same house.

In Proverbs 27:18, the Holy Spirit tells us that a master sometimes needs to speak harshly, but true leadership commands with nobility and authority. A master can act kindly and punish gently with a blameless and tender heart. The Holy Spirit does not forbid scolding or punishment but does not permit the excessive punishments that masters carry out today, including beating, burning, flaying, and killing. I do know many who are not like this, because they treat their slaves like sons, proving that it is possible to treat them well and according to God's will.

Chapter 3. The blacks' spiritual suffering.

How does this chapter explain why masters do not baptize their slaves or educate them in basic Christian doctrine? Sandoval believes that slaves must be baptized and gradu-ally receive the other important sacraments of the Catholic Church, especially confession and holy communion. The Catholic sacraments are religious ceremonies performed either regularly, as in confession and communion, or at important stages in life, for example, baptism, marriage, and last rites. Last rites (or extreme unction) is a sacrament meant to prepare Catholics for death and the afterlife. If masters do not permit their slaves to marry, they prevent the slaves' participation in another Catholic sacrament. Sandoval is disturbed that masters do not help their slaves fit into the Christian system, since their Christianization is meant to morally justify why slaves are brought from Africa, accord-ing to papal decrees from the 1400s.

Although he believes the Jesuits must help correct this problem, masters have more power over slaves' daily lives, so they must also be held accountable and take a pater-nalistic, caring role to help and protect their slaves. This fits into the standard colonial hierarchies: there may be inequalities in society, but the elite should protect the weak, who will be grateful for paternalistic help and patronage by their betters. How does the anecdote of the poor old woman illustrate Sandoval's belief in this system? No one in his society denied the social hierarchy of African slaves on the bottom level with masters and colonial authorities ruling over them. However, slave masters' desire for material gain might conflict with Sandoval's more benign paternalistic approach of educating and caring for one's slaves. Sandoval also sees the practical side and views it as illogical for masters to abuse slaves who represent a significant monetary investment.

---

10. A word used throughout the book to refer to Spanish-speaking slaves who have lived among Europeans for a significant amount of time. Sandoval often contrasts *ladino* Afri-cans with *bozal* slaves.

The blacks' spiritual plight is lamentable. It is very common to justify slavery by arguing that it gives them the chance to learn how to go to heaven through our good example. However, masters believe in two things that contradict this argument. First, they value slaves less if they have been baptized, because if they have received a Christian education, they are thought to be *ladino,* or residing with us for a long time. This means they have less value, because they might have already been sold several times because of their bad character. Thus masters do not want to have baptized slaves and prevent their slaves from being baptized by hiding them from those who want to teach them about Christianity.

Second, the devil has convinced masters that slaves are incapable of understanding our faith, that it is all nonsense to them. Masters believe it is a waste of time to try to teach slaves the catechism, that baptism is pointless, having slaves make their confession[11] is a joke, and giving slaves communion is blasphemous. Masters believe this applies to both *bozales* and *ladinos.* But I know from experience that some *bozales* are not incapable of understanding confession. Is being ignorant and crude a reason not to receive baptism, confession, or communion? Or maybe we should spend most of our time and energy teaching ignorant and crude people? Having a limited potential does not prevent an individual from receiving baptism, nor should any baptized person who has received preparation and instruction be excluded from confession or communion.

I once asked a *ladina* black woman if she had taken communion before. She said that she had not but that she did want to take communion now. I scolded her for being so careless. She understood what I meant and responded with words that made me feel sorry for her miserable master, because this master pushed her slave into sin. The woman said: "Father, after I take confession the priests always give me a piece of paper to prove that I am prepared to take communion, but I have never done it, because my mistress prevents me by taking the paper from me as if I were not capable of receiving God. Although a long time has passed, I have come secretly to take communion now, so please give me permission so that I can change my fate." The Bible tells us of those people who cried when their idols were broken, so we should not be surprised when black men and women complain of their masters' great cruelty because these masters take God away from them and pointlessly deprive them of such a great treasure. How can we compensate them for this theft?

---

11. The sacrament of confession is a secret conversation with a priest in which the person confessing lists their sins. Confession and the absolution of sin must precede communion or receiving the body of Christ in the communion wafer. Confession and communion for slaves is discussed in more detail in Book 3, Chapter 20.

Because slaves have trouble understanding instruction, their masters must give them plenty of time to be taught Christian doctrine in order for them to receive legitimate baptism, sanctioned by the grace of God. To make up for their shortcomings, we must provide them with good examples and teach them with our actions as well as our words. This way they will see that the law of God is sacred, and a better way than how they lived before. Insufficient instruction and bad examples prevent them from becoming good Christians, and they continue to live like brutes and seem incapable of improving. Since they learn so much about how to sin, they must go to confession. Even during Lent, their masters will not let them leave work to go to confession.[12] Masters are even more careless when their dying slaves need extreme unction. We have to ask doctors and surgeons to tell us when blacks are close to death so that we know to go to them without being called by their masters. A doctor once told me to go to a certain house. When I arrived, the master turned me away because he said there were sick people inside. When I returned later, I had to confess eleven people just before they all passed away.

What can I say about marriage? Slaves live together for many years without being married. Their masters do not permit them to marry and will beat, imprison, or sell their slaves in order to prevent it. But they do allow their black women to live as concubines so that they will have children. If some slaves marry, masters give them fewer privileges than they give to unmarried couples. For some reason, masters like to keep women and their children forever apart, selling them separately.[13] Finally, masters do not try to teach their slaves; some slaves who have lived here for twenty years do not know how to make the sign of the cross. I am so hurt by this that I must describe even more miseries.

God, who is a merciful father, asks those who have power over others to care for them. Thus masters are obliged to care for their slaves. This obligation is especially important for slaves on the ships, because this is when their salvation is most at risk. If slaves set sail without receiving baptism and the faith, they will probably stay that way. Bread must be rolled out before it is baked, and the slave ships are the paddles for placing this bread into the oven of the Church. Masters of slave ships must be very careful that the slaves receive simple, indisputable baptisms. Masters must feel confident that this will not prevent the slaves' sale, or stand in the way of their profit. Why not give slaves enough food

---

12. Traditionally, in the 1600s, most Catholics went to confession only during Lent, the forty days before Easter. Because confession was required before they could eat the communion wafer, this meant they took communion only once a year.

13. The Catholic Church in Latin America often protected slaves' marriages by forcing masters to keep slave couples together. While illegitimacy was very common in colonial Latin America, in general the Catholic Church encouraged marriage whenever possible.

to live? Why not provide them with adequate shelter? Why not cure them when they are sick? I hear people say: "I will pay a bag of *reales* for this broken down slave," so, if they are so valuable, why throw slaves in the mud and abandon them? Woe is me—is a slave bought for a bag of *reales* not worth more than a beast? Why don't masters care for slaves? Why don't they keep them healthy and reward them for their hard work? I cannot believe that men will cross the sea and travel many leagues on land, risking their fortune, honor, life, and soul to bring slaves here and try to make a profit from them, but when they have the slaves, they treat them badly when they are healthy and even worse when they are sick. The following anecdote will prove how little masters care for their slaves' salvation.

One day I entered the house of an honorable man. I saw a very old and sick black woman working in the house as if she were a healthy young girl. I wanted to question her to see if she was Christian. I heard that she was not Christian, because it was too hard to teach her. They said she was a *bozal* and did not understand anything, so no one bothered to teach her about Christianity. When I spoke to her, I could tell from her words that she was not as crazy as people said, although I had to teach her the catechism using an interpreter who spoke her language. For three days, I asked her questions and taught her the catechism, using several different interpreters. After this I knew she was not Christian, so I baptized her. But up until then, after thirty years as a servant in that house, no one cared enough to make her a Christian. By having such a low opinion of her, her masters proved that in our miserable era people forget God and lack a conscience. Even though this woman was partially crippled, every time she saw me she stood up as well as she could. She asked for my hand and my companion's[14] hand to kiss them, thanking us and condemning her masters for leaving her so long in such obvious danger of eternal condemnation.

Chapter 4. How slaves should serve their masters, and how masters should serve their slaves.

In this chapter Sandoval ponders how masters and slaves fit into the Christian view of the world and the afterlife. Not surprisingly, this seventeenth-century Jesuit tells slaves that it is their duty and fate to work and suffer in this world, in hopes of reward in the next, using biblical passages to support his argument. On the other hand, Sandoval promises slaves that cruel masters will suffer in hell unless they follow a godlike model of benign paternalism, and he argues that God has expectations and standards for masters' behavior as well. Sandoval's Baroque worldview was very hierarchical, but slaves did have a place in that hierarchy, especially if they understood the value of Christlike

---

14. Possibly a reference to Pedro Claver.

humility and obedience. Slave masters were not at the top of the hierarchy, living above all morality; they were also subject to a more powerful ruler. How does Sandoval apply the role of a father to both God and slaves' masters? What does Sandoval mean when he says that all people on earth are truly equal?

Masters must open their eyes and see their obligations; they are masters, not absolute lords living outside of the law, nor are they kings commanding their slaves. They must exert their power in moderation. When they act immoderately, their slaves have good reason to ask: "How can a Christian act like this?" On the other hand, slaves should know that they must be obedient to both strict, cruel masters and kind, gentle, and friendly masters. If a servant has a clear conscience he will attain God's grace and friendship. He must have patience to endure the sadness and pain caused by his master's unjust fury that comes even when he does his work well. Saint Peter asks the question: "How can someone win God's grace if he only suffers when he is punished for his sins?" But if you try to do your best and obey as you must, and you patiently endure your masters' insults without complaining, you will receive God's grace. Your vocation is to obey not only kind masters but also masters that harass you and treat you cruelly.[15] Christ, the Savior of the world, suffered injustice and cruel punishment for your sake, so you, out of love for the Savior, must obey your masters, even if they show you no mercy.

Saint Paul has this to say to servants who are punished just for doing their work: "Continue working without complaining, because you know you will be rewarded by God in heaven."[16] In other words, masters on earth do not appreciate your work, but God will not forget to reward you for all you have done for his love. If you are not compensated on earth for your work, you will be compensated in heaven. If your master is tyrannical and unjust, do not lose patience or seek revenge, because God knows what is happening—he will avenge you and punish everyone who deserves punishment. If this does not happen in this life, it will be done in the next. Those who had the most power on earth will receive the worst punishment after death. People who had great power but used it to do evil on earth will be sent to the eternal flames, but powerless servants who lived humble lives will enter the kingdom of heaven.

Servants must serve their masters as if their masters were God, because God wants servants to be obedient. Masters that are fair rule over their servants in God's name and command their servants in a way that pleases God. God is an absolute lord, but he does not rule like a tyrant; instead, he is like a father who

---

15. Sandoval cites I Peter 2:18–20, which discusses servants' duty to submit to their masters.

16. Sandoval cites Colossians 3:22–24.

commands his servants with love, tenderness, and friendliness. He asks them to do good things, and his commands are justified, like the commands a father gives his family. If someone is ordered to do something that God would not approve of, they do not have to obey. This applies to the commands that a lord gives to his subjects, a master to his servant, an owner to his slave, and a father to his sons. A master's demands must take into consideration what his servant is capable of achieving, without going beyond his strength. A master must also have good timing, show sympathy to his servants, compensate them appropriately, and be patient with their shortcomings and weaknesses. In this way, masters on earth model themselves after God, because even the most powerful people have to be obedient to God. God wants masters to be like fathers so that their servants will act like obedient children.

People who rule over others here on earth should do it fairly and always remember that the ultimate master is in heaven. Masters should never command their servants to do anything that violates God's laws. Even when a master asks his servants to do something that is fair and just, he cannot ask them to do more than they are capable of doing, and he should not rush them or force them to work until they faint. A master should listen to his servants' grievances and let them rest when they complain of being overworked and tired. Masters should not be like Pharaoh, who tyrannically oppressed the Hebrews [in the Old Testament]. Although they screamed out their complaints, he showed them no compassion and continued to abuse them. If a master refuses to listen to his slaves' complaints, God will judge him, because God judges everyone. If a master hurts his slave, how will he respond on Judgment Day when God asks him why he did something so evil? Maybe the master will say that this person was his slave, so he deserved to be punished. God will not accept this excuse because his laws protect slaves, and even someone who is a master on earth must be an obedient slave to God. God will not allow anyone to break the laws he made in favor of slaves so that masters will not become corrupted with their own power. God will judge and punish unjust masters for the sake of their abused slaves.

In his secret plan for us, God created masters and slaves, but all of us are really the same even if some are important on earth and others are not. This is why everyone should be humble and keep in mind that everyone on earth is equal. Masters should not take pleasure in ordering others but should try to improve themselves first and then rule over others, without losing either their humility or their authority. They can have a commanding outward appearance but still stay humble inside. God created us all, so why would someone want to go against him by harming another one of his children? Everyone must carry out God's laws by treating their fellow human beings with respect. Servants must serve their masters obediently, and masters should not harm their servants. Leviticus 25 says, "The servants are mine," meaning God created servants and made laws to protect them.

Chapter 5. Quotes from sacred scripture about how masters should treat slaves.

The passages cited here show that the Bible acknowledges the existence of a system where masters rule over servants and slaves, but a set of rules and obligations exist to make this relationship tolerable. How does Sandoval say masters should treat their slaves? How does the way in which masters behave affect their slaves' behavior?

The holy apostle Paul says: If a person does not care for his own, especially his servants, he rejects the faith and is worse then an infidel [1 Timothy 5:8]. A master who acts carelessly is not faithful to divine law and Christian faith. He should remember that he is like a shepherd over his slaves and that they are his flock of lambs. Someday he will be asked to account for his livestock. No slave is too lowly to be made free and noble by Christ's humanity and blood. The master should be very careful in anything he does with regard to his slaves' bodies and souls. He should make sure they know the Christian doctrine and how to follow the Church's rules. They should go to Mass and observe official fasting days if at all possible. They should take confession and communion at the proper times, following the guidance of their confessor. Masters should try to figure out if their slaves are not Christian and try to help them. Anything related to the soul is very important, but the body also has needs that masters must fulfill fairly. They must provide a fair daily wage or decent food, clothing, and shelter. They should remember the Golden Rule—do unto others as you would have done unto you—and love their slaves as they love themselves. If you were a servant, how would you want your master to treat you? If you are a master, treat all your servants as you would want to be treated. If you are cruel, they will curse you and cry out to heaven for justice. God will hear their cries, and you will be punished. Moses said: Do not deny the poor and needy their daily wages, whether they are your own people or aliens among you, but pay them their wages because they need them to stay alive [Deuteronomy 24:14–15].

Ecclesiasticus tells us: do not be cruel or punish your slaves too harshly, because they are also made of flesh and blood.[17] They should be treated kindly and with care. Punishment should not be done in anger or vindictively, because if you go against Christian charity, you commit new sins while you are punishing old sins. If you insult and curse your slaves, you are more to blame than they are, because they probably have only committed very minor sins. When you angrily chastise their sins, you only offend God more. You should not punish

---

17. The quotes from Ecclesiasticus are from the book of Ecclesiasticus or Sirach, written two centuries before the time of Jesus. This book is not accepted as part of the Old Testament but is considered part of the Catholic tradition. The sections Sandoval quotes come from Chapter 32, directions on how to treat servants, and Chapter 4, encouraging acts of mercy.

others in a way that makes you deserve to be punished. Instead of correcting a sin, you make it worse with your bad example, and the servant will want to commit more sins because of your anger. Ecclesiasticus says, do not act like a lion in your house; do not oppress the servants and slaves. Do not rule tyrannically, filling the house with your furious shouting, threats, and violence, ordering people to do the impossible. By acting like this you corrupt the servants and make the good servants turn bad, and loyal servants will become disloyal and want to run away. If you have a loyal servant, love him with all your heart and soul, love him as you love yourself and treat him like a brother, as the blood of your soul and the comfort in your home. If you unjustly oppress him, you give him motivation to leave you, and you will lose the benefit of what he does for you. Try to restrain your anger so that you do not lose good slaves and then must try to discipline the bad ones.

Saint Augustine[18] said, do not punish servants and slaves too harshly, but speak kindly to them, reward them, and cherish them. We are obligated to love our slaves even more than our own children. Saint Augustine ranked the love we must feel for others: love God first, then your parents, then your children, and lastly your slaves—unless your slaves behave better than your children.

We should think about all the evil and misery endured by these cursed people: the devil leads them to worship false gods, and their masters mistreat them. This helps us see the terrible and disastrous state of their souls. The devil disdains them, and the entire world rejects them, but God Our Lord, the most holy Virgin, and the sacred apostles greatly esteem them, as I discuss in the following chapters.

Chapter 6. Our Lord God values the blacks and this ministry.

In this chapter Sandoval uses biblical references to argue that Africa was chosen by God to be the first nation of the world to convert to Christianity. This connects to the title of the entire work, De instauranda Aethiopum salute *[On Restoring Spiritual Health to Ethiopians], because Sandoval believes Africa can return to what he sees as its glorious Christian past, after a period of what he views as a serious decline into sin. Sandoval uses these examples in hopes of inspiring other Jesuits, whose order is modeled on the apostles. How does he argue that teaching Christianity to Africans is just as important as missions to the indigenous people of the Americas? In this chapter, how does Sandoval try to convince his readers that a mission to Africans in Cartagena is important, necessary, and valuable work, through the use of biblical examples? The story of*

---

18. Augustine was a very influential early Christian philosopher and theologian who lived from 354 to 430. Although educated in Rome, he was African and spent most of his life in North Africa.

Iphigenia's connection to an apostle and to strong Christian beliefs proves to Sandoval that God favors Africa and that Africans can be good Christians.

God has always valued the Ethiopian nation, as can be seen in divine scripture. This love shows us that we do an important job when we minister to the Ethiopians and try to save them. David says: Ethiopia will be the first to give her hand in marriage to her husband God [convert to Christianity; Psalms 67:32], because Ethiopia was the first nation to enjoy the fruits of Christianity in those glorious early days of the Church. This is the best praise we can give to this nation. God reached out to the blacks to join his Church and receive the Gospel, so Ethiopia is a model for other nations. This nation joined God's flock first and guided the rest on the straight and certain road of evangelical law, teaching other nobler nations. Although God reached out to this nation, now its salvation is hidden from them. Ethiopia's sins must have been very serious to bring them such great misfortune.

Many churchmen work to bring Christianity to the Indians, and I envy them for working on such a glorious task, but their enthusiasm also discourages me, because our work with the blacks is just as important. No one speaks in their defense and no one runs to help them. I believe I am not exaggerating in saying that the poor blacks are more desperate than the Indians.

David also said, regarding the foundation of the church, that the Ethiopian nation was one of the first stones used to construct this divine edifice. This stone, although black, was lustrous and strong.[19] Among the three kings that adored Jesus Christ, one was black.[20] God revealed his high opinion of Ethiopians when he chose Simon, a black prophet, to take part in the founding of his Church, as is written in Acts 13:1. God does not look down on any color, because what is important to him is that souls find spiritual good.

We also see God's esteem in the stories of the life of the holy apostle Matthew.[21] Working great miracles, Matthew converted the Ethiopian king and queen, their children, the court, and a large part of the kingdom, including, it is told, a princess called Iphigenia, who was very beautiful and wise. Iphigenia heard the holy apostle speak highly of those who remained virgins, so she was determined to consecrate herself to God and enclose herself in a monastery. She

---

19. Sandoval refers to Psalm 86 and Song of Solomon 1:5. Many scholars have discussed the line "I am black, but beautiful." This line could also read "I am black and beautiful."

20. European Christian tradition portrays one of the three wise men as black. The black magi is a common image in European paintings from the 1400s, signifying a vision of Christian Africans as part of European empires after Portuguese expansion into Africa. The lavishly dressed and bejeweled black magi also represents Africa's wealth. The black magi is not specifically mentioned in the Bible.

21. The story of Matthew and Iphigenia is not in the Bible. Here Sandoval uses other early Christian sources.

carried out her plan along with two hundred other maidens who wanted to join her. In this way, the virgin Saint Iphigenia founded the first and most important monastery for religious women in the world. Out of love for the Lord, this praiseworthy, saintly woman ruled and governed her monastery for twenty-three years, during the time that Saint Matthew was in this kingdom helping her. She also continued on after he left. Her monastery is the world's first order of nuns accepted by the Catholic Church. It is an important fact that an apostle actually founded this monastery and governed over it for many years.

Saint Matthew considered this monastery and its founder so important that he sacrificed his life for it and died to preserve Iphigenia's chastity. We learn from historical sources that when the king of Egypt died, his brother Hirtaco came to power. Hirtaco wanted to marry Iphigenia, both because she was very beautiful and because he wanted to conquer Ethiopia. He asked Saint Matthew to persuade her to be his wife. The holy apostle preached to Iphigenia and her religious women in front of the king and his court. First he discussed how God instituted marriage and how necessary it was for preserving the universe, but then he added that remaining a virgin was much better than being married. He also said that a servant would be punished for taking the king's wife from him. His sermon implied that Iphigenia was the wife of Christ and that Christ would be angry if Hirtaco took her from Christ or forced her out of her monastic life. Hirtaco left the church in a fury and sent his ministers to stab the apostle with a lance as he was saying Mass. They left his dead body on the altar, which was stained red with his blood. Hirtaco continued trying to persuade Iphigenia to marry him, but she would not submit, so he commanded that the monastery be burned down. In this fire, the apostle was seen in the flames as they blew upward. This proved how much he valued this convent, although many others cursed it.

Chapter 7. A recent strange event confirms God's love for this ministry.

Through the story of a Jesuit and an Indian convert living in the town of Salvador de Bahia in Brazil, Sandoval again juxtaposes indigenous Americans and African slaves: he believes the miraculous story shows that God wants Indians to be baptized properly, and therefore the same applies to African slaves. Sandoval tells the story of this miracle as a way to show divine encouragement for Jesuits working with Indians and, by extension, Africans. To Sandoval this miracle is a clear sign that God wants the Jesuits to do missionary work in the Americas. A miraculous or fantastic event is not unexpected, inexplicable, or illogical for Sandoval—it simply reiterates God's involvement in the day-to-day events of life.

The story of the life of Father José de Ancheta, a Jesuit in Brazil, tells of an Indian called Diego who died in Bahía de Todos os Santos. Diego was known to be a baptized Christian who died in his Portuguese master's house. After he died, he was covered in a shroud and put in a coffin. But then the mistress of the house reported that she saw the body move. The Indian, who had seemed dead a moment before, asked why he was in a burial shroud. He said he would explain what happened to him only to Father José de Ancheta.

When the father arrived from the Jesuit college, the Indian asked to see a reliquary[22] that he had seen before when they were walking together. When the father took out the reliquary, the Indian was very happy to see it and paid his respects to it, and then he wanted to tell the story of how he had died. He said that as he entered the next life, he left the road leading to heaven because he had not been baptized, and this fact made him come back to life. The Indian confessed that he had not been baptized during his lifetime but had just been given the Christian name Diego by the Spaniard who captured him.[23] However, he had always been very careful to follow God's commands, so everyone thought he was a Christian. But now Father José had to baptize him, because he knew he would die again soon. Father José refreshed his memory of the Christian doctrine and quickly catechized and baptized him. The priest felt that he had achieved something that made his time in Brazil worthwhile, because he had helped at least one soul go to heaven. Diego was now ready to die happily. He asked that his simple possessions be given to some poor person and requested that two masses be said for his soul. He held a candle and asked Father José to remain with him until he passed away. Soon after this, surrounded by prayers, this happy soul abandoned its body and joined its maker. God showed great mercy in allowing Diego's soul to be reunited with his body so that he would be baptized and then go on to eternal life.

Diego's story and the information I have received from both Jesuits and Dominicans working here proves that Indians were baptized just as carelessly as the black slaves are baptized now. Saint Luis Beltran,[24] a Dominican who worked in Cartagena de Indias, felt very upset by the cruelty of the *encomenderos*[25] who not only killed Indians for no good reason but also prevented him from preaching to the Indians. Once when the saint was preaching in front of

---

22. A container for remnants of a saint's body or clothing.

23. The fact that he had a Spanish or "Christian" name would make people think Diego was baptized. Although Sandoval says this story took place in Brazil, apparently Diego was captured in a Spanish slave raid, perhaps near the border between Portuguese and Spanish territory.

24. A Dominican saint who lived from 1526 to 1581. He preached for several years in New Granada, now the country of Colombia.

25. *Encomenderos* were people "entrusted [*encomender*]" with royal grants to the labor of American Indians in the early Spanish conquests of the New World. In exchange for Indian labor, the *encomenderos* were meant to teach the Indians about Christianity. This anecdote

many Indians, an *encomendero* entered the church and forced the Indians to go back to work. Diego's miraculous story shows us that the Lord supports the ministry to the Indians and that we should be inspired to overcome all of the challenges in order to convert them and help them go to heaven. Thus, for the sake of the Church, we must also examine and question the baptisms of *bozal* blacks as well as *ladino* blacks and Indians. Every day we discover more people who have not been baptized or who have been baptized very carelessly.

Chapter 8. The most holy Virgin Our Lady's great esteem for the black nation.

A few selections from this chapter provide examples of how Sandoval tried to prove that Africans have divine favor through the intermediary of the Virgin Mary. Several different Marian statues in Spain, Portugal, and the Canary Islands (including the image of the Virgin in Guadalupe, Spain) portray her with dark skin. Sandoval does not mention the famous Virgin of Guadalupe in Tepeyac, Mexico. How does the story of the black woman and the bull show that Mary helps Africans? How does Sandoval try to connect this woman's experience to the fact that she was a member of a black brotherhood that was founded in a Jesuit church and dedicated to a statue of the Virgin? Such fraternal organizations, also mentioned in Chapter 2, provided social and charitable opportunities for Africans and their descendants once they became members of the Catholic Church. What else does the woman do that Sandoval might perceive as earning her the Virgin's special favor? Again, this miracle makes perfect sense to Sandoval as a sign of God's role, through the intervention of the Virgin, in the Christianizing of African slaves.

The most holy Virgin, Mother of God and Our Lady, clearly loves the black nation, because certainly her Son Jesus Christ loves it, and she loves everything that He loves. But beyond this, I can prove the Virgin's love in two more ways. First, she is known to love the color black. Many of the oldest and most miraculous images of the Virgin are colored black. Black Virgins include the great image of Our Lady in the main church of Lisbon [Portugal], which is called *la Candelaria* [candle mass]; an image of the Virgin on the island of Tenerife in the Canary Islands; the Virgin of Guadalupe [Spain]; the Virgin of Montserrat [Spain]; the Virgin of the Pillar of Zaragoza [Spain], and the Virgin of Loreto [Spain]. We think that these last two images were made while the most holy Virgin was still alive. Because she wanted to be shown as black, she showed how much she loved the black nation. Black people feel a great love for these images. Also, the Virgin often wore a black robe and veil. The Virgin also loves the black nation because a black king came to worship her only Son, not long

---

from the life of Luis Beltran is an accurate depiction of how enthusiastic churchmen con-flicted with *encomenderos* seeking money and power in the New World.

after his birth.[26] She must have spoken to this king and promised that she would help his nation in whose name he came. Because her child showed great mercy to this nation, she became its protector. First loves always have first place in the soul, and the Virgin felt love for these kings who were the first to visit her Son and the first to recognize her as the Mother of God even though she sat in the hay, surrounded by mangers and animals. It is said that the first church that the Abyssinians built in Ethiopia was dedicated to the most holy Virgin. This church was called Holy Mary of Mount Zion, and it was built while this sovereign Lady still lived.[27]

I know a strange and entertaining story about how the Virgin works to convert the Ethiopians and how God chose her to do his work. Not long ago, I knew a very devout black woman who was a member of the black brotherhood dedicated to honoring the image of Holy Mary the Great, founded in the Jesuit college in Santa Fe de Bogotá. One day this woman was walking alone on a narrow mountain pass. Suddenly she saw two terrible and ferocious bulls racing out of the brush to charge her. She prayed for the help of the most holy Virgin and the Christ child. Just as the bulls were approaching, she hid in the bushes. Then she saw a vision of the child, similar to the one honored by her brotherhood. This vision was so beautiful and lovely that it stole her heart, and she no longer felt afraid. Her heart was consoled and filled with joy, and then somehow the deadly bulls disappeared. Thus the bulls, threatened by that great child, fled, leaving the black woman with a vision of the Son of God and the knowledge that the Virgin helped her. This strengthened her faith a great deal.

Chapter 9. The sacred apostles' great desire to help the blacks; Saint Augustine.

The early Jesuits thought of themselves as new apostles, because they aimed to move around constantly and preach all over the world; thus Sandoval offers the biblical apostles as models for his fellow Jesuits. Chapter 9 discusses how the apostles Matthew, Bartholomew, Phillip, Andrew, and Matthias preached the Gospel in Ethiopia and succeeded in converting some people there. Matthias apparently survived preaching to a group of cannibals but was ultimately stoned and beheaded. Sandoval also mentions a story about the Apostle Thomas, who observed that Ethiopian priests were very strict about remaining chaste even if they were married. Sandoval argues that many Christian priests do not "control their own nature," but heathens manage to "do this to serve and honor demons." The next two chapters discuss the work of the Apostle Thomas in India. Sandoval calls the East Indian natives "Ethiopians," presenting this land as

---

26. See note 20.

27. See Introduction for more information on Christianity in Ethiopia.

*populated by blacks. Such a viewpoint shows how Jesuits always work with black peo-
ple around the world, reinforcing the importance of his mission to Africans in Cartagena
and demonstrating the Jesuits' connection to Iberian expansion around the world. The
numerous stories about Thomas and other apostles highlight the Jesuits' desire to imitate the biblical apostles and how the Company continues work begun in the early
Christian era, as presented in the New Testament.*

*Miraculous events mark this worldwide Jesuit mission. Sandoval claims there is
some evidence that Apostle Thomas preached to the Brazilian native people. Although
Sandoval does not mention it, colonial Latin American churchmen also believed that
Apostle Thomas journeyed to Mexico. In Chapter 11 Sandoval discusses the cross that
might mark the grave of the martyred Thomas in Meliapor, India. He describes a miracle: the cross bled and changed color from white to yellow to black. He interprets this
event as symbolizing the apostle's preaching in Europe, Asia, and Ethiopia.*

Chapter 14. Motivation to remedy the miseries of such cursed souls.

*The next chapters give more examples of the rewards and motivations for preaching to
and converting black slaves. As Sandoval says, "working for the love of God and our
neighbor, we are motivated by rewards in this life and the next." Sandoval believes that
God and Jesus help the most miserable people on earth, so the Jesuits should do the
same, imitating the saints and apostles and earning themselves the reward of an afterlife
spent in heaven. Because everyone else ignores them, the slaves are like "weak, thin lost
lambs" in need of charity. Doing charitable acts for them makes a person a true friend
to God, an important motivation in Sandoval's view. In the paragraph below he suggests that Jesuits in the Americas seem to gravitate toward working with wealthy Spaniards. The rich might seem a more tempting audience, but why does Sandoval believe it
is easier to preach to African slaves?*

God has given me the responsibility to reach out to the poor and dejected of the
world. God's message is to help the poor, shelter those in need, and bring
together the outcasts to share the good news of the Gospel with those who need
it. Trust me: working with the Spanish by teaching and confessing them is a
more luxurious ministry, but it is dangerous, insecure, and not as beneficial for
us. Those that help the rich nobles and people who live in luxury take on their
very heavy burdens of conscience. These poor blacks do not have burdens for us
to carry; they carry fewer burdens than we do, so we can easily carry both their
burdens and our own.

Chapter 15. This ministry is necessary and excellent because it takes these souls from a miserable state to a very secure and happy one.

This quote from Chapter 15 sums up Sandoval's very negative assessment of the way in which the Ethiopians, in his view, have "fallen from God's grace" by deserting the Christianity they once practiced. How does connecting skin color to moral decline move toward a more hardened view of Africans as natural slaves and other race-based generalizations?

The black nations are now so abandoned, miserable, cursed, and unfortunate that they are in a dangerous state with little or no way of improvement. What caused this? What curse made such an abundant and rich people, so favored by God himself, so alone and sick without God? The white color that shone from those souls has disappeared so that even if they want to, they cannot change the black and ugly color of their bodies.

Chapter 16. This ministry gives honor, glory, and spiritual delights to his ministers, and dignity and nobility to fallen souls.

Despite his negative description of blackness in the last chapter, Sandoval does not view Africans as inherently or permanently irredeemable. Instead, as he repeats throughout De instauranda, *they have strayed from Christianity due to the influence of the devil. According to this passage, who can rescue Africans from their fate?*

There is nothing better than working to save souls, in liberating captives not from the Turks or the Moors but from the power of the devil. This ministry does this by baptizing those who have not been baptized because they are unloved, not because no one would give them this holy sacrament. . . . This holy ministry is a fountain of life and health, gathering together souls that lack any knowledge of the doctrine or the true God. . . . The sacred scripture says that the best possible work a person can do is bringing needy souls to God.

Chapter 17. This ministry is excellent for the great benefits it gives to its ministers.

The main idea of this chapter is "God most loves and desires the salvation of souls, so there is no other occupation more agreeable to His Majesty or beneficial to us than this ministry." Sandoval compares God's reaction to the "harvesting of souls," a common Jesuit metaphor, to the way the king of Spain might feel if one of his subjects brought him a valuable nugget of gold or silver from one of the mines in the Americas. What kind of reward is promised in the passage below?

Preachers who work with souls will shine in glory like stars in the heavens, because they are illuminated by the light of all of those that they have saved. And how about those who work with desperate and hopeless people? Saint Augustine says that one star shines more brightly than another, and so do priests, depending on what they do. So what light and rays shoot forth from our work? Each person who works in this ministry will receive, from the hand of God, a beautiful kingdom and a resplendent crown [in heaven], bringing certain security and secure tranquility, tranquil tenderness, gentle happiness, happy blessedness, blessed vision, and unending praise for God.

Chapter 18. This ministry is excellent for practicing theological virtues to a superlative degree.

How does Sandoval try to make the mission to African slaves appealing in this chapter? How does Sandoval explain how a priest practices the virtues of faith, hope, and charity in this chapter? Sandoval repeats his conviction in the inherent goodness of Africans, and he appeals to the Jesuit appreciation of hard work, self-sacrifice, and martyrdom for a good cause. At the end of the chapter Sandoval goes deeper into exploring the essence of charity and how a charitable person must act, using a biblical quote from 1 Corinthians 13. He explores this theme in greater detail in the next chapter.

If you view the black nations as a piece of land where God has buried his richest treasures, as an evangelical minister you will strive to acquire this land and immediately start digging it up. The treasures found in this field are the most heroic virtues and blessings. This is one of the best arguments I can make for this ministry: it forces us to continually exercise the most excellent virtues. I will begin this discussion by speaking of the greatest virtues of faith, hope, and charity. Those who work in this ministry constantly challenge their faith. The workers must also continuously feel hope that their efforts are saving souls. And no other work is so charitable. We practice all of these virtues only for God's benefit. Only for his sake will a person decide to no longer deal with the rich and powerful, for the sake of overwork, fatigue, and even death, as they try to help these rejected, poor, coarse people.

What other ministry practices faith more? We need very strong faith in order to bring life to dead souls. Faith consumes the life of those who work with the blacks, especially in dealing with the *bozales*. Doing this work out of strong faith means a happy life and a peaceful death.

No other ministry forces one to constantly draw on the virtue of hope. Here we hope for so much, because our task is so arduous and difficult. We constantly strive to feel hope in so many ways: we hope to help people who have neglected the faith for so long, and we hope we can overcome their ignorance, their difficulty with our language, their rebelliousness, and their tendency to reject the faith even when they are free in their own lands.

Although they are barbarous and uneducated, when slaves come to Christian lands they are willing to receive the faith and work hard to protect their faith. I also believe, and others who understand these nations agree with me, that in their lands they might try to practice our faith, but they often commit many errors. This is because they lack priests, not because they are naturally evil. The Abyssinians have been Christian since ancient times, but because they have no priests, they have degenerated from their excellent beginnings. Nubia was Christian in ancient times, but it lost the faith when one of the country's bishops died. The Nubians worried about this, so they wrote to the Ethiopian emperor and asked him to appoint a bishop for them. Two Augustinian friars lived in the kingdom of Congo. They spent their lives baptizing, and when they died, the king wrote to the Portuguese king and asked for more priests. When none were sent, he rang the church bell himself and brought the black people together to talk about God. He spent the rest of his life trying to preserve the Christian faith.[28]

The two poor friars mentioned above must have had great hope and confidence to believe a mission could succeed among barbarous infidels carrying bows and arrows and lacking any knowledge of God. Some men have had great success in trying to convert barbarous people, but others have lost their lives or suffered a long captivity. God makes some of them into martyrs, and others stay hopeful as they preach to thousands of souls. This work is like constantly carrying a heavy ebony cross, but the rewards make it easier. Merchants and sailors are brave enough to endure the sea and huge waves. Laborers work through storms and tempests, and soldiers fight through wounds and defeat. So we, who work to bring spiritual health to so many people and help them reach heaven, must not let hard work scare us.

Most of all, this ministry practices charity. You cannot do this work without charitable feelings, because while you work with the slaves, it is impossible to feel pride, envy, ambition, impatience, and, above all, self-love. This ministry forces you to constantly practice the virtues and never indulge in any vices. In this work you must constantly exercise all of the following elements of charity: charity is patient and kind; it is not envious; it does no harm to anyone; it is not proud, nor ambitious, nor self-interested; charity does not brag; it does not become angry easily; it does not remember evil; it does not celebrate evil or dis-

28. See Introduction for more information about Christianity and Catholic missions in Africa.

honesty; it endures everything; it has unending faith and hope and perseveres forever.[29] We will discuss each of these points in the next chapter.

Chapter 19. This ministry is excellent for exercising all the virtues of charity.

Using a rhetorical style that recreates preaching a sermon to a group of Jesuits, Sandoval breaks down each of the lines from 1 Corinthians 13 mentioned at the end of Chapter 18 to explain in detail how working with African slaves fulfills each one of these listed individual characteristics of charity. Sandoval tries to directly engage his readers as if they were in his presence by addressing them as "you." While arguing his points, Sandoval uses various examples and anecdotes, bringing to life many details of his day-to-day work experiences, which are explored in greater detail in Book 3. To Sandoval, charity, also translated as love, is the most important Christian virtue. A person who wants to go to heaven must practice this virtue, and he argues that the best method for priests to set themselves on this path is to work with the African slaves. What models does Sandoval encourage the Jesuits to emulate? How does he characterize Africans here? What pedagogical methods does he recommend? How does he contrast, juxtapose, and evaluate scholarly and missionary activities in this chapter?

Charity Is Patient

Working to help these poor people exercises a basic virtue of charity: patience. Through our love we endure much suffering and we must always be patient. We travel at all hours, even under the burning sun of midday, without thinking about our personal comfort or health, worrying only about the needs of others. It is very tiring to work in this hot country, so we must be patient even when we are sweating and exhausted.

We practice patience looking for interpreters. We often cannot find interpreters, but we can do nothing without them. We must be very patient when the interpreters do not want to come to help us or when their masters will not let them help us. We must be patient with the interpreters, because they also get tired of this work and hide to avoid it. Sometimes the interpreters lose their patience and ruin all the time we have spent looking for people to bring together to catechize, which can take five or six hours running all over town. We must be patient when it seems that the slaves do not understand and will not want to respond. We must be patient with their barbarity and difficulty with our language. We should instead seek out the loving language of the Holy Spirit. This is how the apostles attracted converts. We have to be patient with

---

29. This famous passage is often used in marriage vows.

the masters, because instead of appreciating the help we give their slaves, they hide them and try to make them avoid catechism. They force them to work or even sell them to keep them away from us. These are just a few of the things that could make us lose our patience. But we cannot get angry and speak harshly. We have to always remain gentle and supportive so that they will eventually surrender themselves to our efforts. This entire nation of people tries a man's patience. Without patience, mercy, and love, our efforts are useless. As everyone who has experience knows, whenever you want to do anything well, you have to suffer and be patient. This is especially true when you are working with souls: it is like the patience that a fisherman has to have when he waits an entire afternoon for a fish to bite his hook.[30]

In conclusion, a great deal of patience and tolerance is extremely necessary when working with these people. For their own good, we must make them listen to us. Two great saints, Saint Francis Xavier and the patriarchal saint of Ethiopia, Andrés de Oveido, worked with blacks.[31] Through their patience, they opened up China, stopped the persecutions in Japan, penetrated almost all of Guinea, and converted many kingdoms.[32] All we have to do is try to convert a few black slaves! Patience is a rock that breaks the waves and undercurrents in this sea of difficulties. Spaniards have many more vices, and it takes much more patience to work with them. We ask so little from people who are new to the faith. Our Lord only wants their salvation. Remember that patience is born from love, and nothing can cool the love of Christ in your heart.

Charity Is Kind

The charitable worker is kind, gentle, and friendly to everyone. God is very good and gentle when he sets his attention on the poor. His kind eyes turn to the black slaves because they are poor unfortunates that need his gentleness and goodness. God favored and honored human beings, his servants, because he made one of them the Mother of his Son, as a blessing to all of us. In this way, God favored us and made us great. We take advantage of God's favor when we show our compassion and kindness by passing on this favor to others through instruction, doctrine, and the sacraments.

If we face opposition in our work, from either slaves' masters or anyone else, we must not give up but instead feel even more motivated, exchanging bad feelings for positive action. You must always have a happy, positive spirit to endure

---

30. "Fishing for souls" was a common phrase the Jesuits used to describe their work.

31. Andrés de Oveido was a Jesuit who worked in Ethiopia and lived from 1518 to 1580.

32. An optimistic summary of international Jesuit missions. Many of these missions would suffer reverses in the 1600s.

all the difficulties you face in carrying out this charitable ministry. We must treat the blacks kindly and help them by showing them generosity and mercy. We must speak gently and be willing to repeat ourselves. Sometimes, in order to save someone's soul, I have to repeat myself a thousand times. I know someone who has enough patience to repeat one point for six hours before he moves on to another issue.[33] You will need to be very friendly all the time, because this is the best way to soften even the hardest heart. We must speak to slaves as if they were our sons or brothers and promise them that we will force their masters to give them medicine, clothes, and rewards and treat them well. We must not be disgusted when they do not understand us. We cannot show our anger or worries. We must bring them gifts that they can enjoy, because "a spoonful of sugar helps the medicine go down." We must give them clothes to cover their nudity. We must tell them about the Gospel when they are sick and let them know that God will bring them peace and well-being.

Charity Is Not Envious

There is no envy in charity. If you truly love another, you desire only good things for this person. It is impossible to be kind and gentle if you are envious. The worker who is dedicated to this holy labor is content with his fate, because he is imitating the saints in heaven. None of the saints envy each other because they all enjoy each other's glory. If we are doing God's work, why should we envy others? What could be a better occupation for us? The Son of God gives us nothing but love and help here on earth, so we should do nothing else but give love in return, for the greater glory of God. We must not do this unenthusiastically but walk quickly and purposefully and begin climbing the gentle mountain of converting souls for God and the angels.

Charity Is Not Proud

When we practice charity, we do not speak poetically but use simple and direct words to set hearts alight and burning. In the ministry to the blacks we must go directly to the point without affectation or pompous words. We speak differently from our usual speech in order to make ourselves understood. We might have to speak barbarically, in a way that would enrage a grammar teacher. Saint Bernard[34] spoke with admirable eloquence and sagacity. He accommodated his words to his listeners' level of understanding. When he talked with laborers, he spoke as if he were a servant in the field; with gentlemen, he spoke like a court-

---

33. Sandoval is probably referring to Pedro Claver here.

34. It is not clear which of the many men who are named Bernard, and who have been made saints—Sandoval is referring to here.

ier; with idiots he used simple and crude metaphors; but with pedantic sophists, he could argue subtly and with great ingenuity and wit. Like any good fisherman, he had different hooks and bait for different kinds of fish, because he showed great charity and only wished to win souls for the Lord.

Those who work with the black slaves must say no more than absolutely necessary. Any verbal ornamentation or elegance is superfluous. The slaves are like invalids with no appetite for food, who must be given something simple and nutritious. They can only comprehend the most basic points, and more details only bother or embarrass them because they do not understand them. Or, if they do understand, wordiness distracts them from the main point. The minister does not need to use elaborate rhetoric or many subtle arguments and intricate ideas because this subtlety will drown them in things they do not understand. You must organize and present the doctrine in a way that suits each listener, giving milk to the infants and food to the adults. If you hope to teach and preach to vulgar people, you do not drown them in mysteries that they do not understand.

Our holy father and master Saint Francis Xavier provides us with many examples of this kind of teaching, and I find these examples very helpful. Because he had a gentle and effective sense of charity, he would walk through an entire city ringing with his own hand the little bell sent to him from Rome to East India. He stopped in the plazas and crossroads to proclaim: "Faithful Christian friends of Jesus Christ, I call on your sons and daughters and all of your slaves to receive the holy doctrine, for love of God." His kind words were sent from heaven and made many people run to the father and enter the church with him. Then, with his eyes and spirit elevated to God, he made the sign of the cross and spoke aloud, very softly and with great devotion. He spoke so his listeners would understand. He thought only of God's glory and helping their souls, so he spoke Portuguese, which was what they spoke.

There is no waste in charitable acts. This is especially the case in this ministry to the black slaves. You must proceed very cautiously with those who have been converted recently. When you ask them if they are baptized or not, ask the question very delicately so that they do not retreat in shame or anger.

You must be modest to be charitable. This is a very important virtue practiced in this ministry. We work with humble people, and so we must also be humble.

This ministry is free of anything false or superfluous. We can only concern ourselves with things related directly to our goals. Without doubt, no one is richer than those that work with these miserable people: before God our rags are fine brocade; horrible smells seem like sweet incense; filth and mud are turned into a golden treasure. Helping a soul in such extreme misery is not done in vain, nor is there any part of this work that is not full of grace and glory.

Charity Does Not Brag

One of the most essential properties of charity is that it does not promote itself. The worker is charitable partially because he is not arrogant or boastful. Vanity and self-complacency destroy good works. The Gospel of Matthew 6:1–5 says, do not perform good works in front of others to hear them praise you, or you will not be rewarded in heaven. The hypocrite has no hope of entering heaven. Human praise runs out when life ends. If you think about it clearly, how can you compare the kingdom of heaven with the vain praise of people? Look at what you do in life: you plant much and harvest little, you eat but you are never satiated, you drink but you are not satisfied; you cover yourself but you are still not warm. All you do in your time on earth achieves nothing—it is as if you put something in a sack full of holes or poured wine into a leaking cask. Do not exaggerate your charity, because although your efforts are very meritorious, it is best to focus on God, not the vainglory of exterior things. Working in this ministry completely absorbs the worker, but you will receive no public recognition. No one will praise you for working for four or six hours teaching the blacks what is necessary for their salvation. Without the Lord's help, we could not overcome these physical and spiritual challenges. But despite these challenges, this work passes pleasurably, even happily and delightfully.

Charity Is Not Ambitious

Do not practice charity out of ambitiousness. This mission is a perfect demonstration of this point, because everything good comes from within this divine enterprise, and there is nothing else to desire beyond it. It is a pleasure to be without ambition. When you deal with such humble people, you gladly accept the help of others, not because you want recognition but just because you enjoy it and do not want to do the work alone. The holy father Master Francis Xavier thought that people who worked to convert infidels and catechize recent converts should be very humble and not have ambitions for other work besides this very humble ministry. He chose men from Portugal to help him, rewarding the most serious, virtuous, and talented priests for their long service and work. Xavier knew from experience that this work made men face the temptations of the devil and other bothersome things, so only very holy and careful people could work with him. Clever or wise priests were not suited for the work. However, he said that men who combined both virtue and learning could serve as the ideal ministers of the Gospel. Those who were more scholarly than virtuous might not be satisfied doing this work, because their high level of learning meant that perhaps they should not concern themselves with such thieving, low, barbarous, and vulgar people, although doing this would offer a great sacrifice to God Our Lord. Charity only sees the good. No ministry, however lowly, should be disdained if it makes a man work to imitate Christ's example. These ideas are important for maintaining a charitable heart, because many things in this ministry seem indecent and provoke fastidiousness in ecclesiastical persons. Charity embraces everything, from souls full of sin to poverty and bodily indecency. Thus charity is not ambitious.

Charity Does Not Seek Rewards

Those who do charitable work do not look for their own personal benefits. This is especially the case in this ministry to the blacks. In place of the comforts and gifts that you naturally seek out for yourself, comfort them and give them gifts in order to save them and heal their bodies and souls. This point is proven throughout this book. Do not seek personal rewards, because charity offers all that it has for the good of other souls.

Charity Does Not Anger Easily

Do not become irritated or angered in this ministry, even when other people seem to stand in the way of doing things for the glory of God. When you are absorbed in this work you will take little notice of anger. Having a bad temper and making accusations only exaggerates unimportant problems. When one hard object hits another, you hear a noise, but when something hard hits something soft, no one hears or feels anything. A bullet can make a great deal of noise if it is shot into solid stone, but when the bullet hits a sack of wool, the softness blocks its trajectory and it loses its force. Therefore, a soft and gentle answer can calm anger, while a bitter and sharp answer provokes anger, like throwing wood on a fire. Your charity will prevent you from acting angrily or being unwilling to work, even while you are experiencing very crude things and dealing with the extraordinary lack of understanding in these people. Showing patience and modesty when faced with the intolerable stench and brutal nudity of these people only serves to enlarge the soul.

Charity Does Not Remember Evil

In doing charitable work, you suspend your judgment many times every day. In this ministry, we see rational men, redeemed with the blood of Jesus Christ, suffering great misfortune and misery in their bodies and souls, lacking help for their salvation. They are naked, abandoned, almost without food or drink, and abused. Still, you must refrain from judgment. Charity is so simple that it not only does no evil but never even suspects evil. Doing charitable work means attending only to your own concerns, not noticing how masters do not care for their slaves or even scorn them. Do not be injured from insults, and concern yourself only with matters pertaining to God.

Charity Does Not Celebrate Evil

In doing charitable work you often see things that are painful and sad: people who have died without learning anything, without receiving baptism or any of the sacraments. We must use these negative occurrences to inspire us to work more and improve the situation. Charity also suffers from its own faults and imperfections. Some kinds of people find shortcomings in themselves, but knowing your own imperfections does not mean you should give up. Even those who work for religious goals do not have to be perfect but should just strive to improve themselves. Everyone has something they can improve in themselves, but slowly, as we work, we can lessen our faults and weaken the devil inside of us. Doing works of charity gradually diminishes our own imperfections. God is loyal to us, and he will not permit us to be tempted by more than we can resist. He helps us in overcoming and defeating our personal demons and carrying on with our service to him.

Charity Is Honest

Evangelical ministers who work with poor people can feel happy in the fact that they work for truth. They feel joy when they see those that they have helped leave the path of lies and enter the true path of the faith, the certainty of the sacraments. They save so many souls that would have otherwise been condemned to hell, so God offers them the reward of heaven in return for their hard work. Even if the work seems too difficult, we should not give up, because eventually this work becomes enjoyable. Discipline and practice at first seem difficult, painful, and sad, but soon they are easy and agreeable. At the end of the day, I can look around and see four or five slaves who I have been instructing about to be buried. I think to myself, I worked for three hours with one of these people, surrounded by a terrible stench. I felt heartfelt anguish for two hours, trying to overcome the ignorance of another person. I wasted four hours looking for an interpreter for another individual. Of the remaining two, one was baptized and the other received extreme unction. Now all of them lay dying, but I have instructed all of them and given them the sacraments, so I am happy, knowing that Jesus Christ's blood was shed for the salvation of their souls.

Charity Endures Everything and Has Endless Faith, Hope, and Perseverance

Doing charitable work practices these four virtues: patience, faith, hope, and perseverance. There is no patience without suffering, and in this ministry we must endure constant suffering. But after all of our labor and tribulation, we will be rewarded with great happiness and rest in heaven. Be happy, because it is certain that you will receive great treasures in heaven. Even if all the earth turned into gold and all the rocks and stones became precious pearls, this would not compare to what you will receive. We must have great faith and hope in order to believe that we can succeed in converting the black slaves. We must also endure many things in order to help our brothers.

Chapter 20. This ministry is excellent for practicing works of spiritual mercy.

Jesuits working with African slaves spent all their time involved in charity such as "teaching, advising, correcting, preaching, confessing, and administering the sacraments." The sections included here focus on one of the most basic Jesuit conceptions of their charitable mission, what they called consolation, or providing comfort for those they perceived as in spiritual need. How does Sandoval characterize the emotions felt by African slaves? How does he assess their behavior? Are slaves presented as individuals here or does he generalize about all Africans?

These people respond best to someone who treats them with love and friendliness, because they are very confused and afraid about their new life and the work they must do. We try to give them good advice and calm them.

In this ministry we often work to comfort sad people. All the blacks are very sad and feel very disturbed by their painful state of captivity. No free person outside this ministry knows more about these unhappy people, their worries, and the pain they suffer. We are the only people who regularly interact with them, so we have many opportunities to console them with the love and mercy of God. We try to make them feel better by speaking of the afterlife. This usually encourages them and makes them feel better.

The person who works in this ministry faces many challenges and annoyances. Almost all of the slaves are very ignorant. They do not know how to work for their own salvation. They do not understand the concept of confessing their sins, so we must ask them many questions. Some are very crude. We could say something a dozen or more times without them understanding it. Some slaves will deny that they have committed any sins, so the confessor has to prompt and question them very carefully. Others give contradictory confessions. They confess one thing and then deny it, so the confessor does not know the actual sin. Some are very long-winded and waste time with vulgar talk. Others are very afraid, and we can do nothing to calm them down. Still others act very rudely and contradict what the confessor says to them. Some slaves are very hard and insensitive. They show no reaction, no sadness or repentance, no matter what we say to them. But we must be patient with all of this because we can only appeal to them through our love. We have to speak softly and tenderly, and act kindly and friendly. If we get angry with them, they will become exasperated and irritated or just sad, and then it is impossible to convert them or help them in any way.

Chapter 21. This ministry also excels in works of bodily mercy.

To the most basic list of human needs (water, clothing, and shelter) Sandoval adds "a good death." Preparing individuals for their death and burying them afterward was one of the charitable acts most valued by the Jesuits. The point of summarizing these charitable actions is to show how working with slaves strengthens a Jesuit's chance of an afterlife spent in heaven. However, describing the charity also reveals the experiences of African slaves. Does the issue of the clothing focus more on Sandoval's ideas of modesty or the slaves' needs?

There are many opportunities to help these poor people. Normally they are sick when we visit them. We preach the Gospels to them, but before that we give them a gift and cool them down with a little drink of water. They often say they will not receive the holy sacraments until they have water. They are very thirsty when they leave the slave ships. It seems like their insides have been burned by the salt water. They are forced to drink salt water because their masters forget to give them fresh water, and they are afraid to ask for it, so they are left to die of thirst. This happens most often to women and children. They feel much better after drinking cool water and will sometimes drink huge quantities because they are literally dying of thirst.

The slaves cannot provide clothes for themselves, so we beg their masters to at least cover them decently. But often we have to bring them some rags to wear, and they are so grateful that we might have given them the most elegant brocades. This gratefulness proves that they feel ashamed of their nudity, but they cannot do anything about it. We also try to help improve their living conditions. We beg their masters to house them decently and treat them like humans, not beasts. We also try to make the *cimarones,* or runaways, return to the service of their masters.

Finally, we work in this ministry to help provide the dead with shrouds and a decent burial. After the slaves die, we place them in a decent position and place so that priests will come and take them to the church, where they are buried like Christians. Otherwise, their masters throw them out with their garbage, without a shroud.

Chapter 22. This ministry practices poverty, chastity, and obedience.

Sandoval struggles with the subject of chastity because he cannot be very specific in this discussion. Openly and directly describing how working with slaves challenges the Jesuit vow of chastity would mean discussing sexuality, exactly what Sandoval wants to deemphasize. He argues that in the mission to the slaves, it is not difficult to maintain the vow of chastity, despite the fact that the Jesuit priests often work with naked and, in his perception, immodest people. He supports this idea with the argument that because they are working so hard to do good deeds, the priests do not think about the fact that they work with people who are naked. Sandoval advises them, "One must be careful not to look [at their bodies] in order to avoid anxiety and distraction in one's heart. Good works are a great remedy against Satan's temptations and lead to purity in the heart." In fact, Sandoval says that if male priests really want to show how strong they are in resisting temptation, they should not hide from women, considered the "gateway to hell" in the early modern Catholic vision of sin and temptation. (In contrast to the last chapter, here it seems that the slaves are to blame for the fact that they do not have any clothes.) He notes that a saint once said it is possible to be chaste even around Roman dancing girls. The idea is that it is morally superior to resist blatant temptation instead of simply avoiding sin by hiding from it. Sandoval assures his readers that if a priest is doing something good, God will protect him from submitting to his temptations.

Although Sandoval is quite vague about providing details of what kind of temptation the slaves offer the Jesuits, he says that priests who work with them will both see and hear "things they do not want to see and hear." But he advises them to ignore or forget these things, focusing their minds on the spiritual rather than the physical, a difficult task because the physicality of Africans, as hard workers who were often without clothing (especially in Africa), was the focus of European perceptions of them. Sandoval judges the Spanish to be more physically attractive and appealing (perhaps he is also thinking of their more familiar European mannerisms and elegant dress), so in his opinion, Africans offer fewer temptations to the Jesuits. Africans were viewed as physically stronger than Europeans, and African women as less attractive, in order for both sexes to be more suited for hard work and less capable of intellectual activities. This kind of thinking about beauty and physicality provided the foundations for later racial stereotypes and generalizations.

Our minds and vision must be like the rays of the sun, because the sun's rays shine down on garbage and other disgusting and filthy things, but they always stay pure and clear. We are the rays of the Sun Christ Our Lord. We look at human bodies with an honest freedom and a free honesty, as if they were souls without bodies and inanimate corporeal things. It is more risky to work with Spanish men and women, because they have a better outward appearance and a more presentable way of speaking, so we deal with them without noticing the danger too much. If there is temptation in seeing the blacks naked, that very nakedness and the disgust that goes along with it are a very effective remedy against temptation. If we truly give our spirit to this holy ministry and to the glory of the Lord, trying to do everything perfectly, we will not be distracted by what we hear and see.

Chapter 23. This ministry practices humility and other virtues.

Sandoval concludes Book 2 by explaining how working with slaves will make a person humble, continuing the theme of how Jesuits will receive moral benefits and God's favor by taking part in Sandoval's mission. He provides several reasons for why this work is so humbling. First, no one praises or even cares about working with slaves, so a person cannot become arrogant or proud. Second, Sandoval lists three behavior traits that he says the Virgin commands because they help "practice humility in order to please her Son and conquer the enemy." These are eating the worst food, wearing the simplest clothes, and seeking out the most humiliating work. Sandoval says his work with slaves fits all three requirements, and "although it is shocking, virtue and the highest perfection can be found in the filthiest jobs." In this approach, doing the "dirty work" is morally superior to holding positions of power or being a great scholar. Sandoval says that God would advise "scholars, preachers, and teachers" to "leave the books and clever ideas, the applause of the pulpit, and the estimation of men. Put your learning and talent toward helping the blacks, a miserable and unfortunate people who are treated like animals." People who work with the slaves become kinder, gentler, less selfish, and more patient, and therefore they have more virtues and a better chance of going to heaven. Finally, Sandoval says that this ministry may seem poor, but it is actually very rich because "We easily find God's presence in it, and His Majesty gives his riches with full hands to those employed in this labor. . . . In the darkness, gloom, and obscurity of Ethiopia hides the majesty of God, and he lives happily in these nations. He does not hate this dark and obscure land."

END OF THE SECOND BOOK.

Book 3

METHODS FOR PROMOTING THE SALVATION OF BLACKS IN THE PORTS OF AFRICA AND THE INDIES

Book 3 highlights the fact that Sandoval viewed De instauranda *as a manual for Jesuits who wanted to join his mission baptizing African slaves in Cartagena. This section is full of practical advice for those who want to take part in Sandoval's ministry. With step-by-step instructions, he carefully details his approach to baptism, catechism (teaching Africans the basic precepts of Christianity), confession, and communion. As the specific details accumulate, Sandoval shows his absolute conviction in the rightness of baptizing Africans, his lack of recognition of any other belief systems, and the further development of his vision of Africans. How does Sandoval prove, in Book 3, that he is an "ecclesiastical imperialist," as mentioned in the Introduction?*

Argument of the Third Book

This third section presents the fundamental goal and purpose of the book. The success of this entire enterprise depends on working with an organized method. If we do not use the right methods, our entire project, so valued by God, will fail. The natural condition of those we are working with demands a method and a plan. If we do not follow our plan, we will reverse the good we have already achieved. In Book 3 I explain the methods I have developed after researching many different nations [African ethnic groups]. I have learned how much variation there is amongst them and that what works for one nation will not work for another. We must have a methodical system to go directly to the truth and make progress toward baptism, and I have developed a system to catechize them, take their confessions, and administer the sacraments. Here I describe some successful cases, in order to provide a model for future success. I also present situations that will help guide you in making the right decisions. I explain how to prepare the slaves to receive the holy sacraments, which are the divine channels of life. But the sacraments can be corrupted when they are administered unsystematically, and then the sacraments might fail to fulfill God's expectations.

I could have discussed these issues in a more scholarly or intellectual way (as I have tried to do in the other books) in order to amuse the reader, but instead I have chosen a clear, straightforward style to best convince and persuade. I decided that I must strip my ideas of their eloquent and rhetorical clothing, so that, thus naked like ancient athletes in the arena, they can engage in hand-to-hand combat with their contradictions and defeat them. Simplicity is the most effective way to defeat confusion.

Chapter 1. Important Observations to Aid in Ministering to the Black Slaves.

The warnings provided here give the reader a sense of the urgency Sandoval feels about baptizing African slaves, highlighting disease and death. Why would a slave hide the fact that he or she was sick? What role do masters and doctors play, according to Sandoval, in helping or harming their sick slaves? What kind of emotion does Sandoval expect his readers to feel when they work with sick and dying slaves? In this chapter Sandoval describes his activities and quotes sources that appeal to the ideals of the Company of Jesus, reminding his Jesuit readers that, from the foundation of the order in the mid-1500s, Jesuit writings stressed active ministries and also portrayed the Jesuits as "doing battle" for Christianity. Sandoval's concern with the Jesuit mission, goals, and image becomes central in Book 4.

Before getting to the specific details of how we practice this holy ministry, I must emphasize that all ministries that help souls for the glory of God are worthy of our efforts. However, I believe that confessing, converting, teaching, baptizing, and guiding these poor black *bozales*[1] and putting them on the road to heaven is the most meritorious work, of the greatest glory to the Lord, and the most advantageous and useful for us.[2]

I want to give you some warnings that I have learned from many years' experience. The first is that we cannot wait to be called to help people who need us. We must travel around constantly, looking for souls who need our help. When we hear that fleets of slave ships have come to the port, we must not wait until we find out they are sick and dying. Instead, we must meet the fleets, if possible, before they sail off to the isolated places where they offload the dead slaves and bury them to protect the cities from the plagues they are carrying. We cannot trust their masters. When we go to masters homes to ask about their slaves' sicknesses, they tell us that their slaves are perfectly well or not very sick at all. Since the masters only care if their slaves are alive or dead, a dying slave seems very healthy to them. Because I used to believe masters' stories about their slaves' sicknesses, occasionally I would arrive at their homes and find the black slaves already dead, missing out on baptism, confession,

---

1. See p. 5, note 6 or the glossary for a definition of *bozales*.

2. Sandoval reiterates the central message of Book 2: that charity and good works create merit to lead to a heavenly reward.

and instruction before they died. We must only believe what we see with our own eyes, and we must not fear being humiliated for the sake of helping so many souls.

My second important warning is that when you see a sick slave, help him immediately, even if he does not seem that badly off. Alexander the Great said: "To achieve great victories, do not put off for tomorrow something that could be done today."[3] Suetonius said that Julius Caesar wrote or studied every day, even when he was fighting a battle. He was so ambitious that he held his lance in one hand and his pen in the other.[4] If non-Christians act this way, aren't we, as Christians and priests, even more obligated to get our important work done, especially when we are working with such needy people? If we want to succeed in our mission, no day should pass without work.

The reason why we must always be alert and hard at work is because if we back down for one moment, a forest full of terrible thorns will instantly appear and we will not be able to find a path through it. Another reason is that these people are so barbaric that it requires so much work to catechize them and prepare them for baptism and confession, especially when they are cramped by sickness and so disgusting that nature itself abhors them. If we cannot persevere, of course our interpreters cannot stand to continue, either. If the slaves manage to live, they will have the benefit of the sacraments, and we will have achieved something good by administering them. Then we can relax and drift in the ocean of this ministry, not drown in the sea of worries. We can become overwhelmed if we dwell on the fact that so many of them are always so sick, that we must work day and night without reward or enjoyment, and that often we cannot find dependable interpreters. The blacks themselves regularly hide the fact that they are dying on their feet. When they finally explain their sickness, they are very badly off. Because they had not known how to explain or indicate their sickness, they are now about to die. So we must give them spiritual help as quickly as possible, assuming that any illness they have is very serious. This is the best way to avoid a thousand disasters every day.

My third warning is also very important. We must tell all the medical doctors and surgeons to let us know which slaves are sick so that we can minister to them and prevent the carelessness of their masters. We must make the doctors remember to inform us when they find someone with an incurable disease. Masters, overseers, priests, and curates must also call on us for our help, and

---

3. Alexander was a Macedonian conqueror who lived from 356 to 323 B.C.E.

4. Suetonius was a Roman historian who lived from around 70 to 130 C.E. In one of his most famous works, *The Lives of the Caesars*, he describes the life of Gaius Julius Caesar (100–44 B.C.E.), a great Roman leader and military general.

then we will come to remedy the sickness and help the priests who are confessing the very sick.[5]

Ultimately, we cannot think only of successful conversions. We should dwell on the will of God. We can do nothing more than our best to please God. We must spread our good intentions to everyone who works in our ministry, because our purity gives us great peace and prevents anything from standing in the way of our success.

Chapter 2. Of the necessity of multilingual, faithful interpreters and linguists.

In this chapter Sandoval refers to Pliny the Elder, a Roman scholar from the first century, to observe that a person who does not speak another's language seems to be a subhuman barbarian. Sandoval used the term "barbaric" to describe uncomprehending Africans in Chapter 1 of Book 3; thus he both perceives how language difficulties dehumanize others and falls into this mindset himself. What practical tips does Sandoval suggest here to overcome the challenge of language difference? Unlike the apostles in the Bible, Sandoval must depend on African interpreters. When it comes to interpreters, and Sandoval used numerous Africans for this job, perhaps here he introduces some variety in his generally negative view of the slaves' mental capacities. Why would he sometimes not trust the interpreters to communicate Christian doctrine correctly, even though he believes them to be quite dependable when it comes to not revealing sexual secrets told in the slaves' private confessions? How can the attitudes Sandoval demonstrates regarding sexuality and the confession be connected to the argument that sexual violence is always present in slavery?[6] Race and sexuality are also linked in this chapter when Sandoval compares walking around town with an African interpreter to Loyola's being seen with prostitutes.

Since they do not understand our language and we do not understand theirs, the information in the last chapter is useless unless we have interpreters who understand the language of the sick or healthy adult who, with our help, is to be catechized, baptized, or confessed. Masters do not use interpreters, nor will they help us find them. And it is virtually impossible for us to learn all of these numerous and very distinct languages, especially with no one here to teach us.

People who work in this ministry must walk around the entire day looking for linguists and interpreters, because if they do not, the entire structure of this

---

5. People gave their final confession as part of the last rites. This was done in hopes of having sins absolved before death in order to open up the possibility of going to heaven.

6. See Chapter 19 for further discussion of this issue.

work will collapse. As Pliny writes, those who speak different languages do not view each other as fellow human beings. The use of linguists and interpreters for the conversion of infidels is not a new practice. This method was used by the apostles and other saintly men, even though the Lord communicated with the gift of all languages on the day of Pentecost.[7] If the sacred apostles had such success saving souls with the help of interpreters, even though they did not really need them, we must understand that we desperately need interpreters to achieve anything in this ministry. The apostles traveled around looking for interpreters, so we should not be ashamed to walk around a city doing the same. It is an effort but not so much so, and we perform much more difficult tasks as part of this ministry. It is not undignified for a priest to go from house to house looking for translators. After he finds them, he should not be ashamed to walk with them, even if they are black. Ignatius himself walked with the prostitutes in Rome.[8] By looking for interpreters, we are adding to the sons of God and bringing souls into the Catholic Church.

It is helpful to have a little notebook or some other record in the form of an alphabetical list that includes all of the castes and languages and the known interpreters. Write down their names as well as where they live, the names of their owners, and how many languages they understand and speak. This way, when you need someone who speaks Angolan, Arda, Caravali, Bantu, Mandingo, Biojo, or one of the more than seventy other languages spoken in Angola, Sâo Tomé, the rivers of Guinea, or one of the other ports, you know where to look for them and can find them quickly and easily in order to use them to translate catechism lessons and help with baptisms and confessions of the sick. Without this notebook, you risk failure no matter how hard you try. I often failed to find interpreters after an exhausting day searching before I started working on my notebook.

We should also find out who speaks several languages so that we can avoid extra work and the hassle of finding several different interpreters. *Ladino* interpreters often speak several languages. The *bozales* also often speak and understand many languages, so they can be baptized, confessed, and helped in whatever language they understand, without us having to be forced to look for interpreters who speak every different language. I have frequently experienced cases where, for example, a sick Nalu speaker does not understand the language

7. On Pentecost, described in the New Testament and celebrated as a Christian holy day, the Holy Spirit visited the apostles in the form of a flame. A crowd of listeners suddenly understood everyone who spoke, despite their different languages, because each language spoken was heard as their own. This led to the baptism of three thousand people.

8. Ignatius Loyola founded a charitable house in Rome in 1543 as a ministry to prostitutes.

the Biafra interpreter is speaking. I must find a Nalu who speaks Biafra and thus catechize one person through three or four or even more interpreters.[9]

Some interpreters do not understand the catechism and will not repeat what is said to them, so we must have them repeat it several times in their own language. Some say whatever they please in their own language. We must look out for this and fix it before everything gets confused. When the interpreter does not understand what we are saying, this stands in the way of our getting the point across, because we have to repeat each question three or four times. Intelligent interpreters understand us immediately, but many do not—usually only one in ten is a good student. The best method is to make the interpreter repeat the mysteries of the faith that we are teaching, as can be seen in the following exchange:

I say, "Tell me, son, is there a God?"

He responds, "Yes."

"How many gods are there?"

He responds, "Only one."

"Tell me, who is God? Repeat to me the mystery of the Holy Trinity, and then as you have said it to me, repeat this to your relative in your language."

You must patiently and gently proceed in this way with all the mysteries of the faith in order to catechize successfully through an interpreter.

We have a few favorite interpreters whom we try to find whenever we can. These include both men and women, because both are needed to interpret confessions. If at all possible, to avoid difficulties when they are confessing their sins, principally lascivious ones, men must translate for other men, and female interpreters must be used in women's confessions. But sometimes we do not have enough interpreters to keep the sexes separate. Then we must tell the interpreters that they have to keep all secrets that they hear during confessions. I have never found this to be a problem.

We have to ask the interpreters' masters to let us use their slaves free of charge. Usually the masters do not want to volunteer their slaves to work as interpreters, so we have to persuade them that the slaves need to be catechized. We tell them that loaning us their slaves pleases Our Lord and that they are doing a great service. We give the interpreters devotional objects as a reward for working so hard on this task. All of these trivial details add up to a very beneficial ministry that saves many souls. A painting can be perfected by a tiny brushstroke, just as our task consists of humbling yourself, looking for interpreters, and putting into practice all the other trivial things I describe throughout this

---

9. See Book I, Chapter I, and the Glossary for more information on these language groups.

book. As Saint Jerome says,[10] little things matter a great deal, because they accumulate into something important.

Chapter 3. Of the blacks' potential to understand our holy faith.

This complex chapter reveals the several facets of racial ideologies in Sandoval's era. Sandoval purposefully and somewhat defensively positions himself in opposition to those who view teaching Africans about Christianity as a waste of time, attitudes held by slave masters, traders, priests, and perhaps even other Jesuits. Three interrelated elements of early modern race thinking are highlighted here: free will (in this case to accept or reject Christianity), language and the perception of barbarism, and the African performance of roles assigned to them versus European interpretations of African behavior. In the discussion of free will, Sandoval asserts his stance on a debate that began when Spaniards first discussed how to philosophically frame their role, referring back to ancient and medieval philosophers, as conquerors in the Americas. The terms of this debate were often defined by how "civilized" different groups of people were. Spanish philosophers and jurists in the 1500s debated these questions: Are some people "natural slaves," virtual animals living outside civilization? Or do they belong to nations that are so barbarous that they can be conquered, enslaved, and converted forcibly? Or do non-Europeans have free will and the ability to make decisions so that, once instructed, they will sensibly pick the best possible option, which is, in the minds of early modern thinkers including Sandoval, acceptance of Christianity and European domination?

Sandoval views Africans as being in the last category, using examples from personal experience to show that language does not represent a fundamental or permanent division between rational human beings and barbarous subhumans. Language, not their essential selves, their minds, or their intelligence, is the communication barrier here. It is as if he wants to sever the links that had begun to connect African slaves' language differences to inherent inferiority, a burgeoning racism fueled by other perceptions of African physicality that made them suitable slaves. For Sandoval, Africans have free will and thus cannot be forced to be Christian against their will. Sandoval also feels confident that, due to their inherent humanity, Africans will accept Christianity. His proof in this chapter is their behavior.

What can be learned from Sandoval's description of the positive reactions he sees after working with African slaves? It is too simple to relegate these descriptions to wishful thinking on his part. While his enthusiasm and conviction might have made Sandoval look for slaves' acceptance of Christianity, did African slaves also perform roles they

---

10. Jerome lived from approximately 340 to 420. He is considered one of the great scholars of the early Christian church, especially for his work translating the Bible from Greek and Hebrew into Latin.

believed would help them survive this new situation—having a preacher speak to them through an interpreter? Some historians argue that successful slaves constantly played roles for the sake of survival. In fact, surviving slavery, becoming ladino, *means losing the self in an imposed role.*[11] *Did Sandoval give the slaves any reason to demonstrate happiness, or were the slaves acting? Is it likely that slaves were so eager to accept their new names and, as Sandoval says, become "different people"? Did those slaves Sandoval mentions in the final paragraph simply perfect their performance until their masters viewed them as saints, or did there come a point when they actually became devout Christians?*

Our Lord God, the Catholic Church, the pope, the monarchs of Castile and Portugal, and the Company of Jesus have shown that they value black people, because they work to convert and save them in Ethiopia, Guinea, Congo, and the Philippines.[12] I believe that black people are worthy of all this effort. The time spent teaching them and administering the sacraments to them is not wasted. Those who say that these people are barbarous and rustic, lacking the potential to understand our faith, should remember that the apostles also preached to those who they now call incapable of understanding the faith.[13] In those days, they did not understand more nor were they any smarter than they are now. If the apostles and other saintly men found them to be so barbaric and believed that they wasted their time preaching to them, they would not have bothered to give them the good news of the Gospel. If the glorious Saint James the Great had judged the Spanish to be stubborn and rustic, he never would have gone to them to preach the gospel. Even after he made a huge effort, he did not convert more than ten Spaniards.[14] But even though we are not apostles, we convert many more people, which shows that the African nations have the potential to be Christian.

Here are a few examples of the many experiences I have had that show African slaves' potential to understand much more than what they are told and taught. Once I went out to baptize a black man because he told me he had not

---

11. Alex Bontemps explores this issue in *The Punished Self: Surviving Slavery in the Colonial South* (Ithaca, NY: Cornell University Press, 2001).

12. Of course only the Jesuits traveled to these places, but Sandoval wants to show that all the authorities *approve* of their efforts.

13. A reference to biblical apostles in Africa. See the Introduction for more information.

14. Saint James the Great is said to be an early disciple of Jesus who preached in Spain. He is also referred to in Spanish as Santiago Matamoros ("Saint James, Moor-killer") because of his miraculous appearances during battles between Christians and Islamic forces in the medieval Iberian peninsula. Sandoval makes an interesting comparison here, implicitly paralleling the ancient Spanish to Africans.

been baptized. I talked to his master to try to figure out why this was the case and if both master and slave were in agreement about his baptism. The master told me that his slave was deceiving me, because he himself had taken the slave to be baptized. I did not believe this and felt that the master was the one being deceived. I told the master's story to the black man, and he denied it so strongly that everyone believed him, even his master. He said that it was true that his master had taken him with the rest of his companions in a small canoe (something the master had mentioned) to the priest so that they would all have water poured on them [in the baptism ceremony]. However, this slave had not received baptism. When he was captured in Africa, his guard told him that when he was about to be baptized, he should say that his name was Miguel. He wanted to be baptized, so when the priest here asked his name, to try to figure out if he was already baptized, the slave said it was Miguel. The priest replied, "Then your name is Miguel, and you are already Christian."[15] Miguel said, "I left quickly, and soon my master came to take us on board the canoe. I did not have water poured on me." He concluded by saying that whatever his master said, he was not Christian, if being Christian meant having water poured over you. The master began to believe his slave. Miguel feels so much gratitude for the benefits of baptism that to this day, whenever he sees me he stops before me, falls on his knees, and claps his hands as a sign of joy. Then he asks me for my hands and puts them over his eyes, and then he gets up and goes on his way.

With the help of five interpreters, I baptized another who was on the brink of death. This man was so grateful to me for having saved his life that each time he met me on the street, he approached me, his face full of laughter, and bowed to me twice to show his gratitude, so deeply that I felt inspired to laugh and praise the Lord, because the man acknowledged the help I gave him in his own unique style. Many others do the same, and they are grateful not only to me but also to my companion [Pedro Claver?] and to the interpreter that translated for them.

Another black man told the interpreter to tell me that his soul felt very comforted after catechism and confession. He begged me to return another time so that he could speak to me more. A woman also asked me to return, saying that the words I said to her had consoled her very much. Another man was so happy when he heard what I told him about the immortality of the soul and the resurrection of the body that he kept clapping his hands to show the joyfulness in his heart and the fact that he no longer feared death. After I taught another slave the mystery of the Holy Trinity, he asked me, through the interpreter, what I

15. The fact that Miguel had a Spanish or Portuguese name made it seem like he had already been baptized, because these names were given or imposed on slaves before they were sold. As this example shows, the fact that slaves had a non-African name did not mean they had been baptized.

meant by three in one.[16] I appreciate these kinds of questions from a black man like him because they prove to me that these people are not really *bozales*. When they speak in their own language, they seem as intelligent as if they were *ladinos*. They complain about their work; they describe how uncharitable their masters are; they describe the inhumane treatment they receive when they are sick, and they beg me to help provide them with shelter or gifts because they are so abandoned and needy.

The slaves often say the sweet name of Jesus over and over again when they are punished or ill and especially when they want to die. This makes them feel comforted, and it also shows how well they understand what we teach them.[17] I have heard many slaves do this, even when they do not know another word in our language. One man, as he was about to die, said in his own language, "God created me and God takes me now. What can I do?"

Once I was catechizing a black man to prepare him for baptism. I asked him if he wanted to become a Christian. He responded that yes, he did, very much, because his father and mother were already dead. I asked another man if he wanted to be baptized. He looked shocked and said, "Of course!" He was happy to be baptized, saying he must be baptized in order to go to heaven and be a son of God, as I had told him. I asked another group that I was catechizing if they were happy to learn all the things I taught them. They all said that my lessons made them very happy. This response seemed very natural, so I reacted with happiness myself and showed them how joyful I felt. All of us were comforted, and we continued the catechism in a celebratory, friendly mood. One person said, after being baptized, that God was the sun and he was so great, and that he wanted God to dwell in his soul, and other words along these lines. All of us sitting there felt happy and joyful to hear this.

I love to see them after they are baptized. The women are especially enthusiastic. They congratulate and embrace each other and brag to their Christian friends about their new names. They laugh if coincidentally their friends have the same names. They consider people with the same names to be their friends and relatives. The way they act, showing that the divine grace has entered their souls, proves to me that they understand what I teach them. Before I preach to them, they seem indifferent, sad, and melancholy. They can hardly raise their

---

16. The Christian concept of the Holy Trinity is that the Father, Son, and Holy Spirit are three separate divine beings but only one God.

17. Slaves were often observed to call on God, Jesus, or the Virgin Mary when they were being punished, but the reaction was not always as positive as Sandoval's, and in fact this habit led to the slaves being questioned by the inquisition. See Javier Villa-Flores, *Dangerous Speech: A Social History of Blasphemy in Colonial México* (Tucson: University of Arizona Press, 2006).

eyes, open their mouths, or say a single word. After I baptize or absolve them of their sins, they become different people, and their behavior shows it. They laugh and celebrate amongst themselves. They embrace each other, and the men embrace the priest and all the translators and godparents, asking them to come to their house to visit them. They show such extreme joy that their reaction contradicts the idea that happiness does not prove one has a good conscience and is in God's grace and friendship. I say this because they are so sad before baptism and afterward so happy and joyful that this happiness must come from having a good conscience and enjoying the grace and friendship of God through holy baptism. This reaction proves they are able to understand enough to be prepared to receive the holy sacraments.

Although I have proved my point, it would be a shame not to mention a few other cases that so clearly demonstrate what I am arguing. These poor people suffer so much violence in these miserable times. It seems they are not capable of receiving the sacraments because they are thought to be *bozales*. Because they do not understand our language, they are left to die without the sacraments, as if they were beasts. I know one black *bozal* man who is certainly not a beast. I could not find a translator to help him prepare for baptism, so I brought him with me for three days while I searched for one. When we stopped to rest, he said, impatiently, "Baptize me, Father, because I cannot sleep all night from terrible headaches. My companions sleep the whole night through so peacefully, while I toss and turn, looking at that beautiful necklace on their necks, the one that you have not given to me." He was referring to the medals that I put on those that I have recently baptized, to show that they are Christians.

I know a black woman of the Nalu caste [ethnicity] who is a *bozal* but surely not an animal. I separated her from the rest of the catechism group three times because she did not understand what the translator was saying. Finally, not wanting to make me angry, she spoke to her companion, another *bozal*, who understood her well. When I separated her again, she repeated back to me everything I had been trying to teach. These actions helped me by giving me an idea for a new method for how to deal with similar cases in the future. She was so happy and joyful, and she became even more so as her friends learned the catechism. She told them how they should answer so they would not suffer her confusion.

We conclude this subject with one more happy case: an exhausted black man, worn out with a terrible sickness, could not hear or respond to anything I said to him. He was laid out on the bed with a cloak over him to comfort him. He finally spoke out and expressed his gratitude. Then he surrendered, and he died after receiving the sacraments, knowing he was saved.

These cases prove two points. First, these blacks are not the beasts that some people like to think they are. These people *want* them to be incapable of Christianity. The blacks should not be considered infants, either. They are adult men, and as such they should be baptized after being instructed and giving their free consent. When we instruct them, we have to consider what nation they come from and how much they might understand, because every nation differs. Second, these people cannot understand us as quickly as Spaniards do, so pastors and ministers must teach them slowly and spend a great deal of time on their catechism. However, they do possess free will and exercise it in all of their actions, like any other human being. They have wars and make peace, they marry, buy and sell, barter and exchange just like we do. Sometimes, very rarely, the slaves do not want to be baptized. They refuse to leave their sect and false law.[18] But usually, like bestial people who live among us, such as captured Moors [Muslims] or Englishmen,[19] the slaves simply do not understand our language.

I conclude by rebuking those who say that the blacks are incapable of receiving the sacraments and living by God's law or that blacks cannot understand these concepts. Instead, motivated by charity and zeal for the glory of the Lord and the desire to help abandoned souls, we must look for proper interpreters and translators. I confess that when a black person speaks to me in his language, I do not understand a word and seem more *bozal* than he does when I speak to him in my language. I believe that all people confess the same. Why do we think that a black person should understand our language? Why do we use their ignorance as an excuse to avoid working with such needy and hopeless people?

When a black slave lives for a long time among the Spaniards, he can show similar understanding and devotion to our own. Some of them are even more virtuous than the average Spaniard, and many black slaves live completely pure lives. One man who lives in the city of Quito [Ecuador] is so rude and uncivilized that he hardly understands our language, but he is so saintly and good that his master set him free. He is now employed as a humble lay brother for the Franciscan friars, and he frequently takes the sacraments. Everyone knows that he has done many miracles, and the people revere and honor him like a saint. In the city of Huamanga in Peru, all the noble and devout ladies honor a virtuous black woman. She is admitted to the parlors of all the noble houses. Everyone wants to speak to her because she lovingly discusses Our Lord and her speech fills her listeners with divine love. Her masters revere her so much that they do not treat her like a slave but worship her as a saint. She governs over their house. God honors those who serve him. In plain, black vessels, he stores the precious liquor of the virtues and his divine grace.

---

18. Sandoval is probably referring to Muslims here.

19. Several English pirates and sailors were put on trial for their Protestant beliefs by the Cartagena inquisition court. In the case of the "captured Moors," Sandoval might be referring to Islamic prisoners in Spain, because the only Muslims in Cartagena would have been African slaves.

Chapter 4. How the blacks are baptized in their lands and in the ports from whence they came.

Building on his arguments in Chapter 3, here Sandoval presents more evidence in support of his work with African slaves. His descriptions climax in a denunciation of the standard baptisms received by slaves and his proposal for a new system, which is outlined at the end of Book 3.

Instead of depending on ancient and medieval sources or scholarly accounts from Sandoval's contemporaries, this chapter cites letters he has received containing different eyewitness accounts of baptisms in African ports. Sandoval reveals a complex web of informants in Africa, South America, and Spain. These reports come from the rector, or chief administrator, of the Jesuit college in Santiago on the Cape Verde Islands, from Jesuits working in other parts of South America and Africa, and from several captains of slave ships. Sandoval wrote these authorities asking for information and contacted the slave traders in Cartagena to give their sworn testimony before a notary about the baptisms they had witnessed personally. Despite his account of the horrors of the slave trade in Book 1, here he trusts the words of the traders. Note how Sebastián Gómez, the Jesuit working in the Cape Verde Islands, seems quite defensive about the way baptisms are done in Africa. Sandoval might find this dismissive attitude toward African slaves frustrating, but why would he choose to publish the letter? What are some of the most common attributes of the African baptisms? How do the attitudes expressed in this chapter contrast with Sandoval's conception of how Africans react positively to Christianity in Chapter 3 and his acknowledgement and understanding of their free will? Who is ultimately to blame for the careless baptisms?

Ethiopians that come here via the port of Luanda [Angola], which includes Angolans, Congos, Angicos, and Malembas,[20] and those that come via the island of São Tomé, people such as the Araraes, Lucumis, and pure Caravalis,[21] ordinarily arrive here with a legitimate baptism. It is rare to find that these people do not know what baptism is, especially those that come through the port of Luanda. As a general rule, the opposite is true for slaves from the other nations of the Guinean rivers; however, sometimes the knowledge of baptism varies depending on when the slaves left and who was in charge of the ministries in Africa. We often find people who come from São Tomé with careless, invalid baptisms, just as bad as those of the slaves that come from the rivers of Guinea. In this chapter I provide eyewitness testimony of these baptisms. The first testimony comes from two letters from Father Sebastián Gómez, rector of

---

20. Peoples from the Bantu-speaking cultures of Congo and Angola.

21. For more information about these castes and their languages, see Book I, Chapter I, and the Glossary. The Introduction discusses the Portuguese slave trade and attempts to establish the Catholic Church in West Africa and the Atlantic Islands.

the college of the Company of Jesus on the Cape Verde Islands. I have translated the letters from Portuguese to Castilian below.

The first letter, dated April 19, 1614, says:

> I will now address the question that Your Reverence[22] asked me about how slaves are baptized here. This is a very good question. In Cacheu [Guinea-Bissau], the baptisms are done in the same way as they are done here in the Cape Verde Islands. A priest goes to the ship and asks the black brutes if they want baptism. Some of the people in the boat shout "yes, yes," because of course they know what the word "yes" means. They are baptized without learning any catechism. I have frequently tried to improve this situation. I even brought up the issue in the bishop's synod,[23] which did achieve some results. Unfortunately, the bishop died before he could confirm my suggested changes. We were all very sad about his death, because he was an extraordinarily devout member of the Company.

The second letter is dated April 20, 1616, and says:

> As to the problems with baptisms, your concerns would have already been addressed if the lord bishop had not died, because the synod had proposals designed to address this issue. I am confident in Our Lord that we will come to some solution. I will do everything I can to help. Right now, I am doing everything possible to catechize the black slaves who leave in slave ships from this port. Unfortunately, the proposals I made at the synod did not go into effect, so I hope that they will be baptized later, because at the moment, many of them do not learn the catechism before baptism.

I have another letter from a Jesuit priest working out of Cordoba de Tucuman [Argentina], dated December 21, 1622. This letter confirms that baptisms are administered in an inconsistent fashion, even in the ports and lands where we think it is done more carefully. Quoting from the letter:

> I have testimony from the slave merchants themselves that in the Angolan port called Luanda, black slaves are simply lined up in the plaza one day before they set sail. This is done by ministers or priests. Up until this point they have been in prison. They do not learn the catechism and do not even know anything about God. The priests tell the slaves their names and give them pieces of paper with their names written on them so that they do not forget them. After this, the priests put salt in all of the slaves' mouths.[24] Next, they throw water on them several

---

22. A common title used to address a person with a position of authority in the colonial Church.

23. A meeting of Church leaders.

24. In Catholic baptisms a small amount of salt is put in an infant's mouth during the ceremony. Documents relating to the Council of Trent explain that this procedure symbolizes a taste or relish for good works and divine wisdom.

times with an aspergillum[25] to do it as quickly as possible. Then the baptism is done. Later they give this speech and have an interpreter translate it: "You have become sons of God; go to the Spanish lands and learn about the holy faith. Forget everything you have learned in your own country. Go there willingly, and do not eat dogs, rats, or horses, etc." When the slaves are asked what they think baptism means, some say that it puts a spell on them so that the Spanish can eat them. Others think that this is how the Spanish get them ready to make them into gunpowder. Those slaves who have a pretty good understanding of it say that when they were baptized "their heart said nothing to them" (using their own words). They add that they were *bozales* when it was done, so they did not understand it at all.

The above letter was written by four of the most respected and wisest Jesuit fathers, based in the province of Andalusia. Their names are Diego Granado, Diego Ruiz, Cristóbal Ruiz, and Matheo Rodríguez. The lord archbishop of Seville, Don Pedro de Castro y Quiñones, ordered them to carefully question many slaves about their baptisms.

Father José de Acosta[26] writes that often black slaves who come to the Cape Verde Islands are asked if they are Christians. They usually respond that they were only children when they were captured. They were lined up in a crowd on a boat or on the beach. They remained entirely ignorant of what was going on as a priest or a soldier sprinkled them with water. Later on they found out that they were Christians, without being taught or understanding what this meant. They remained completely ignorant of the meaning of baptism, as if they were utter barbarians or animals, just because no one bothered to teach them anything.

I also asked several ship captains who bring slaves to this city of Cartagena de Indias to make a sworn legal testimony about their experiences. This is what they said:

> We, the registered captains of ships that navigate the rivers of Guinea and the port of Cacheu, buying slaves to take to the Indies, testify that the fathers of the Company of Jesus of this city of Cartagena asked us to give a statement about how the blacks are baptized. We swear by God Our Lord and on the sign of the holy cross that this testimony is true. Two or three days before the boats leave, a priest or his representative comes to the ships and puts on his surplice and stole.[27] He commands the blacks to stand. They come forward, still imprisoned in their chains

---

25. An instrument, such as a brush or a perforated container, used for sprinkling holy water.

26. Acosta was a Jesuit who lived from 1540 to 1600. His works had a great influence on Sandoval. See the Introduction for more information.

27. A stole is a strip of material worn around the neck, hanging down on the chest. It is about four inches wide and usually decorated. Wearing this means the priest is performing the sacraments of the Catholic Church. A surplice is similar to a long, loose shirt.

and shackles, and they are baptized two at a time in couples of a boy and a girl. Then they call forward the *bozal* men and women and put water on them, saying the official words of the ceremony of baptism, while the slaves remain in chains. Neither before nor after the ceremony do they try to teach them anything or tell them what baptism is. They do not have enough time to do this, because no one speaks the same language. They do not ask the slaves' consent, nor do the slaves give their free consent, because they do not know what holy baptism is. People are scandalized by these baptisms because they believe the slaves should learn what they are receiving and be asked if they freely wish to receive it. We sign this statement under oath in Cartagena de Indias, July 19, 1610. Signed, Alonso de Proenza, Pedro Fernández Daveyra, Felipe Rodríguez, in the presence of Andrés de Campo, notary public.

In the city of Cartagena de Indias on May 25, 1613, Domingo Fernández, captain of the boat named Our Lady of the Piety, which came to this port from the rivers of Guinea, also appeared before a notary and said he agreed with the report given in the above document and also said that in his ship the children were not baptized. I swear this before God and make the sign of the cross.

In the city of Cartagena de Indias on June 1, 1613, Alvaro Núñez de Sosa, captain of the ship named Our Lady of the Piety, which sets sail from the San Domingos River, appeared before the notary. Having read the above testimony, he agrees with what was written and testifies that on his boat, the children were not baptized. Sworn and signed, Alvaro Núñez de Sosa.

In the city of Cartagena on July 13, 1613, Marcal de Sylva, captain and master of the ship called Our Lady of the Rosary from the rivers of Guinea, appeared before the notary. He also swears under oath that the above accurately states what happens in the rivers of Guinea.

In 1620 and 1621, the lord Don Diego de Torres y Altamirano, a Franciscan friar and the bishop of Cartagena de Indias, investigated the issue of the slaves' baptisms in his court.[28] In fulfillment of the duties of his position and inspired by his own zeal, he sought to improve this evil situation.

The illustrious lord Don Pedro de Castro y Quiñones, archbishop of Seville, also examined this issue on November 28, 1613. I received documents relating to his investigation just a few days ago. Here I will briefly quote from these documents. The archbishop received the declarations made in Cartagena de Indias by all of the aforementioned ship captains. He also questioned several captains in Seville. All were in agreement about how black slaves are baptized in the Cacheu and the Guinean rivers before they embark on their voyage to the

---

28. Bishops ran ecclesiastical courts in colonial Latin America. These dealt with disputes within their diocese including moral issues, divorce, church property, and church organizations.

Indies or Spain. They said that when the slaves are baptized they are not asked their consent, nor are they instructed in the faith, nor do they understand what holy baptism is, nor are interpreters there that know their languages. They receive baptism blind and utterly ignorant to its meaning. The captains Martín Vázquez de Montiel, Baltasar López de Setubar, Gaspar López de Setubar, and Alvaro Serrano de Setubar also said that after some of the slaves are baptized, the traders continue buying and selling them so that everyone is mixed together on the ships and no one knows who is baptized and who is not baptized.

The archbishop also asked Captain Gaspar Carvallo if the blacks were asked for their consent when they were baptized. He testified that he has been in the port of Saint Paul of Luanda in Angola twenty times in twenty years of working in this region. The baptisms he saw brought a group of slaves together to listen to a priest, who says the following, using an interpreter: "Until now, you have been condemned to live under evil laws, but with this baptism you will be saved. If you die after being baptized, you will go to heaven." The captain does not remember anything else that the priests say to the slaves, but he testifies that this is how they usually baptize seven hundred slaves at a time. Just this year, he witnessed six or seven hundred people baptized like this in three or four hours. Sometimes slaves arrive after the speech is given and are baptized anyway. The priest works as quickly as possible because he wants to get out of the heat.

Captain Carvallo was asked if the blacks often leave the ports without being baptized. He said that usually if a ship only contains thirty captives, the slaves are not baptized, because no priest wants to travel a league outside the city just to baptize twenty or thirty slaves.

Alvaro Perea also testified that the merchants in the city of Luanda often delay bringing their captives to the fleet so that they frequently arrive after the baptism is over. Thus, an unknown number are not baptized and are sold with those that are baptized.

Another letter comes from Father Geronimo Vogado, rector of the Jesuit college in the city of Angola. He wrote this letter to Father Diego de Torres, Jesuit Provincial of the province of Paraguay, Tucuman, and Chile. This learned, saintly, and talented father has dedicated his life to the ministry to the black slaves. He says that although he is old and weak, he still works in this ministry, serving God. The father rector writes that the slaves are not baptized and should be rebaptized, *sub conditione* [conditionally], because they are so carelessly baptized right before their ships leave. He also says, "I have told the bishop many times about this negligence, and I hope that the new bishop will help us work to catechize them and oblige their masters to bring them somewhere where they can comfortably learn the catechism." The letter was written in Angola on November 18, 1621, and proves that local bishops and priests determine how well slaves will be baptized. The lack of a little care puts the salvation of so many souls in danger.

I want to add to these testimonies other accounts given to me by people who come from these lands and by people who have done these baptisms. One priest from Cacheu brought a great band of black slaves to Cartagena de Indias. He said they were baptized and demanded that they be taught the catechism here. When I questioned them, I could tell that they understood nothing and were as bestial as all the rest. I mentioned this to the priest and humbly asked him to tell me what he had said to the blacks before he baptized them. He said that when he boarded the slave ship he asked for the most *ladino* slaves to come forward, and he asked them if they wanted to be like the whites, by having water poured on their heads. (How would they understand him? He would be speaking two or three languages to people who speak more than sixty different languages.) The priest continued, "The interpreter said they agreed to this, so I baptized them." He then permitted me to catechize and baptize them.

A ship captain and the black slave who served as a translator on his ship gave me another description of what happens at the slaves' baptisms. The interpreter swore that he would honestly repeat what he said to the slaves, which is the following: "Relatives, listen to what he [the priest] says to you, open your eyes: here is sweet water and there is the salty sea. You do not have to drink that salty water, because it makes you sick. Drink this sweet water, because it is the whites' water." He said that neither the priest nor the captain said anything else, and the priest baptized the slaves after the interpreter said this statement.

Another witness confessed that sometimes the blacks arrived while the curate or vicar in Cacheu was eating, so the priest commanded them to kneel together near his seat. Then he poured water on their heads from the pitcher on the table. He did not explain anything to them, nor did he repeat the words that are supposed to be said at a baptism. This witness was a layman, but even he recognized that these baptisms were not valid.

I conclude this chapter with a story I heard from a man who came here from the port of Sâo Tomé Island. He reported that a priest came to the slave ship and took water from a pail in his hand. He then put the water on the slaves' heads, without washing them or cutting their hair. This meant that the water did not touch their skulls, because usually all captives have thick, greasy, dirty hair. This witness also told me that so many people were baptized in one day that the priest became tired of baptizing them standing up, so he sat down and continued on baptizing from a seated position. His arms became tired from moving them to do the baptism, so, according to the words of this witness: "When the black slave approached the priest, he kneeled before the pail and the priest grasped him by the neck and dipped him in. After he raised him up, the father put his hand above him. Some passed with such speed that the father did not even touch them." This is how black slaves are baptized in their land, and this evidence alone shows that their baptisms are invalid, but I will provide more proof of this in the next chapter.

Chapter 5. The value of these baptisms.

This chapter takes the accounts from Chapter 4 and turns them around in search of the African perspective on the hasty baptisms described above. Moving quickly from the theoretical to the specific, Sandoval again uses evidence from personal experience and his interpretation of slaves' understanding of baptism. Arguably, this chapter provides the most complex exploration of African actions, reactions, and feelings in De instauranda. How does this chapter further explore Sandoval's understanding of free will, intelligence, and knowledge, as they apply to Christianity and African slaves? Although generally Sandoval only grants slaves the right to free will in a very narrow way, of course not extending it to freedom from slavery or from Christian worldviews and morality, how does he show some sense of Africans as historical actors and subjects in this chapter? By acknowledging their logical rejection of Christianity as something coming from their enemies, something likely to harm them, does he implicitly criticize the way Christianity goes hand in hand with imperialism in his era, or he is just criticizing the careless priests working in African ports? Why might he object to Africans describing their captors as whites instead of Christians? How seriously does Sandoval judge shortcomings in baptisms at the end of the chapter?

This chapter will present the most important topic of this entire book. I begin by explaining my philosophical arguments. The baptisms that black slaves receive in Guinea and in other lands and ports, when they are done in the way that I described in the last chapter, are usually null and invalid. If nothing else, the validity of these baptisms is in doubt. The reasons why I believe this come from the works of the most important theologians. I can sum up all of their opinions in one statement: all Christian laws, Church councils, and Christian scholars and authorities agree that when adults are baptized, they must willingly and knowingly agree to being baptized. Otherwise, their baptisms are invalid. This point is made in the following quote from Father José de Acosta:

> If this barbarian (speaking of one of these Ethiopians) has no comprehension of the meaning of the baptism that he receives, or if he does not understand that there is any difference between regular water and holy water and is ignorant of the Christian faith and the Christian church, we cannot presume that this man agreed to being baptized. This kind of baptism is the same as a baptism done while he was sleeping or unconscious, because he knows nothing about it and has not willingly accepted it. I have no doubt that in such a case an individual has not received a valid baptism.

Acosta explains that you cannot want something if you do not understand it— you cannot love something that you know nothing about. There is a difference between adult and infant baptism. Infants do not have to understand or consent to baptism, but adults do, because they are free men and they must consciously accept it. This is their entrance to the Christian church, and by entering and surrendering to Christ, they must willingly agree to follow Christian laws, and they must exercise their free will. Theologians argue that if you baptize someone who is sleeping, this is not a valid baptism because the person has not given free consent. A baptism is valid only if a person willingly agrees to it, and the same applies to black slaves. Their baptisms are invalid if they have not freely consented to them. The next section will show how the black slaves do not give their free consent to baptism.

The first issue is teaching each person about baptism. All must be instructed before they can be baptized. Baptismal water is just water on the body, providing no spiritual benefit if the soul has not received the faith.

How can we decide how much the black slaves need to know before they are baptized, and how do we know if they understand what we have taught them? They can agree that they want to receive the water that the Christians receive, but they still do not know what this water means. Every day I talk to many black slaves who know that pouring water on a person's head is something the whites (this is what they call Christians) do, but they do not know, nor does anyone tell them, what the purpose of this water is or why Christians or whites pour it on themselves. They think that the water is for bathing or washing, just like any other time when they wash themselves. They must understand that baptism is a ceremony connected to religion and a belief in God and that it makes them friends or sons of God, takes away their sins, and helps them go to heaven. They must at least realize that it has something to do with the Christian religion. They cannot only say that it is something Christian, Portuguese, or white, without knowing what the word "Christian" means, other than that it refers to a person who has taken away their liberty. This is not enough information!

So if these points represent the absolute minimum level of understanding in order to say that baptism is valid, do the black slaves reach this level of understanding when they are baptized on ships, in port, and in other places? The eyewitness testimony I gave in the last chapter, where people swore that nothing is said to the slaves on the ships about baptism nor do the slaves give their free consent, indicates that these baptisms are invalid. People say that the priests only go to the slave ships out of courtesy or personal interest, so the slaves receive no catechism, faith, hope, or penitence. The priests disregard everything and commit sacrilege in doing these invalid baptisms.

Even if the priests made an effort, circumstances and difficulties make valid baptisms impossible. Remember, on each ship there are more than six hundred blacks from many different backgrounds, without anyone understanding the differences between them. They do not understand if someone catechizes them in only one of their languages, such as Bran, Mandingo, Fula, or Biojo.[29] People

---

29. See Book I, Chapter I, and the Glossary for information about these languages.

who speak other languages will neither understand nor have any concept of what has been said to them, and in consequence, they will not be baptized. Everyone is rushing to have the ship leave; they have no time to show if they understand the catechism. Even if someone explains the catechism to them in their own language, how do we know if they listen willingly or understand well enough to retain the information, and if they will continue to live a Christian life? Even Spaniards can listen to a sermon and remain utterly ignorant of what they have just heard.

How many do not understand just because the ship is so noisy? Or maybe they are too far away from the priest to be able to hear. They might be distracted, melancholy, and sad, as they sit thinking of their captivity and how they have been imprisoned for no reason. They might miss their native lands and what they have left behind: father, mother, wife, children, and the friends that they love with all their heart. Many of them, especially the boys, will be sleeping or playing. We know that boys will not listen quietly to sermons until they are grown up. The mothers are probably distracted by their children's anxious cries, so they cannot hear or understand.

Even if all the other conditions are perfect, I know from long experience baptizing black slaves here in Cartagena that we must be very careful to ensure that they understand what is said and taught to them. This requires much exhausting work, effort, and sweat. You have to battle with them for a long time, trying to enlighten them on the concepts of faith, hope, pain, and charity. This is very difficult for people unaccustomed to paying attention or memorizing things that they have never heard before. I work with each person individually, so in this case they are not afraid and know that what I am doing will not hurt them. When so many disturbed and frightened people are packed together in cruel captivity, crushed against their worst enemies, determined to return to their homes (all common conditions on the slave ships), how can we believe that they understand enough to be baptized, especially so quickly? I do not believe that it is possible that the black slaves generally understand enough to know that this is a ceremony of the cult of God, for the good of their souls.

I also do not believe that they give their consent to be baptized, and I see much proof that they do not willingly receive baptism or understand that this water is a holy thing. They are not explicitly asked for their consent. If someone asks them if they want to have this water poured on them so they can be like whites, and so on, I am certain that they not only reject this but detest this water and all other things connected to the whites from the bottom of their hearts. Whites are their worst enemies: they take the slaves from their homelands, separate them from their parents and siblings, take away their liberty, put them in chain gangs, shackles, and prisons, and then confine them in a ship to take them to distant lands, without hope of returning to their own. They are badly fed and treated and threatened with poor examples. It is much more likely that God has lost them rather than gained them with holy baptism—no surprise, considering the imprisonment and abuse that takes place. Therefore, I do not believe that they consent to baptism. Instead, they are forced into it because they cannot contradict their masters who cruelly imprison them. They know that if they do not obey, they will suffer even worse punishments. Would anyone else put in a similar situation willingly agree to something their enemies did, something they did not understand? From the way they are treated, they would assume that it is something harmful or at least not useful to them. The blacks feel the same way. Not only do they want nothing to do with the whites' water, but they abhor doing something that makes them like the whites, because the Spanish have earned their great spite and hatred. The blacks hate and deeply reject anything that they believe will unite them or make them similar to their worst enemies: the whites. They are superstitious, so they also have the superstition that baptism is evil. When they see a priest come to baptize them, they are surprised and fear that this is one more thing that threatens their life. Some people argue that if the slaves do not openly hate or contradict the Church, they implicitly agree to joining it. But I say that this is not enough. Think about how they do not fight off the burning brand used to mark them and permanently imprison them in their masters' power to be abused and threatened.[30] Branding hurts them, and they do not want it, but they passively receive it and suffer through it, meanwhile detesting it on the inside.

The absurd answers we get when we ask the slaves if they understood their baptism or what was meant when their heads were washed are another form of proof that they do not receive legitimate, voluntary baptisms in their lands and are even unaware that they were baptized at all. Some respond that they are afraid of this water and believe the whites do this to kill them. Others think that the water is like a brand, a mark put on them so that their masters know who they are when they buy and sell them. They think this because often they are marked with a burning brand at the same time that water is thrown on them, making them think that one thing goes with the other. Some say that water was poured on them to wash their dirty heads or to wet their hair in order to shave it. Others say the water was meant to cool them or think that the water prevents them from having sexual relations with the women on the ship during the voyage. Still others say it is a white ceremony that must be obeyed, or that it prevents sickness, especially headaches, similar to a practice in their own lands. One slave told me that water was poured on him to enchant him, to prevent him from rising up against the whites in the ship in the course of the voyage. He also thought that it was done so he would live many more years and bring

---

30. Slaves in Latin America were branded with a mark that stood for their owners' names. Sometimes several words were branded on their faces. This practice was banned in 1784.

gold to his masters. The slaves rave on in this way because they are not told that baptism is a holy ceremony, and they do not understand that it is sacred.

Even here some slaves are Christianized only enough for them to be confused. This especially happens to slaves who are thrown into the mines or the pearl fisheries,[31] or to women made to be nurses and give milk to the infants. Their masters and priests do not improve the situation by teaching them using interpreters, so they still do not understand baptism. We cannot say that this misunderstanding comes from their ignorance, or that they cannot learn, because, in more than eighteen years of practicing this ministry, I know that some blacks can understand and explain baptism. Almost every black slave that comes from Luanda, where they are catechized, understands and can explain who gave them the water, how it was given, what they said before it was done, who said it, and in what language and for what purpose. They say that they were told it was the water of God and that it would make them sons of God so that they would go to heaven when they die and that they must now live like whites, not eating dogs, cats, serpents, and so on. They also say that they received it willingly. So when we question these slaves, we do it not to baptize them but instead to see if for some reason, some of them have not received the water, or have not received it willingly. We usually can say that they are Christians, because they explain things well and in a way that agrees with the testimonies given by ship captains. This is not always the case for slaves who come from Cape Verde and the rivers of Guinea and sometimes São Tomé and even Luanda itself. In these cases, all of them are baptized but have not been catechized or instructed in any way, and the captains can confirm this.

These are principal arguments that prove that these baptisms are null due to a lack of understanding of what baptism is and the will to receive it. Consider just the physical fact that often water sprinkled on many people at one time will not touch every single person. Most people only receive a few drops and are not completely washed by the water, especially if it just touches their thick hair, not their heads.

Thus it can be inferred that priests and masters commit serious sins in Guinea, on the ships and in other places where they carry out these baptisms. They commit sacrilege by administering a sacrament that is morally null and evidently doubtful, and very certainly without its principal effect, that is, grace, because adult slaves are not prepared for it by having the necessary faith and penitence. We must improve this situation from now on.

I conclude by saying that the baptisms done in the ports in Africa are merely a fruitless, sinful, sacrilegious ceremony, with no effect or value. These

---

31. African slaves worked as pearl divers on the Pacific coast of what is now Ecuador and Colombia.

futile rituals mean that people may not have a legitimate baptism later to help
in the evil done to them. This is enough discussion of adult baptism.

Chapter 6. Of the value of the baptisms of the children that priests baptize in the African lands or ports of Guinea, and so on.

*Sandoval consistently argues that slaves must give their free consent to be baptized.
How does his emphasis on the slaves as adults with free will affect his thinking on
infant baptism, done before a baby can possibly understand the meaning of the ceremony? Sandoval's opinions on this issue are in line with the paternalistic, expansionist,
imperialist Catholicism of his era, arguing in favor of baptism in almost every possible
scenario. The Council of Trent enforced its tradition of infant baptisms, a practice challenged by Protestant reformers such as the Anabaptists. In the case of African infants
and children who were transported alone to America, Sandoval believed that the Catholic Church became their parent. The Church protected them and embraced them so that
they would know no differently than to become a part of it. Catholicism also insists that
water poured on a person in baptism must directly touch their bodies, so babies held by
their mothers are not necessarily baptized simultaneously. In Sandoval's time Catholic
doctrine decreed that unbaptized infants could not go to heaven, although, because they
had committed no sins, they might dwell in limbo, in a state of happiness. However
protective the Church was of infants as new members, its doctrines also guaranteed the
rights of parents, recognizing their authority and their rights to exercise their free will.*

In the last chapter I argued that adult baptisms are only of value if adults give
their free consent to receive baptism. However, children do not have to explicitly agree to their baptisms, so I discuss this topic separately. Because we rarely
know who the fathers are, and their masters assume that babies are baptized
when their mothers are baptized, we have to discuss the issue of the validity of
infant baptisms done at the same time as mothers' baptisms.

I doubt that many children's baptisms are valid, because when we ask the
mother if they put water on her child when they put it on her, she says yes, they
poured water on her, but not on her child, unless it fell down from her head to
that of her child. To help get a clearer understanding of this, we give her a pail
of water and a jug and ask her to demonstrate how the water was poured on her
and her child. Some of the slave women take the jar full of water from the pail
and pour it on their heads, and then they pour more on the heads of the babies,
demonstrating that was the way the priest did it when he baptized them. If they
do this, we know that they have both been baptized, especially when the mother
pours water on her baby first. Other women take the jar full of water and pour
it on their head and then put it on the floor. When we ask why they do not
pour water on their babies' heads as the other women did, they say that the

priest only let water fall from the mother's head to the child's head. In this case, we assume both were baptized. We must do all this investigation in order to explain such a serious thing to such brutish people, for the salvation of their souls requires covering such an important subject slowly and carefully. If a priest is ignorant and careless enough to baptize a mother without telling her anything about the catechism [the Christian doctrines], he would probably be just as careless in baptizing her child.

There are several theological arguments that support my approach to baptizing slave children. First, children of infidels [non-Christians] who live in a Christian kingdom should never be baptized against the will of their parents.

Second, a child of a Christian father and an infidel mother, or of a Christian mother and an infidel father, can be baptized, with the approval of the Christian mother or father, even if the infidel father or mother does not agree. We need the approval of the Christian parent so that the Christian parent will carefully educate the child, to prevent the infidel parent from perverting the child.

Third, in cases where both parents, either Christian or infidel, impede the baptism of their child, the Church can baptize the child against both of their wills. The reason for this is that a Christian father has the obligation to baptize his child, and the Church can force him to do it. If he does not want to fulfill his obligation, the Church must remedy the situation by baptizing the child against the parents' will.

Fourth, the children that come from Guinea without their parents should be baptized here without their parents' consent. This kind of baptism occurs every day on the slave ships. These children are like orphans because their parents are so far away. They are under the control of the masters who buy them, who stand in the place of their parents. God demands that these masters care for them and bring them up well. Slaves who were taken captive in a just war, captured during violence or looting, bought from someone selling them legally, abandoned, or are in Spanish hands via any other method must be baptized and instructed in the Christian faith. Even though baptism is probably against the will of their parents, these children are no longer in their parents' care but are in the care of the Christians, and we must ensure their spiritual well-being. If the parents can be consulted, we must ask their consent, because in this case the children are still subject to their parents' authority.

Fifth, according to the Church authorities, infant children of infidels, even if they are slaves of Christians, cannot be baptized against the will of their parents. This is because infants must be under the authority of their parents, especially regarding issues that affect their souls. The Church has never baptized infants in this position against the will of their parents. If the parents want to remain forever outside Christianity, they might pervert their children who have become Christians.

Sixth, if children of infidels are baptized without the approval and consent of their parents, their baptisms are valid, firm, and true, even if the sacrament does injury to their parents because their children have been baptized against their will. If this does happen, the children should be separated from their parents for their upbringing and education, to avoid being perverted by their parents' arguments and tricks. Being with their parents could lead to damage to the sacrament of baptism.

Seventh, if an infant is dying, I always baptize the infant. If I have to choose between taking away the eternal life of the soul and harming the physical life of the body, I choose to protect the soul, because physical death will then give them eternal life. Baptizing in these cases harms neither the parents nor the sacrament of baptism, because the child will die soon and will no longer be under the influence of the parents, so they cannot pervert or trick him.

Eighth, if the children of the infidel parents can already think for themselves, they can be baptized without the consent and approval of their parents, even in contradiction to their parents' wishes. Because they can understand baptism, their souls are no longer subject to their parents' power. If you are not sure whether they can understand or not, baptize them without their parents' approval.

Ninth, when we say that children cannot be baptized against the will of their parents, we use the word "parent" also to mean guardians that take the place of parents. However, it is not as serious for a guardian as for a parent whose child is baptized without their permission.

Tenth, I must discuss the issue of the age at which we can consider infants to have become adults, in order to determine when they can consent to their own baptisms, understand what they are accepting, and become true Christians.

In general, I think that children have the use of their reason when they are seven years old, because this is the age when their adult teeth come in. At this age they can be baptized as adults, and we can baptize them by teaching them the catechism as we do for their parents. They may seem like children in all other ways, and they are not yet old enough to receive the sacrament of penance.[32] I follow this rule in all the cases that come before me.

Sometimes we have difficulties when we question children who have already been baptized. Their answers show that they do not understand what is happening. They cry, hide, and act afraid, ashamed, and bashful. They will not speak, making it very clear that they either are innocent or lack understanding. In these cases, if water has already been poured on them in Guinea, we consider them baptized before they had the use of their reason. But if we decide that they

---

32. In other words, they cannot take communion because they are not mature enough to confess their sins, feel true regret from them, and resolve to act differently in the future.

have not been baptized, we do not try to do it until they have rested, have lost their fear and shock, have grown up a bit, and are better prepared to be catechized. Then we ask their consent and teach them what they need to know about baptism. In conclusion, regarding children that come from Guinea, we must examine their mothers to find out if the children have been baptized. If they are not baptized, we can baptize them. If there is any doubt, we baptize them conditionally.

Chapter 7. How to treat the blacks when they disembark from the slave ships.

This chapter discusses how a large number of both black slaves and Indians have received invalid baptisms in the past, due to the carelessness of priests and friars. In the case of slaves, this applies not only to recently arrived slaves but also to Africans who have lived among Spaniards for many years. Sandoval says that some slaves know a great deal about baptism, but this is information they have learned over years of living with Spaniards, and it does not necessarily mean they understood the meaning of the baptism ceremony at the time when they were baptized. Sandoval's concern is that priests give these non-Christians the sacraments of communion and confession as if they were Christians. In doing this, these priests are unknowingly committing a sacrilege. Another point made in this chapter is that some priests fear baptizing a person two times. Sandoval assures those concerned that by using the method of conditional baptism, priests can avoid worrying about this issue. He ends the chapter by emphasizing that priests in the ports from whence the slaves leave are the ones responsible for baptizing them. Slave traders in Africa must help carry out the obligation of baptism before slaves board the ships. Otherwise, when the slaves are sold in the Americas, everyone will assume they have already been baptized. Sandoval also criticizes how the indigenous people he worked with who lived outside the city of Cartagena have been similarly neglected by the Catholic Church.

This point should also extend to all older adult Indians, because in the past [the 1500s] they suffered the same carelessness in instruction in the catechism that the blacks now experience in their baptism. The priests now dedicated to the instruction of the Indians have assured me that they have revalidated more than a thousand Indian baptisms (after hearing about the invalidity of the blacks' baptisms), including for Indians who confess and take communion as Christians. I also speak from personal experience in this matter, because I have examined Indians in the same way that I examine blacks, and I found many non-Christians. In a mission to two farms in the Rio Grande de la Magdalena,[33]

---

33. That is, near the Magdalena River.

I baptized more than twenty Indians in one night. The next night I baptized another fifteen elderly Indians because after examination I found their baptisms as invalid as those of the blacks.

Chapter 8. How to examine the blacks when they arrive at port in slave ships, and other prerequisites that must precede catechism.

In this chapter, which is full of practical, organizational details, Sandoval explores the metaphor of the soothing, cleansing water of baptism. Because slaves are literally dying of thirst when they arrive in American ports, he can take advantage of their desperate craving for water as a symbol of his vision of the spiritual healing provided by baptism. Throughout this chapter, what general demeanor or style of behavior does Sandoval recommend when working with slaves? How might this approach take advantage of their physical and mental condition after enduring the horrific voyage across the Atlantic and the Caribbean? How does Sandoval explain the benefits of baptism in this chapter? What role do ladinos *have here?*

Many years' experience has taught me how to question black slaves to find out if their baptisms are valid. These examinations must be done very carefully. You must follow every trivial point of the method described below, because everything is essential in order to successfully work with such crude, sad, timid people.

First, as soon as the ships arrive and the black slaves disembark, we must go to the port and determine how many slaves there are and where they come from. We also need to know what sicknesses they have, how many are dangerously ill, and how many children there are. We must know exactly who needs water so that we can bring it to those who are dying, which is usually most of them. This is heart-wrenching because they do not know how to ask for water. The mothers are so discouraged that they are afraid to ask for water for their children. When slaves cry out for water during the catechism, we pour it directly from the jug into their mouths. Many times I have seen people drink one, two, or even three full jugs of water. If you can endure all of the shouting, you should first determine who needs water and baptize them later. We also have to find out who is sick and see if they have been taken somewhere to be cured. [. . .] Some slaves cannot leave the ship because they must stay away from the town in order to avoid infecting it or the slaves that are still healthy. We have to find out how many healthy slaves remain on the ship to take care of the sick ones. We have to find out where the slaves that have left the ship are living and who has bought them. We must write down all of this information so that we do not forget it, and we must and remind ourselves what we need to do, in order to get it done quickly. We gradually question the new arrivals and then look for *ladino* interpreters. We have to assess what kind of baptisms the slaves have received and help them according to what we found out and how needy they are.

The answers they give to our questions reveal the great variety of baptisms the slaves receive. If they come from the rivers of Guinea, almost all of them will not be baptized. Some might have had water poured on them before they left but without explanation of the meaning of holy baptism either before or after the ceremony. They do not know why this water was poured on them, and they have not accepted it willingly because no one told them about it in a language they can understand. Other slaves have not even had this rudimentary baptism because no water was sprinkled on them whatsoever. Some were not there when the water was thrown on the rest, perhaps because they were hidden for some reason. Very few arrive with a valid baptism according to the rules of the Church. The *ladinos* that work on the ships guarding and protecting the *bozales* usually have been baptized after living for years among Christians, and they know what they received and why. Some *ladinos* were baptized by priests who go on missions inland, working for years to convert the gentiles. Some slaves have heard the sermons of these missionary priests, making their baptisms legitimate.

The black slaves that come from the island of Cape Verde also have different kinds of baptisms. All of these slaves are originally from the Guinean rivers and do not learn much when they pass through Cape Verde, even if they have spent some time there before arriving at Cartagena, unless they were raised there since childhood. Those who were raised in Cape Verde are called Creoles.[34] We must assess their baptisms like all the rest unless they were born in Cape Verde. Cape Verde natives do not have to be examined because they are baptized as children in the Holy Church, like people that are born here in our Christian villages, because Cape Verde is a Christian land.

If they are from São Tomé, being Ardas or Araraes, Caravalis, Lucumis, Minas, or one of the many other castes that come from this island, we also find they have received a wide variety of different kinds of baptisms.[35] Many people have not been baptized whatsoever, others have had baptisms that might not be valid, and others do not understand the catechism at all. Many ships do not go through the island of São Tomé, where some baptisms are done carefully, but

---

34. The word "Creole" often means "born in America," referring to people of African descent with a new American identity. As Sandoval mentions here, the Portuguese also used this word to refer to people from the islands of Cape Verde and São Tomé, generally of mixed African and Portuguese ancestry, so the concept of "Creole" extends beyond the Americas.

35. The island of São Tomé was an important slave trade market where slaves from mainland Africa were sent to be shipped elsewhere. See Book I, Chapter I, and the Introduction for more information.

leave directly from the mainland. The slave traders buy slaves on the coast and then set sail for the Indies immediately, without passing through São Tomé. Slaves on ships coming directly from the mainland are usually not baptized. São Tomé also has both native and Creole residents. The natives do not have to be examined, because they were born among Christians and should be Christian, but we must question the Creoles, because they come as children from Guinea and are raised among Christians but might not have been baptized adequately.

If the slaves come from Luanda and are Angolans, Angicos, Congos, Malembas, and so on, they usually have been sufficiently instructed in order to be considered validly baptized because they are asked their consent before the water is poured on them. In Luanda, men and women, and the children, who are called *moleques,* are separated into groups when they are baptized. This concern for orderliness avoids confusion and assures more understanding of the catechism, which is said in their language. The only slaves who are not baptized are those who missed the catechism, those who were too far away or distracted to hear it, or those who did not freely agree to baptism and were only doing what their masters commanded. Some outwardly consent but contradict their agreement in their hearts. This variation in baptisms is normal among the black slaves who arrive at our ports. All of those who come from Guinea must be examined to avoid neglecting or rebaptizing a person who is already baptized.

The various castes must be grouped together and given gifts so that they feel motivated to take part in the examination and catechism. Women and men should be put on separate sides of the room, but first they must give their free consent to baptism. They must be wearing decent clothes, even if it means bringing them an old rag to wear, because this small act of charity helps us carry out the ministry calmly, decently, piously, and modestly. Sometimes the slaves share jugs of fresh water amongst them and drink many jugs of the most brackish water because they are parched with thirst. Women and children are very thirsty and have a great appreciation for water. I have seen something several times that I would not believe if I had not seen it myself. When I am about to baptize some people in a silver font, I ask them to pour the leftover water away in a corner or other decent place. They tell me not to pour or spill any of the water. They stare at the water as it falls over the head of a person being baptized and onto a plate, and then they drink it up without leaving a drop. This shows how thirsty they are and how much they are suffering. I should also mention another incredible occurrence that I have experienced several times. I wrote down a description of this event so I could refer to it later. Once I could not, no matter how hard I tried, learn anything about one man's baptism, even after pleading with him and giving him presents. Then I saw him staring at a jug of water, and I asked him if he wanted a drink. He said yes and then drank insatiably. When he was satisfied, he stood up in a happier mood. He spoke and answered my questions, so then I could baptize him. Everyone in the room felt very comforted by this. What else can I say that proves my point better than this incident? It also inspired me to create a method to use while catechizing. I say:

"Tell me, child, do you remember that jar of nice, sweet, fresh water that you drank when you were parched with thirst?"

All respond, "Yes."

I continue, "However happy your body felt to receive that water, your soul will be much happier when your head is washed with the holy water and when I tell you about God and heaven. This will take away your sins and make you His child."

When you teach the catechism, it is much easier if you speak kindly to the slaves. Show them that you love them in your role as a father and a priest of God, whom all men respect and revere. Explain that your tonsure[36] is like a crown, because they find this kind of visible symbol very important. Make them listen very closely when you speak of God's greatness. Tell them that their master loves them very much and that they must do what he says; they must ask and beg him to treat them well, give them gifts, and heal them when they are sick so that they will have a good master with whom they can live happily in their captivity. Make them understand that the Lord did them great mercy in bringing them to a Christian land. It is better to be a slave here than free in their lands, because here, even though the body suffers working in captivity, the soul rests in the liberty that is attained through the holy water of baptism. Tell them that in this land they have family and that if they serve well, they will have a good captivity, and they will be content and well dressed. Tell them to give up their sadness and pain and be happy. Sometimes, intelligent *ladino* interpreters tell them that the catechism is the truth and anything else they know from before is a trick. From long experience I know that they want to accept salvation in their hearts. They feel so depressed because of their sickness and because they feel unwanted and overworked in their cruel captivity. But the law of God enters them and makes them feel calmer and happier. This can be seen in the pleasure they show when they hear what we say to them. Their custom is to applaud and show their great joy by clapping. This shows that they are ready to receive the sacraments.

It is extremely important that we question the slaves kindly and patiently. We must bear with their slow and contradictory replies, even when they stray from the point we are trying to make. When they answer a question incorrectly, they seem to be disturbed and ashamed, so we give them time to think about the question and calm themselves. If we rush them and make them respond too quickly, they will not understand how important it all is. Sometimes we have to

36. A partially shaved head that signified a man was a monk, priest, or friar. The tonsure is no longer a standard practice in the Catholic Church.

ask the same question in several different ways to see if they always provide the same answer. Reassure them that speaking the truth will mean that they will live happily with God forever. If that does not calm them down, leave them alone and try to teach them the catechism another day when they feel more comfortable and will learn more easily. Sometimes it helps to use another interpreter, to see if they understand better. Do not harvest the fruit before it ripens but instead cultivate the tree carefully so that it bears the healthiest fruit.

Chapter 9. More details on examining the blacks and preparing them for catechism.

What are some of the ways in which Sandoval develops his organized and regimented approach to baptism in this chapter? According to Sandoval's words here, determining where a slave comes from, that is, his or her nation or caste, is the most important step in judging how to proceed with the baptism. Pressing physical needs, such as thirst, as explained in the last chapter, and the slaves' state of health are also primary concerns. Sandoval views it as sacrilegious for a person to be baptized twice, so if he is not sure if an individual has been baptized or not, he gives a conditional baptism. The idea of a conditional Catholic baptism is still considered legitimate today in cases where a priest doubts the validity of a person's first baptism. Sandoval believes that true baptism only exists when an adult understands the meaning of the ceremony and accepts it willingly. How does he try to baptize dying slaves? How is he at the mercy of the slaves who work as his interpreters?

After organizing the slaves into their different castes, as described above, I ask them their names, in case that will show me that they have been baptized. If they tell me a Christian name, this might indicate that they have already been baptized. However, Christian names can be deceiving. Many slaves have Christian names but have not been baptized, and many more do not know what their baptism means. Next I ask if they were present when the other blacks were baptized on the ship and if, along with all the other slaves, water was poured on their heads. Sometimes the slaves are given salt when they are baptized, to help them remember that water was poured on them.[37] This is common in Luanda, the port of Angola. Many say that they did not have water thrown on them, but this is not always true. Even if they have been baptized, they might not have been paying enough attention to understand it. Sometimes asking where they came from helps us figure out if they have been baptized. If they come from Cacheu, they normally have been baptized. If I think they definitely have not been baptized, I try to get them to tell me why not. Some explain it well, but

---

37. See note 24.

others are less convincing, so you should find out more by asking their friends and companions.

If they do mention having water poured on them, you must carefully ask if they were spoken to in a language they understand, and if they accepted the law of the whites and their God by their own free will. You may have to ask this several times or change the way you ask. For example, if they say they received the water of God, ask them if this water means they will go to heaven as a child of God and are no longer of the devil. They must also understand the Holy Spirit. I have no simple way of teaching this concept.

You must be convinced that they were baptized properly, with words said in their own language, and with some understanding of the purpose or meaning of baptism. Even the roughest and most confused person must understand that it is the water of God for the children, captives, and servants of God, in order that they may do what God commands and clean their souls of sin, allowing their souls to go to heaven and bringing them into Christian brotherhood with the whites. All of these kinds of statements show that they received a legitimate baptism, especially if they freely consented to it.

We hang a metal image on a cord around the neck of those who we believe are Christians. If they do not have Christian names or have forgotten the ones given to them at their baptism, they are given another name and separated to one side in order to learn the catechism. Learning the catechism prepares them for confession. They need to confess through interpreters if they are sick. If they are very sick, catechism prepares them to receive extreme unction. They can also take the holy sacrament if they are decent and capable enough to receive it. If the answers they give to our questions definitively show that they are not Christians, because they either say they have not been baptized, or respond with ridiculous answers, or express negative feelings toward baptism, then they are separated to one side, men and women separate, for us to baptize them unconditionally when the time comes.

If we are not sure whether they have been baptized, or if we suspect that some aspect of the ceremony was left out when they were baptized, for example, if no water was poured on them—if we have even the slightest doubt—they are separated off to one side with a thread tied to their index finger so that we know who needs to be baptized conditionally later. Those who have learned about baptism after their arrival here also must be rebaptized conditionally. Those who say they have been baptized but admit to not remembering much about it or understanding its purpose, other than that it means they are Christians, must also be baptized conditionally.

When all have been organized and separated, the interpreter sits in a place where all can see him, especially if he must catechize three or more different castes and nations at the same time. Because some interpreters know so many languages, the catechisms can be combined so that more people hear it in a shorter time period. We must speak clearly, briefly, patiently, and energetically to the translator. The priest must be alert and answer all the questions coming from people speaking different languages. He must help them stay calm but at the same time keep them interested and lively, welcoming them through the interpreter, being prompt, but not passing from one question or point to another until he is satisfied that everyone understands.

We cannot complete a catechism successfully without an interpreter who accurately translates everything we say in all the different languages. It is very difficult to find a *ladino* who has a good nature and is religious enough to clearly state the truth. Often interpreters will not translate what we say or will say things more simply when they feel like it. Some are tied to their obligations to their masters. I know more than fifty interpreters, but I have struggled to find them. Some only want to catechize on certain days at certain times. Some are healthy and, with good reason, fear catching contagious diseases. Some do not want to travel very far and will slip away and put the priest off with jokes so that he has to give up and find another interpreter. Sometimes they tire and become fatigued in the middle of the catechism, believing that they have said enough, and they tell the priest to hurry up and do the baptism. If he does not agree, then they leave, and we cannot find another interpreter to finish the catechism, especially considering the risk of catching an illness. Many masters will not allow their slaves to work as translators, or if they do allow it, only on very specific days and for specific lengths of time. If these limits are exceeded, the masters will not loan them again, and another translator must be found.

Many times sick people have not been definitively baptized, so, while sick and infirm, they join in the larger catechism groups with healthy people. They are divided up by caste and examined together. This helps the sick ones understand better, because with repetition they become more familiar and comfortable and can be baptized quickly. Some of the sick are failing quickly, and their infirmities do not allow them to be questioned and baptized in a group with the rest. In this case, we go directly to the sick person and at the same time try to bring together everyone we know on the ships or on land that is of the same nation or caste. This prevents a rush to find interpreters. Sometimes the interpreters help in the catechism and baptism of a group of black slaves of the same caste who are gathered together in one house. Or the blacks of one particular caste can gather together in the interpreter's house if the interpreter cannot or does not want to leave it. This is the best way to help him do the job.

Usually I decide what catechism must be done in a given day by going through the lists of castes: Banhuns, Biafras, Fulupos, Biojos, and so on. Going by my list of castes, I check my note of where they have been sent or if they were not included in the large baptisms on the slave ships. Then I bring the slaves of a particular caste together—one day Banhuns, another Biafras, and so on—until all are done. When they are green and *bozal,* they do not know how to get back to their houses, so guides and guards bring them back to their masters after the baptism. The guide also reminds them of what they have just experienced and what their new names are.

Chapter 10. The catechism and instruction that must precede baptism.

Why does Sandoval believe that African slaves cannot be taught the complexities of the Christian religion before they are baptized? What must they understand about their baptism and the actual purpose of the water? Recognizing that he believes Africans have free will, how does Sandoval try to make baptism appealing to the slaves? What attitudes does the model dialogue indicate toward other belief systems? How does Sandoval assess the beliefs and culture of Africans? How might they have reacted to these questions internally, regardless of their answers? Did the slaves necessarily reject their African culture when they answered these questions the way Sandoval wanted them to answer? Sandoval recognizes that almost everyone in the world fears death and wonders about their fate after death. What terrible fate awaits those slaves who do not agree to baptism, according to what he tells the slaves? How does Sandoval explain the idea of the Christian God and the Trinity? Hierarchy, difference, and power play a role in this catechism: how does race become an issue in Sandoval's teaching methods? The explanation of heaven and hell clearly equate good behavior with reward and bad behavior with punishment; how does he use metaphors that relate to slavery? How does he pare down his teachings even further in order to quickly baptize very sick slaves? How might their current sick, weak, and terrified condition make the slaves more ready to agree with Sandoval's teachings?

In the Catholic Church, sufficient catechism must precede holy baptism in order for the baptism to be valid. We must follow this standard set by the great theologians. However, we have to work quickly with these needy people, even though they understand so little. At the very least, they must understand the law of Jesus Christ before receiving baptism and becoming Christian, and they must give their consent.

A lack of understanding and consent makes so many baptisms null. It is also a great sacrilege because it condemns so many souls to a terrible fate. The mysteries of the faith must be taught quickly and simply due to the slaves' ignorance, so it is best not to explain it in too much detail. Instead, we say very little in a simple way. We avoid complications and give them time to understand and repeat simple points. This is sufficient.

The slaves must be taught that without baptism, they cannot go to heaven. They must receive enough information so that they can agree to the baptism freely. They must be told what this water means, and they must be attentive, because they have to answer questions later. If they do not answer correctly, they will not have the water poured on them.

Second, they must be told that the water is not for washing their heads or refreshing them, nor is it poured on them in order to cut their hair. Instead it is God's water, and baptism is a great thing that Jesus Christ commands to renew humankind. It puts them in God's grace and friendship and provides them with all its benefits. They go from being slaves of the devil to children of God. They are no longer sinners. Baptism cleans the soul of all stain of guilt but also frees them from the pain of hell and purgatory. If they die after being baptized, they go straight to heaven, as if they had never committed sin. This is how they will become Christians, like the whites, and how they receive the law of Jesus Christ in order to adore him and remember nothing more of the idols and false gods of their land. We repeat this point as many times as is necessary for them to understand, until they give the correct answers to these questions:

What is this water that will be poured over them?

They respond that it is water of God.

Do they want to receive it with all their heart?

Yes.

Where will they go if they receive it?

To heaven with God.

Whose children are they after receiving that water?

Children of God.

If they receive the water, will they be children of the devil or of God?

Just children of God.

Which gods should they have from now on, the true God of the whites, Jesus Christ, his Son, or the false and lying gods of their land and of witchcraft and superstition?

Only the God of the whites.

Do they want to be Christians, obeying the law of Jesus Christ like the whites, living like them, serving and obeying the great God of the Christians, or be Moors [Muslims], gentiles, and barbarians, like they were in their land?

Be like Christians.

Also say to them at this point that the whites are important because they have accepted this water that makes them Christians. If they had not, they would be unimportant and without value. If the slaves receive the water, they will also be respected, and they will be able to go to the temples and houses of God, to associate and eat with the other Christians. If they are Christians, when they die they will be buried in the church. If they are not Christians, they will be thrown in the rubbish dump, where they will be eaten by dogs.

[Third,] they are taught the following mysteries: God is watching us, even if we cannot see him. He is in heaven, on earth, in the sea, in this land, and in all places, and his eyes are always watching. This God has always been and always will be great and powerful. He made all: heaven, earth, land, sea, food and drink, themselves, and all people. This great God created many things they see and many they cannot see.

[Fourth,] we must teach them the mystery of the Holy Trinity: Father, Son, and Holy Spirit, three persons in one God. We must teach this by comparing it to something else. For example, we show them a cloak, just one cloak. We then fold it twice so it has three parts and unfold it to show that it is only one cloak. This is how we explain that God is Father, Son, and Holy Spirit but also is just one God. They enjoy this and it satisfies them. They even ask us to fold and unfold the cloak again so they can see the demonstration more than once.

[Fifth,] we tell them that this great God has a son, also a God like him, who is the second figure of the three we mentioned. We say he was made into a man like other men, in order to save them and take them to heaven to be with him and with his Father, and he is called Jesus Christ. We teach this lesson in a way that appeals to their rough and coarse level of understanding. We say: "Look, children, don't you see how the son of the white man is white, the son of the black man is black, the son of the mulatto man and Indian man is mulatto and Indian: thus also the Son of God is God." This satisfies them. We warn them that God did not need to have a woman to have his Son, like white, black, mulatto, and Indian men do, because he is a great Lord and he can do anything he wants, and thus he can have a son without a woman.

Sixth, we tell them how this Son of God became a man and was born of Saint Mary. We tell them that Saint Mary, the Mother of God, never knew a man, like other women that have children, because even though she conceived her Son Jesus Christ, she remained a virgin. She was still a virgin when she gave birth, because she was the Mother of God, and he can do great things.

Seventh, we tell them that this great and all powerful God has two houses. One is very beautiful and is always full of happiness and is located up in the sky. Those who have water poured on their head will go there, with their children, if they do what he commands. They must believe that we are teaching them God's commands so that they will go to heaven, where they will be happy forever. But God has another house below, where there is nothing but fire, whips, and punishment. Those who do not have water poured on them and who do not want to serve him go there, where they are tortured forever.

Eighth, the Son of God died because he loves them and wants all of them to have their heads washed. After he died, he returned to life. The door that had been closed was opened, and he was in glory. He wants Christians who willingly have had their heads washed and who do what he commanded to be there with him. They must not kill, fornicate, or steal. Those who do not want their heads to be washed, who steal, fornicate, and kill and who are not content with only one woman, are thrown into the lower house, where they will be punished by burning in fires forever.

Then we question them to see if they understand what we have told them. We ask them which of the two houses they want to go to when they die and God calls them to him. If they understood, they point their hands upward and look to the sky, to show that they want to go to heaven, where God is. Some even grow angry if they are asked if they want to go to the inferno, because they know it is very evil. They should know that when they are baptized a second time, their souls will become white and washed clean of sin, and they remain children of God. They understand this when we say it is like the brand made on them with the mark and sign of their masters. When they are baptized, they become children and slaves of God, and when they die they will go to heaven, where God is, to live happily with him forever. Their masters always have their slaves with them, and God is also always with them, because now they are his slaves. He bought them by dying for them and with the water that now is poured on their heads.

Ninth, we tell them the mystery of the Resurrection.[38] They feel very consoled by it. We tell them the soul never dies; only the body dies when it is sick. The body returns, resuscitated, and lives again, uniting with the soul. The body and soul go together to heaven, if they die with the water of God on their head and if they were friends of God. Without these things, they will go to hell. These people struggle to understand the idea of resurrection, so we try to explain it to them in terms that they seem to understand. Afterward, they seem to be grateful and happy. We tell them that dying is like going to sleep. If someone calls them while they are asleep, they will wake up, move around, and return to doing what they were doing before they fell asleep. We explain that this is how it will be when they die. They will lie dead until God calls them. When he calls them, they will rise and their souls will return to their bodies. Together and alive, body and soul go to heaven, where they do not have to fear death but instead will be content living always in the presence of God, forgetting their enslavement and sickness. I cannot describe how consoled these new Christians seem after they are baptized, understanding these things.

It is sufficient to teach these mysteries in this simple way, because the slaves are in desperate need and understand so little. If they die, they have learned enough to be saved and to receive the other sacraments. If they live, little by little

---

38. As Sandoval explains, this means rising from the dead, resuming life. Here he refers to Jesus Christ's rising from the dead three days after his crucifixion, as described in the New Testament. In terms of the slaves' resurrection, Sandoval refers to the belief that souls will rejoin with bodies at the end of time, to live in eternal paradise.

they will learn the rest and perfect themselves. After we finish instructing them, we ask their express permission for baptism, before passing to the other actions necessary for faith, hope, charity, and contrition.

We can only explain the aforementioned mysteries when there is sufficient time. When we are very rushed because the person is very sick and cannot understand anything, we only need to tell them the most essential things that they must believe. I believe they must know that there is only one God, who is good beyond anything else in the world. Second, his rewards come in the afterlife, even if we cannot explain the exact specifics of these rewards. Basic to human hope and faith is the knowledge that God punishes evil. Third, they must understand that he is the sole creator of everything. Fourth, he takes away sin and gives grace, so humans look to God for his pardon. Fifth, the soul is immortal, so they must strive for a reward in heaven and fear eternal pain. Sixth, they must understand what sin is. I think that in some cases, it is not necessary to explain faith in Christ and the mystery of the Trinity.

This is how we instruct black slaves in the Christian faith to ensure the correct and fruitful reception and administration of baptism. This is done as simply as possible so that these poor slaves come to understand the mysteries of the faith.

Chapter 11. The other acts necessary for faith, hope, charity, and penitence that must precede the administration of holy baptism.

An important element of Catholic belief is feeling contrition. To Catholics, contrition means that a person despises what he has done that goes against Christian rules and strives to avoid this behavior in the future. How does Sandoval believe he can determine if slaves feel contrition? What process does he think will help him know their feelings, and what signs does he have that they accept the Christian doctrine? The issue of the slaves' sexuality presents another challenge for Sandoval in explaining the basic rules of Christianity to African slaves. What particular doctrine does he fear might put them off the religion all together, although he emphasizes teaching slaves about love? As he did in the last chapter, how does Sandoval compare God to a master or a father figure in this chapter? What role does this give the slaves in the Christian hierarchy? What role does he give himself?

The instruction described in Chapter 10 is accommodated to the limited capacity of these miserable people. We give them the doctrine in small doses and do not tell them any more than they can absorb. Anything else would cause confusion and do nothing to further our goals. When a person's understanding is so imperfect and slow, one cannot provide too much doctrine, or the student will reject it and become confused. In teaching the doctrine we must adapt to our students. Those who are wise and knowledgeable can take in a flood of information, a deluge of thoughts and ideas. Others can only take the most delicate raindrops that fall silently, forming clear and crystalline drops on the leaves of trees and flowers. As preachers we must imitate this gentle mist. We must accommodate the faults and weaknesses of our listeners. The subtleties of the doctrine shrink when it is explained to pigmies and dwarfs, but they still learn something of God. Children learn a little, but as they grow, they learn more of the Christian doctrine.

We should teach them that they can hope for good fortune and joy from God's favor and grace forever if they practice the holy sacraments and good works.

We must make them understand that they should do acts of love for God and love him with all their heart and soul, because he is their creator and redeemer and will take them to heaven. I use comparisons to teach this, saying:

"Tell me, children, do you love me because I work so hard to teach you and I want you to be Christians? Do you love me very much?"

They will all answer yes and make a thousand salaams[39] to show their gratefulness for my effort and their love.

Then I say, "Children, if you love me and show me such love for the good that I do for you and only you, how much love should you have for God, for the many things he has done for you and given to you? He created you and he created the world for you. He became a man and died so that you will live in heaven forever. Now he wants you to be Christians, his children and his brothers and sisters. For this reason, he took you from your lands, where you lived among Moors, gentiles, barbarians, and children of the devil. Leaving your parents, relatives, and friends, condemned to miserable labor, he chose you to teach you the true and certain path to blessedness."

Then I ask them if they love God for doing so much for them, God who loves them very much, whom they should serve truly and obey. Then I make them say "yes" all together and say that they love such a great God and Lord above all things. I also mention parents, because if their parents bore them and raised them, they should love them very much. But they should love God even more, because he created, sustained, and defended them, gave them eyes, language, health, and strength.

Because these people understand very little, it is difficult for them to make the act of contrition for their sins, which is necessary before we can administer

---

39. A salaam is a low bow done with the right hand on the forehead. This gesture is usually associated with Islam, which Sandoval must have realized, although apparently the irony of an African doing a salaam to thank him for baptizing him seems to be lost on the Jesuit.

the sacraments to them. First they must understand sin so that they can describe their own sins and grow to detest them. Of the commandments of the law of God and the Church, they must at least understand that it is a sin to swear dishonestly, to kill, and to fornicate (although specify that this does not mean that fornication is prohibited within licit matrimony; if you do not make this clear, they will think that all fornication is forbidden, and they will reject this rule and refuse to agree to the others). It is also a sin not to hear Mass on holidays, not to fast when you are supposed to, and so on. If they understand the substance of these rules, you can go ahead with the act of contrition. It is sufficient for them to understand some acts of the faith and give their consent. They should also know that they can ask God for everything they need, for the good of their bodies and the sanctification of their souls. This is the essence of the prayer of the Our Father.[40]

In order to motivate these people to feel guilt and contrition for their sins, before giving them confession or preparing them to receive last rites or another sacrament, they must understand that God is angry at the sins they have committed and that they must placate him by speaking with him. They must know that he hears them even if they cannot see him, because he is everywhere. They must say that they understand this. With a crucifix in their hands, they must say the following words in their language, speaking through the interpreter, and feeling pain and sorrow in their hearts for having angered and offended God with their sins: "Oh great God, good God and Lord, my heart hurts me very much for the sins I have committed, sins that offend and anger you. I only want to serve you from now on. Lord, I do not want to go to hell for any reason. Take me to heaven, Lord."

The first time that they repeat these words, they are told that God will be calmed if they say them honestly and show the sadness they feel for having sinned and offended him. Then they slowly repeat these words with the interpreter. After this, we ask them again if they feel pain for having done so many evil things that angered and offended God and if they want to serve him and commit no more sins. We tell them that their sins mean they that will not go to heaven to be with God forever but instead be eternally tormented in hell. If they understand what we mean by eternal pain, they will say yes. If they do not do this, or if they say something unconnected to our point, for example, that their body feels nothing, or that only such and such part hurts, we do not go forward until they seem to understand or they repeat the same words a third time. They might understand the idea of pain and anger if they compare it to

---

40. The most basic Christian prayer. It begins with the words "Our Father, who art in heaven." The words of this prayer come from lines in the Gospels of Luke 11:2–4 and Matthew 6:9–13.

doing something evil to their masters, who become angry with them and punish them frequently. If they ask humbly to be pardoned for their sins, their masters do not punish them but pardon them and ask them to improve themselves. God also might want to punish them for their sins, throw them in the fire of hell and lash them, but if they ask pardon and promise to improve, he will pardon them like their masters do, and he will make friends with them and take them to heaven, because God is infinitely better than their masters. He created all of us, he sustains us and helps us, and we do nothing but sin in return. If, after all this, they do not understand the concept of having offended God, ask the following questions:

"Tell me, children, the sins that you have committed. Are these sins good?"

Usually they respond no (and if they say yes, it is not difficult to change their minds).

"Then if they are not good, do you want God to pardon them and make your souls beautiful?"

They respond yes.

"Now, then, if the sins are not good and you want God to pardon them, are you going to commit more sins?"

They respond no.

"If sins are evil and you do not want to commit more, do you want God to rid you of them? Why do sins offend God? You angered God by doing something wicked. Don't you see what an ugly thing it is to do these sins, because God throws people into the inferno for this? Do you repent of doing these things, because God punishes you so much for them? By committing them you lose your chance to go to heaven—does this disturb you? After this, will you commit these sins and do this wickedness or other evil things again? Do you want to serve a great, good, and merciful God that can give you heaven? If you confess your sins, he will pardon you."

After saying this, I assume that they probably feel contrite for their sins, so I can administer the required sacrament, assuming that they understand enough to take the sacrament in the grace of God. You should not tire yourself or them anymore but go ahead and give them the sacraments.

Some say the slaves will soon forget what they are taught. If they do, this shows that they are only fragile human beings, subject to the same shortcomings suffered by all others. If they understand what we say at the time and agree to it, that is enough, even if they soon forget it. But this does not usually happen. Usually they respond well to questioning. Even today, the day I write this, I have seen proof of this. Today I succeeded in baptizing a black man. More than two months ago, I catechized and baptized another man of his caste. This second man cheered on his timid and bashful companion, told him what he should say in his own language, although he had learned this many days before.

We do not assume they are Christians with a Spanish level of education but merely that they know enough to receive a decent baptism. Baptism breathes life into them—they are only dry bones before they receive it. This is the best we can do, and they will have to learn the rest when their masters teach them to be Christians, if the masters take seriously the obligation they have to indoctrinate them. Some would argue that a few well-taught Christians are worth more than a large number of Christians, but if we only help a few people, a huge number of gentiles and Moors will remain.

Chapter 12. How to baptize the blacks.

Sandoval combines a detailed explanation of his methods of baptizing slaves with a discussion of theological concepts such as grace, concepts that would have been familiar to readers who were priests and members of the Company of Jesus. Grace in this sense means that when people take part in Christian ceremonies such as baptism, God increases their merit, which means they have a better chance of entering heaven.

Note the details of the ritual here. Some African religions placed a great deal of importance on the symbolism of water as a passageway to the spiritual world, a fact historians use to explain the popularity of river baptisms in the nineteenth-century United States. Other Africans, such as the Bambara, took their belief in the power of amulets to the Americas, continuing to both wear and make amulets. Whatever the Africans understood of Sandoval's preaching, the ceremonies described here show that he must have conveyed to them that baptism was a serious ritual. The slaves probably chose to interpret the use of water and amulets in the context of their own beliefs and thus honestly demonstrated the enthusiasm described in this chapter. In a weakened and spiritually vulnerable state, an individual is likely to turn to the traditions and beliefs of family and homeland as a way to frame new, traumatic experiences. It is less likely that the slaves perceived the ceremony as a complete rebirth to a new Christian identity as obedient slaves, interpreting baptism exactly as Sandoval does.

Sandoval compares his mission to African slaves in Cartagena to Xavier's work in India, because following the model of a saint of the Jesuit order gives his own actions greater importance and authenticity. Sandoval does all he can in this chapter and throughout De instauranda *to argue that his mission is legitimate and valuable.*

I have two reasons for describing how the Company of Jesus here in this city of Cartagena baptizes blacks on the slave ships. First, I have criticized how baptism is sometimes performed without the appropriate reverence that such a sacrament requires, so I should carefully describe the correct way of doing it. Second, I would like to provide a standard method for baptizing, in order to avoid mistakes. It is best not to leave out any detail I mention here.

When the adults have been catechized as I described above, they are commanded to thoroughly wash their heads, calmly and quietly, in two or more troughs or tubs of water that we set to the side for this purpose. Washing is essential in helping the baptismal water pass through the hair to touch the skin of the head. When they wash their heads first, they also feel greater reverence for the water that will be poured on them later as part of baptism. They are told that this first washing is not done with water of God, and it only has the effect of cleaning them. Because baptism and becoming a Christian is such a great thing, they must be clean and decent for it.

This done, they return to where they were sitting before. Those that need unconditional baptism step forward first, in groups of ten, first the men and then the women. Following the holy father Francis Xavier's method, they kneel if they are able. Then, with all possible devotion and calmness, they put their hands around a silver font or, if nothing else is available, a trough. The water falls into this container. With his stole on, the priest asks each person the questions we mentioned above, through interpreters, so that we know that they willingly receive baptism with faith, hope, charity, and contrition, or at least attrition, for their sins.[41] When the father judges them to be sufficiently prepared, he gives each of the ten one of the most common names pronounceable. He makes them repeat their names so they do not forget them. Some can remember other people's names and will help them if they forget theirs. Tell them that they must be called and known by that name from this moment forward as Christians and children of God, forgetting their former names from their own land, because these were names for Moors, gentiles, and the children of the devil. All ten of them are assigned a godmother or godfather. A godparent could be an interpreter who served as translator, or another *ladino* black man or woman of their caste who is present, or someone else they have chosen. The godparents must know their obligations to continue instructing the newly baptized individual, according to their abilities and opportunities. Sometimes the slaves do not have godparents, for example when a *ladino* black's baptism has been secretly revalidated. Church scholars agree that godparents are not required in a private baptism. Next, a handsome rosary with a silver medal on it is put around the neck of each person. One by one, holding a lighted wax candle, they approach the priest. He pours water from a silver jar, or the best container that can be found, over each one's head and body (observing all possible decency and decorum), while saying the baptismal words. The water falls into a porcelain or silver font that a companion brother holds for the priest, usually

---

41. While contrition means that a person truly hates their sins because they love God, attrition means regretting sins out of the fear of punishment, so it is sometimes called "imperfect contrition." Catholic doctrine as defined by the Council of Trent stated that attrition was enough to allow for an effective confession and absolution, where the priest absolves a person's sins, helping him or her on the journey to heaven.

kneeling at his feet. These rituals make the neophytes feel more reverence for the ceremony. After they are baptized but before they rise and mingle with those who are not, a medium-sized tin medal is hung around their necks on a strong thread, to clearly indicate who has already been baptized. The baptized slaves then sit down, and another ten come and are given names. This process continues, baptizing everyone who needs an unconditional baptism, women separate from men.

Afterward, we do the conditional baptisms, which are different from the others. We baptize them, saying [in Latin], "If you are not truly baptized, I baptize you in the name of the Father, Son, and Holy Spirit, Amen." We give them a medal indicating that they received a conditional baptism, because this affects how they will receive the sacraments in the future.

Before they leave, we bring them together again, asking them to do their best to obey God's laws now that they are Christians. We tell them some universal guidelines that may relate to their lives and tell them to abide by these rules. They agree and promise to do this.

They all show pleasure and happiness, inspired by the interior grace they have received from the Holy Spirit. When the baptism is over, they seek each other out and embrace each other joyfully, calling each other by their Christian names. They often even cry with happiness. One black woman began to cry powerfully when the priest baptized her, because in her heart she felt the divine grace in her soul. Everyone who was there was very surprised, but they felt admiration for her when they understood that she cried from the happiness of being Christian, a daughter of God, and inheritor of heaven.[42]

It is absolutely necessary and very important to baptize the slaves in this repetitive way in order to adequately prepare and instruct people who understand so little. If they receive better instruction, they achieve greater grace. All receive the amount of grace that they are disposed to receive. The person who is more prepared for baptism receives more grace. The acts of the Council of Trent, when speaking of the baptism of adults, say: "Each person receives grace, which the Holy Spirit divides among all, according to each one's disposition and cooperation." Even though baptism concedes the remission of all sins to everyone, the spirit of the grace is given unequally, conforming to an individual's faith and the size of the purgation or preceding penance.[43]

We also tell them that it is very important not to receive baptism again, in this or any other land they might go to. If someone ever wants to pour water on

---

42. See explanation of the concept of grace at the beginning of the chapter.

43. Sandoval means that everyone can achieve grace leading to eternal life in heaven, but ceremonies such as baptism will be more effective if the individuals fully understand it and feel a strong sense of contrition for their sins.

their head again, even in a church, they must say they have already done this. They must say they are Christians, children of God who are going to heaven. The *ladinos* must especially know that they cannot be baptized again. They believe this baptism is too simple, because it is not as ceremonious as the church baptisms they have seen done after celebrations and weddings. Because we do not use salt or holy oils and no godparents are present, they believe (because they are somewhat fluent and have communicated with those of their former caste and nation) that this baptism is fruitless and without value.[44]

We tell them not to lose the medals we put around their necks, because these show that they are Christians and children of God, so that everyone will respect them and no one can disdain them. It is amazing to see the great value that such crude people give to these medals. A priest once encountered a black man without an image on his neck. The priest recognized the man and thought he had given him the medal, so he asked him about it. The man smiled as if to say, "He thinks he has caught me being careless." Then he took out a little taffeta purse. Opening it, he showed the father a string of ten beads strung like a rosary. He used these to pray to the Lord to the best of his abilities. As a final touch he had also strung the image that had been put on his neck a year before when he was baptized during a serious illness. Now healthy, he had traveled around to different lands, but he had not forgotten the holy principles of his conversion. A black woman lost the image that she had been given at her baptism, so she walked around for many days, looking for the priests who had baptized her, to see if they could give her another medal. She could not find them, so she went several times to the house where she had been baptized, to ask her godmother about the priests. Finally the lady of the house sent her to our college with another one of her slaves so that she could receive another medal. These two cases are not unique. When the slaves who are gathered in the street see the priest who baptized them, they tell him their images have fallen off and ask for others. They follow him until he enters the first house and gives them a medal. We always carry these medals with us in little bronze boxes that have several of them strung on their strings. When we enter a slave ship, they surround us, some asking for an image to replace one they have lost, others asking for a new string because theirs has torn. Still others ask for new medals because theirs are already getting old. Those who are more *ladino* ask to exchange their tin medals for gilt ones because they no longer want white ones. The priest divides the medals out among all of them, first making each of them say their [baptismal] name, to remind them of it. When they know this will get them another medal, they shout out their names with the medal in hand when they want to be given another. When they have a new

---

44. These details were standard for baptisms done in a church.

medal, they are as happy as if they had been given a treasure. They do value it as a treasure in their own way and rightfully so.

Before they leave, we separate off the nursing mothers. They remain alone because they need quiet. They are examined by the same interpreters who helped in the baptism of their children, in the manner I described above. We pour away the water used in baptism in a decent place a distance away from where the people are. This is the most that can be done for baptisms where the water is not blessed.

This is how we examine, catechize, and baptize slaves in Cartagena de Indias. We baptize more than six thousand slaves a year in this way. We do not do anything that shows disrespect for God. Everything we do brings him glory. Saint Francis Xavier, our father, used this method when he baptized his beloved Paravas, also blacks like these people, in the kingdom of Trabancor and on the coast of the Fisheries.[45] The father brought the men and boys together, blessed them, gave them confession, and called on the Father, Son, and Holy Spirit, one true God, three times. He then did a general confession and said the credo,[46] the Ten Commandments, and other prayers in their language, having them respond aloud. He explained the articles of our holy faith and commands of the law of God. He made them beg the pardon of God Our Lord for the idolatries and vices they committed in their past lives. When he asked them if they believed, they all responded by crossing their arms above their breasts and saying that they believed it firmly. Then he baptized them, giving each one a piece of paper with their baptismal name written on it. He catechized and baptized the women and girls separately, in the same way. This erased all the images of the devil in their souls, and they destroyed the pagodas and altars dedicated to their idols, tearing them down and burning the metal, stone, and wood statues, in revenge for the incredible adoration and captivity in which they had been held for many years. The holy father Francis Xavier said that his spirit received ineffable consolation seeing those that until then had kneeled to the devil get on their feet and raise their heads.

Chapter 13. Administering these baptisms.

To Sandoval, the confusion surrounding slaves' lack of baptism is a serious problem that could lead to mortal sin on the part of masters and priests. According to Catholic belief, mortal sin means purposefully committing an act that goes against God's laws as stated in the Bible. The result is that individuals distance themselves from God and risk

---

45. All places in India where Francis Xavier went to teach Christianity.

46. The credo is a statement of belief in the basic Christian doctrines; it is also called the Apostles' Creed.

punishment in the afterlife. Why does Sandoval believe that slaves should not be bap-
tized in churches? How would they need to change themselves before they could go into
a church building? On the other hand, how have some slaves been influenced by Euro-
peans in a way that makes them even less Christian in his opinion? Although his
abhorrence of allowing slaves in church suggests how slaves fit into Sandoval's vision of
the barbaric, it also highlights the fact that he has arranged for the Jesuits to have special
permission from the pope to baptize slaves outside of a church. The way Sandoval
describes the chaotic state of slaves' Christianity in this chapter implies that he believes
that the Jesuits must be entrusted with Christianizing African slaves in order to avoid
the serious consequences alluded to here.

I mentioned at the end of Chapter 7 that priests in ports are responsible for instructing, catechizing, and baptizing the blacks. Now I will describe how this sacrament should be administered. I proved in Chapters 5 and 7 that the baptisms black slaves receive in their lands and on the ships are usually null and at least doubtful, so they must be examined in the ports where they disembark, which include Lisbon [Portugal], Seville [Spain], Bahia, Pernambuco, Rio de Janeiro, Buenos Aires, San Juan de Ulúa, Santo Domingo, Puerto Rico, Cartagena, Panamá, and Lima, Peru, and any other ports where slavers go to sell them.[47] Priests in these ports and towns must examine, catechize, and baptize the slaves that are falsely considered Christians. This must be done as soon as they arrive, before the slaves are sold and separated, because their masters and the priests in the villages where they go assume that having passed through the ports, they are already baptized. Before they are sold to a master, it must be determined if they know Jesus Christ and his Church. If they do not, they must be instructed.

Although priests have this obligation, I realize that it is very challenging for them to carry it out. There are usually so few priests, especially here in the Indies, and they are very busy with occupational and personal matters. The rough, *bozal* blacks need interpreters, which are very difficult to find because they are busy slaves. We do not just need one or two interpreters but a huge number to accommodate all the different languages and nations. Examining and investigating the slaves' baptisms is very difficult. Teaching the catechism

---

47. Salvador de Bahia, Pernambuco, and Rio de Janeiro are port cities in Brazil. San Juan de Ulúa is the fort outside the city of Veracruz, Mexico. By referring to Veracruz, Santo Domingo, Puerto Rico, Cartagena, Panamá, and Lima, Sandoval lists almost all of the legal Spanish colonial ports in the Americas during this era, other than Havana, Cuba. He does not mention Acapulco—mainly a port for the Manila Galleons, trading between New Spain and the Philippines. By adding "any other ports where slaves go to sell them," he alludes to contraband slave disembarkations, very common on the coast of what is now Venezuela and in the port of Buenos Aires.

takes a long time, so all of this work demands a large number of holy, zealous, unoccupied, experienced, and wise priests. Priests cannot baptize the slaves in the church; the blacks that come in slave ships cannot go into the churches because they are too sick, thin, and parched. They can barely stand. They are naked and so disgusting and brutish in their actions after being kept crowded together in the slave ships that it would be indecent to take them into a church, like allowing some filthy animals inside. When they go to church after they have been sold, they are cleaned and dressed, at least well enough to avoid indecency. They must wait to go into the church until they are already instructed, so that they do not behave as brutally inside it as they do outside, not seeing any difference between the church and the sheds where their masters house them. There are many other difficulties and inconveniences that I will not mention so as not to offend anyone.

But these are challenges that can be overcome in order to fulfill such an important obligation. Priests must find ways to conquer these difficulties, in order to save these souls. Masters and slave traders in the ports where the blacks disembark must not hinder or impede the examination and baptism of their blacks. They must tell the priests or other clerics who can help of those who are sick. If they do not, masters should be penalized by not being able to sell slaves that are not already examined or baptized within so many days. (This period would be about how long it takes to instruct and baptize them.) These rules should help, although they are easy to write and difficult to carry out, especially in small villages and other areas that lack priests.

The black slaves are so diverse, crude, and uncomprehending that they cannot remember anything unless it is said to them in their native languages. They must be examined first, to avoid rebaptizing people who have already been baptized, not baptizing someone conditionally who might have been baptized, or not baptizing those that lack baptism. Blacks from Congo are baptized in their lands, as the Indians are baptized here in their lands. Angolans, Angicos, and Malembas come here with good baptisms. Ardas, Caravalis, and Lucumis might have a variety of possible baptisms.[48] Others who are from the Guinean rivers are badly baptized in the ports there. Jesuit priests question them in Cartagena and baptize those who they find have not been baptized or who received an invalid baptism. The examination must be done very carefully, because the nations are so diverse and it is difficult to understand the slaves. You must be especially careful in examining those who are more *ladino* from living inland in Lima, Cuzco, and other places. It is assumed, because they have already passed through so many Christian lands and lived so many years among Christians, that they are baptized.

---

48. See Book I, Chapter I, and the Glossary for more information on these ethnicities.

No priest or confessor should be satisfied when black people say that they were already taken to the church or think that they are already legitimately baptized. We must inquire further, because we have found three ways in which a black slave might not have truly received baptism, even when it was done in a church. First, only holy oils may have been used, not baptismal water. Second, if only water had been used in a slave's native land, the slave might think this is sufficient and want only oil and chrism, not a second baptism with water.[49] Third, having received solemn baptism in the church with water and chrism, the slave might not have understood or consented to what was administered, and so did not become Christian. These are some of the ways in which they might not be Christians, even if they say that they were already baptized in the church.

Confessors must carefully examine *ladinos* who confess without using interpreters. Slaves who recover from the treatment or sickness they suffer on the ships are sold in unknown lands, where they become *ladino* by learning vices and sins, not things having to do with salvation.[50] They understand little about baptism. Elderly black slaves may have arrived before we started checking their baptisms, so some only received invalid baptisms on slave ships. More recent arrivals may not have passed through ports where they would have been examined and baptized. We must avoid committing a grave sacrilege by administering the holy sacraments to gentiles.[51]

Masters should also question their slaves as well as possible to find out if they have been baptized. They should not trust the people who sold them their slaves if the sellers say the slaves were baptized in Guinea. We already know how improbable this is and how wicked it is to lie about slaves' baptisms. If masters discover that their slaves have not been baptized, they must help carry out the Church's regulations or they will fall into mortal sin. If a slave received holy oils but no baptism, the master must explain this to the priest or confessor so that he can determine what must be done for the good of that soul.

---

49. Holy oils and chrism both refer to oil that has been blessed by a priest. Chrism is often olive oil. Oil is put on a person's head during baptism. Sandoval is trying to explain that slaves might not have had complete baptisms, missing one or another element, and the person examining them has to figure out what was done to them.

50. *Ladino* usually means knowing about European culture and language, but here Sandoval uses the word to mean that the slaves only become knowledgeable about immorality through their time among Europeans.

51. Sandoval calls slaves "gentiles" to mean they were non-Christians before baptism. If they receive the other sacraments without a proper baptism, they are still gentiles but are participating in the Catholic Church. Therefore, they are non-Christians taking part in Christian ceremonies, a sacrilegious situation in Sandoval's view.

Priests who do not put some effort into learning what their parishioners need will also fall into mortal sin. Their parishioners will die lacking the instruction necessary for their salvation and for receiving the holy sacraments, especially holy baptism. Priests must visit houses now and then to encourage such instruction and also to see the miserable slaves' ill fortune and desolation for themselves. It is a mortal sin to claim ignorance of the fact that the blacks are not baptized and that each day slaves are buried unbaptized. It is also a sin to not help adult slaves to stay in the grace of God and avoid sin.

It is sufficient to pour water on slaves either conditionally or unconditionally, depending on the answers they give to your questions, without repeating the ceremonies of the Church, such as finding godparents and using holy oils. The baptism is not invalid if you neglect these parts of the ceremony. It would be scandalous for the church of God if numerous people who were already baptized received ceremonious and solemn baptisms. If a ceremony has been performed incorrectly and it must be revalidated, it should be done discreetly and quietly to avoid scandal.

Chapter 14. The privileges given to administer these baptisms.

This chapter describes the special "privileges," or permission and approval that popes have given the Jesuits, as mentioned in the last chapter. Sandoval explains that these privileges allow them to carry out baptisms "outside the church and without the customary ceremonies" and without any interference by parish priests. This means that the Jesuits can board the slave ships or enter the barracks where slaves lived until they were sold, in order to baptize them in these places, as described in Chapter 12. In 1579 Pope Gregory XIII gave the Jesuits broad powers to baptize people in all the American territories controlled by either the Portuguese or the Spanish monarchs. In 1614 Pope Paul V reaffirmed papal approval of Jesuit baptizing rights; Sandoval implies that this was done because people objected to the baptisms they were performing outside a church edifice. These papal privileges are one indication of the special relationship the Jesuits had with the popes, part of their original foundation by Ignatius Loyola (see Introduction). Sandoval says that the Jesuits must have these privileges in order to make up for the shortage in parish priests. Sandoval points out that parish priests do not believe that black slaves are not baptized, and they do not do the extra work to find out more information or to baptize them. Sandoval summarizes the papal privileges: "No one can impede or interfere with the Jesuit fathers in this ministry. The fathers are trusted to judge suitable times and places for exercising this ministry. They can administer the sacrament without the customary ceremonies [applying holy oils, having godparents present] or they can celebrate and administer it with all of them, however they believe will best serve God. All other priests should help them carry out their mission." Sandoval encourages other Jesuits to take advantage of the special rights the popes have given them in order to help the slaves.

Chapter 15. Administering baptisms in cases of need.

A few passages from this chapter highlight Sandoval's presentation of the challenges of his Cartagena mission. Sandoval knew that hundreds of slaves died from illnesses or drowning in shipwrecks. If the slaves made it alive to Cartagena, he believed that they needed to be baptized immediately, before they died of mistreatment, hunger, thirst, and disease. When they seemed healthy, the slaves were quickly sold and sent inland, so again, Sandoval stresses that they must be baptized as soon as possible in the port. Those slaves that survived the passage across the Atlantic and their time in Cartagena's slave barracks faced a very difficult journey to Bogotá or mines outside the Cartagena region.

This trip is difficult due to bad weather, poor food, no water, and impassable roads. The slaves usually travel by sea or on rivers and over a dangerous land route. They are already thin and become very cold on the roads [due to the increasing altitude as they go into the Andean mountain range]. Baptisms need to be done in ports because the slaves run the risk of dying on the road. Some masters will hide the slaves when they arrive in the ports, which I judge to be homicidal to these souls. It is as if a friend had a wound that needed to be treated, but hid it, and you did not report it. Aren't you obliged to reveal the wound so that it will not get infected and kill your friend? This is an even crueler thing to do when the wound is in the soul and the remedy is holy baptism.

Many slaves remain in this city, although it is impossible to know what this number will be when a ship arrives. Usually it is very few, because those brought from Guinea are sold first in large lots to different owners, then these are divided and separated into smaller lots until the divisions are so small that they are bought singly or in groups of two or three. Those who remain serve in private houses, because no one buys twenty or thirty slaves to serve in one house. Thus there is no way to know who will stay here, and it is appropriate to catechize and baptize them all, with the idea that all will go elsewhere, because the majority of them always leave. Not knowing who will stay here, we must consider the spiritual good of all of them and not neglect to instruct and baptize them.

If black slaves who arrive in this port are sold without holy baptism, they run the clear risk of never being baptized for their entire lives. In an emergency, any layperson whatsoever should be permitted to baptize them, even if the baptism is just some idiot saying these words in our vulgar Castilian: "I baptize you in the name of the Father, the Son, and the Holy Spirit, amen." We must consult the authorities of the Church on all aspects of baptism to avoid any doubts or contradictions.[52]

---

52. This paragraph does not seem to fit in with Sandoval's desire for sincere, voluntary baptism but instead shows that he believes that the slaves' souls will be saved through hasty baptisms. Presumably, those slaves baptized by laymen have already been instructed in Christian doctrine.

Chapter 16. Special cases in private baptisms of blacks.

Sandoval allows for a great deal of leeway in determining if an individual understands Christianity enough to voluntarily agree to baptism. When a slave is delirious or unconscious, Sandoval's policy is to assume that this person willingly accepts baptism, because baptism will help the soul go to heaven. This policy might seem to go against his argument of always getting a slave's free consent to being baptized, but Sandoval justifies this by saying that it is an emergency and the soul is in danger. He advises his readers to do a conditional baptism in these cases, in case the person has already been baptized. He also stresses that in many cases, language is the most difficult obstacle to overcome. Even if there is a good translator, sometimes he or she cannot adequately interpret what the slave has expressed. Sandoval encourages his readers to trust that the slaves might have deeper emotions and stronger feelings about baptism than their translated words suggest.

Sometimes the *bozales* are like mutes, because they come from an unknown nation, so no one can figure out their language and they cannot be prepared for baptism. In these cases, I have seen some slaves satisfactorily baptized with signs. For example, take a jug of water in hand and ask them if they want their heads to be washed with that water, while demonstrating to them that with that baptism they will go to heaven. Or take them to the church or other places so that they see others baptized in their presence, and ask them if they want the same. In order to become Christian, they must at least understand baptism by signs, even if this is a very rough and crude level of comprehension. If they just want to receive what they see others receive, if they do not understand something of the goal, purpose, or meaning of baptism, they will not be Christian, and what they receive will just be a wash with water. Thus, one cannot administer baptism licitly to adults, even at the point of death, just by baptizing others in their presence and asking them if they want it also, because they will not understand the value of this sacrament nor the regret they must feel for their sins. However, if there is some indication that they understand or feel contrition, they can be baptized conditionally.

Chapter 17. Administering baptism to a dying infant or adult, when receiving it will accelerate or cause death.

Latin America's colonial port cities were hotbeds of disease spread by sailors, soldiers, slaves, and travelers coming together from diverse regions of the world. Due to its function as an important port from the 1500s to the 1800s, Cartagena was hit by several serious epidemics. Most of the city's colonial hospitals were not occupied by local residents but instead housed sailors and other voyagers. While long sea voyages weakened strong adults, the lack of good nutrition and closely-packed conditions made slave ships far more deathly than normal journeys. Sandoval was one of the few people based in the port who interacted directly with slaves onboard ship and in the city's slave barracks. What appalling moral dilemmas emerge from constantly instructing and baptizing dying people? What justifies baptizing a person, especially a baby, who is so weak that the act of baptism might hasten death?

Baptism is licit if it is administered to the sick when they are about to expire, even if baptism leads to death. However, one must not commit homicide by baptism. For example, throwing a dying baby in a well or a river is not a true baptism, because this action is a suffocation, not an ablution, and the baby is killed, not washed. Baptism must be the opposite: a washing, not a drowning. If one cannot postpone the baptism because an infant or an adult is about to die, and if you have some concern that baptism will push the person toward death, then you should do it without guilt, because baptism very rarely causes death. Do as little harm as possible by controlling the duration of the immersion and the temperature of the water. If a person is near death and is about to die without baptism, even if baptism would accelerate death, it must be administered. Baptism will not accelerate certain death very much. If the person does die after the baptism, it is accidental, not on purpose as in the case of throwing a baby in a river, because the washing is done carefully and cautiously. The point is not to kill but to allow for a good death and the health of the soul. The sick person has a right to this. A soldier should guard his post, even if he knows he will die, because one person's death leads to greater good for the republic. In the same way, a sick person's death is justified because it means the soul lives forever. Finally, we all know that it is right to die for a good cause, such as perishing in a shipwreck in a battle to help your king or your father. If this is true, it is even more right to die for salvation.

Chapter 18. Some special cases of confessing these blacks.

How can a priest understand an African slave's confession without using an interpreter? But then how can the priest maintain the secrecy of the confessional? Sandoval advises his readers to find discreet interpreters who fully understand the concept of the vow of secrecy of the confession. Gossipy, sociable people who have a large circle of acquaintances should be avoided as interpreters. However, Sandoval does not worry too much about this issue because "In many years of experience working with all kinds of men and women from many different nations, I have never heard of an interpreter telling anyone else other than the confessor what happened in the confession. They are a frank, simple, kind, and faithful people, and they are so busy working that they forget things easily. They are very respectful to white people, so we should not worry that they have base morals that other people have." He adds that the slaves confess willingly and do not fear telling their secrets to the interpreters. Because communication is so difficult,

Sandoval says slaves only need to go to confession once a year or when they are sick. They also do not have to confess with interpreters but can do it by using signs. Sandoval also talks about how priests working as confessors have to coach the slaves to confess their sins properly, because even with careful questioning, they might not answer honestly due to lack of understanding. He advises his readers to be patient and slowly try to teach the slaves to feel sorry for their sins so that priests can then absolve them effectively. More details about confession appear in the next chapter.

Chapter 19. How the sacraments of penance and extreme unction are administered to the blacks.

This chapter discusses confession and the absolution of sins. Absolution is the idea that a priest can absolve or pardon a person from their previous sins if the individual confesses his or her sins to the priest and feels contrition, legitimate regret, and the desire to amend themselves. Catholics believe that when a person's sins are pardoned, the soul has a better chance of going to heaven. The Council of Trent made rules codifying the importance of sacraments such as penance because they gave Catholic priests a spiritual authority and connection to the divine (inherited from the apostles, as Sandoval observes) that Protestant ministers could not claim. Sandoval also discusses the concept of penance: after confession, the priest issues a set of spiritual directions, usually prayers, that a person must complete before the confessed sins can be absolved. As he makes slaves discuss their sins, Sandoval tries to move the slaves away from African codes of behavior and toward accepting Spanish Christian ideals of conduct. A significant percentage of African slaves were young male prisoners of war with some fighting experience, a past way of life they had to forget in order to fit into their new lives as slaves in the Americas. How does Sandoval show a sense of his own power, as a priest, when he discusses confession and the outcome of sin? Many of the slaves are near death, so Sandoval believes that their eternal fate may be decided very quickly, and he has a fairly relaxed standard for judging whether the slaves felt contrition for their sins.

Many of the sins discussed in confession have to do with sexuality. Sandoval's vision of correct and incorrect sexuality is molded by the Bible and the fact that Europeans often conceived of African sexuality as distinct from their own in some way, part of the larger conception of African difference and even barbarity. According to this way of thinking, the more Africans were described as embracing unacceptable sexuality, the more they deserved enslavement and needed a civilizing influence. Sandoval's intellectual and cultural background predisposes him to expect sexual aberrations in Africans, so he looks for it in the confessions he hears. His vision of sexuality has been formed by biblical writings such as Deuteronomy 22:5, which says that the act of men or women dressing like the opposite gender was an abomination to God. Sandoval struggles for the words to describe any taboo sexuality, referring to "the sin that offends the ear to hear." He cites sources such as Augustine to suggest to his readers that some regions of Africa had a long tradition of flexibility in gender roles. He also cites long passages in Latin, not translated in the original, that further discuss the issue. Sandoval would not have wanted the casual reader to understand these passages; thus he left them in Latin so that only learned men like the Jesuit priests could read them. What other evidence does Sandoval provide to warn his readers about African sexuality? How might his occupation as a priest under a vow of celibacy affect his perception and discussion of sexuality?

The previous chapter described our obligation to discover the slaves' sins and try to make them confess them. This obligation is especially important when they are near death. Christ Our Lord gave the apostles the authority to pardon sins, but we have to know sins before we can pardon them. People will be eternally condemned if they die without their sins being absolved. The authorities of the Catholic Church demand confession once a year, and those who confess must have pure motivations.

It is very difficult to make the *bozales* understand what confession and the sacrament of penance are. It is even more difficult to confess them and put penance into practice, so I will speak briefly of this. The best way I can think of to teach them about confession is to first make them understand sin by giving them examples of it. I ask the men if they have had many women, because they do not understand that this is immoral, and they say yes. I ask them if they have killed, and they respond yes, because their wars are so continuous and bloody.

"Then, son," I say to them, "look, these things and other actions are what the Christians call sin. Sin is a very evil thing that slaves of the devil do in hell, where God burns and punishes them. But God can take away all of your sins by cleansing and washing your soul with the water of baptism. Even if you do these or other things again after your head is washed, God still loves you. In order to wash away your sins, tell them to me and I will absolve them with words commanded by God. This will clean your soul, and you will remain a friend and child of God. All the Christians do this because it is a great thing that God commanded, so that those who have sinned can still follow this path to heaven."

Then explain to them the role of the priest and the interpreter in confession. Exhort them to tell you the truth without being afraid. Even if they have committed a thousand sins, you will not punish them. Telling the truth will remove the sins and make them friends with God. This method helps them understand this sacrament and its importance.

Then ask them the necessary questions in order to determine if they have committed various sins. The first question is, "After the water was poured on you, did you sleep with a black woman, even just as a temporary liaison?" If you are questioning a black woman, ask if she slept with a black man, and if she denies it, ask if she slept with a white man, and so on, because if the confessor does not specify, they will not state their sin. Sometimes we must carefully ask them specific questions, saying things like, "Did this or that happen to you in the ship?" To which they usually respond, "Yes, it did."

Second, if the men have not actually committed these sins, ask if they desire or think of women in their hearts. They usually deny doing this because they do not understand the question. This is an important issue, because they frequently admit that they had many women in their land. Go on by asking them, "Did you remember and desire these women in the ship and after you became a slave?" If they say yes, ask them, "Then if you desired your own women, did you not desire others?" They will say yes.

One could also ask them if they have sinned by looking at some brazen black woman. They describe this in their own words: "I enjoyed watching her; she made me happy in my heart." This often leads to evil desire, although some people do not even notice that the women go about shamelessly naked as if they were beasts.

Finally, one can ask them about the kinds of sins they ordinarily commit— perhaps they have evil, lustful cravings. Father Hernando Guerrero of our Company points out that some of the histories of Ethiopian nations boast that men do not need women to be good husbands. The Jesuit fathers found many blacks called *chibandos* in the kingdom of Angola. These are great sorcerers, men who dress as women and shave themselves. They sit as if they were women and are very insulted if they are called men. They have husbands like the other women and practice the sin that offends the ears themselves to hear it (even the saints themselves are evasive when they have to discuss it). According to Saint Augustine and other scholars who refer to it as well as preach against it, that abomination seems to be very ancient in Africa. Saint Augustine says that Africa fell into perdition by practicing this abominable obscenity: the men dressed as women, braiding their hair so they seemed to be women, and the magistrates permitted it.[53] I have noted in this city of Cartagena, and even in other places, that some black nations celebrate festivals by having men dress as women. This infernal plague is not widespread but is still serious, even if it is only practiced rarely. Even some slaves who are already Christian participate. Finally, only the wise confessor can decide how he should deal with the sins of the Caravalis. A trustworthy person who spent many years in their land told me that the virgin boys practice bestiality there.

After you ask these questions, as well as asked if they have committed any thefts or if they have cursed, lied, or felt anger toward their companions and masters, there will be enough material for confession. You must then try to motivate them to make the act of contrition or at least attrition. They must say that they feel regret or that it is a burden to them to have done something that offends God. This is contrition. If they say that they regret that God was

---

53. Sandoval continues discussing this topic with a long section in Latin. His approach is typical when discussing what was referred to at the time as the "nefarious sin."

angered, this is attrition. Ask them if they regret sinning for the love of God, or if they regret sinning because God punishes those that offend him with fire. The first shows they feel contrition, the second attrition. This will make them show signs of pain and raise their hands to heaven, saying that they do not want to go to hell, that they want to serve God from now on and they do not want to do anything that angers God, even if they are accustomed to doing these things in their country. In this case, try to motivate them by saying these things to them and making them repeat them with the interpreter.

For example, I say, "Look, children, within your body you have a soul that will never die. God created heaven to reward your soul. Look how great God is: he created you and will take you to heaven if you serve him and repent of your sins. If not, he will send you to the fires of hell. Tell me: wouldn't it be good to not offend God, such a great Lord that has done you so much good? Do you wish that you had not sinned? From here forward will you improve and not sin?"

Encourage them to say yes. If they seem to say it without any doubt, then they feel regret. If even this does not move them, it is more secure and can be more helpful to make them say the words that show contrition, because I believe that when we say something with our mouths, we believe what we say and we cannot internally contradict the meaning of the words we are saying. For example, tell them: "Say this to me, child, 'My Lord Jesus Christ, Son of God, I wish I had not sinned, because of my love for you. I detest my sins. So that you do not punish me with the fires of hell, from here on I will try to be better. This is what you want and help me carry it out.'"

After you do all this, unless a slave specifically objects to it, you should feel convinced that he feels enough regret to be absolved. Then I tell them to repeat three times the holy names of Jesus and Mary as penance. Make them put their hands together, raise their eyes to heaven, and give their hearts to God. Make them understand that the priest speaks words in the name of God to make God their friend. Thus absolved, tell them of the mercy that God Our Lord shows them. Place a colored image around their throat, a pendant that differs from the white one that indicates baptism. This one is a sign showing that they have made their confession. They are happier if they have some material sign that they are Christian children of God and have received the holy sacraments of baptism and confession. It also prepares them to receive extreme unction, in case they fall seriously ill.

Sandoval concludes this chapter by discussing the importance of the sacrament of extreme unction, which is given in the last rites before death. He says that this sacrament serves to cleanse the soul of sin. Priests do not have to worry about administering this sacrament to someone who is unconscious or who has not specifically requested it, and it can be given to a person who has just been baptized. Because of the high mortality of the slaves that Sandoval works with, this sacrament is frequently performed.

Sandoval also believes that sometimes extreme unction helps people recover from their dire illnesses.

CHAPTER 20. How one must administer the most holy sacrament of the Eucharist to the blacks.

A few selections from this chapter bring to light Sandoval's opinions on slaves taking communion, or the Eucharist wafer, which Catholics believe is the body of Jesus Christ. The Catholic mass seeks to recreate the Last Supper with the priest repeating the words said by Jesus: "He broke the bread, gave it to his disciples, and said, "Take this and eat it. This is my body." As mentioned in the Introduction, the Jesuits, following the decrees of the Council of Trent, encouraged people to take communion more frequently. This Catholic sacrament highlights the central role of the priest as a necessary mediator between the sacred and the worldly. Sandoval states that taking part in communion is a fundamental aspect of gaining salvation, and he argues that God made this clear in the Gospels. He also explains that taking communion is also enforced by Church decrees, and he discusses the various debates throughout Christian history relating to how frequently a person should take communion. Different popes and Church councils differed on this point, although Sandoval argues that early Christians took communion every day. He believes that Africans and their descendants born in the Americas should have communion once a month. Because the Church allows delirious, insane, or even possessed people to receive communion before they die, Sandoval argues that certainly slaves should also receive it, especially the many slaves that die on the ships. He ends by saying that those people who think it is improper to give slaves, because of their appearance and actions, the sacrament of the Eucharist, are actually committing an immoral act themselves. How does Sandoval defend the slaves' intelligence in the selections here, and how does this connect to his overall goals in De instauranda?

The Catholic Church commands us to confess once a year, before taking annual communion. This also applies to blacks who have just received the Lord: they must take communion, even if they still go to their dances and parties and drink tobacco [*sic*]. If we forbid the blacks from taking communion for these things, then we must do the same for whites, who do not abstain from tobacco, swearing, gossiping, and many other more serious sins.

By divine law, a black slave who has a small degree of understanding must take the Eucharist at the time of death. Christian scholars believe that there are two kinds of simpletons: some who utterly lack the use of reason and others who are somewhat cogent. The Eucharist must be given to the latter. The blacks commonly do not have less intelligence than the Spaniards that we think of as fools or dunces, and these people always take communion, so the blacks must also. Second, in order to be obligated to communicate, a person must only be able to understand that the Eucharist is not food, and that in some manner they revere Christ in the sacrament. Blacks show how much they can learn and that they are not simpletons when they master accounting, owning businesses and buying their freedom.

Some people believe that it is scandalous to give the sacrament to people whose actions and appearance seem brutal, but the true scandal is not to give them the sacrament. Priests must do their jobs carefully and prevent this scandal. These people do have the necessary intelligence to receive the sacrament, although their lack of knowledge of our language makes it difficult for them to show it.

Chapter 21. The blacks' obligation to fulfill the commands of our Holy Mother Church.

This chapter discusses how African slaves must carry out some, but not all, of the Church's commands. For example, Sandoval declares that slaves must attend Mass on Sundays. He then turns to the rule that commands people to fast or abstain from eating before receiving the sacrament of the Eucharist. He suggests that slaves must fast only to the degree possible, considering their state of health and the heavy labor they must do. He says that slaves are under no obligation to carry out the rule of tithing, or giving one tenth of your income to the church. He observes that it is challenging for slaves to carry out other Christian rules of behavior, because they understand so little of the language. Therefore, they are not sinning if they do something against a rule they do not know. Sandoval wants masters to carry the burden of making their slaves behave like Christians. Sandoval concludes by reminding his readers that godparents, masters, and priests must try to teach African slaves the Christian doctrine, but the slaves can still participate in the sacraments even if they do not know it perfectly.

If their slaves are ignorant, masters must give them time to be instructed, baptized, and given confession. The more careless and ignorant the slaves are, the more obligated their masters are to make them go to Mass and celebrate fiestas. They are also obligated to dress them with Christian decency so that they can enter the church without making a mockery of it. Masters pay so much to maintain their bodies that they should be willing to pay this small price to maintain their souls and carry out a fundamental command of the Church. They should also oblige their slaves not to eat meat on the fast days and have them eat fish, explaining to them in their own languages that at certain times they cannot eat meat, because they are Christians, and this is the rule for Christians. Their masters must give them sufficient sustenance to help them adjust to the days when the Church prohibits eating meat, but they cannot force them to fast.

The master is not obligated to throw slaves who have mistresses out of the house. Slave traders often do this, even when two slaves have contracted legal matrimony. Even if an infidel [non-Christian] slave does not want to change or convert, the master does not have to throw him out, although he must try to make non-Christian men sleep apart from the women, as well as warn future masters who buy non-Christian slaves so that they can also try to help them and avoid offending God Our Lord as much as possible.

Chapter 22. His Most Illustrious Lordship Archbishop of Seville's instruction for all his archdiocese regarding the value of the baptisms of the blacks, in order to assure their salvation as much as possible.

This chapter consists of a 1614 edict given in Spain by the archbishop of Seville, who demands that the hundreds of priests in his archdiocese carry out his orders or risk excommunication (forbidding their participation in any aspect of the Catholic Church). Slave ships came to Seville, although by Sandoval's time they were not required to pass through this port. Most slavers went directly to the Americas. However, the treatment of slaves in Seville could serve as an effective model for other port cities in the Spanish empire. Having the approval of this important Spanish church leader legitimizes Sandoval's work and possibly helped his ideas spread to cities and towns in Spain and the Spanish empire. The fact that Sandoval was able to have a powerful and influential archbishop issue a summation of all of his methods, presented in a more extended form in Book 3 of De instauranda, *proves that Sandoval understood how to manipulate the bureaucratic processes common to the early 1600s. This document is not unlike many other Spanish government decrees that attempted to regulate the empire by listing and organizing groups of people and to provide directions on how authorities must deal with these individuals. However, the existence of a well-organized edict does not guarantee that these official orders were actually carried out; often it simply highlights an ongoing concern.*

By promoting the archbishop's edict, Sandoval is also trying to bridge the gap between the Jesuits' goals and concerns and the secular clergy's activities. The Jesuits derived their highest authority from the general of their Company and the pope, while the secular clergy were meant to follow the commands of local and regional bishops and archbishops. Often these two church hierarchies conflicted. With this decree, Sandoval hopes to get the secular clergy, led by the archbishop of Seville, to support his mission. The archbishop also brings in Seville's local Jesuits as helpers in the mission, directing local priests to seek assistance from the Jesuits based in the Seville Jesuit college called San Hermenegildo. Sandoval was probably able to engage them in his agenda through the extensive worldwide Jesuit letter-writing network.

Despite Sandoval's best efforts and the confidence he expresses at the end of this chapter, it is extremely unlikely that these plans were carried out over the long term. Slavery became much more widespread and concentrated in the circum-Caribbean sugar economy, including in the Jesuit Brazilian sugar plantations. Efforts to discuss Christianity in depth with slaves declined as the African slave trade increased dramatically in

some parts of the Americas (Brazil, Cuba, Santo Domingo, and islands of the Carib-
bean under French and English dominion) and declined in others (New Spain and
Peru).

The following document strongly supports my arguments in this book, so I will include all of it here. The Most Illustrious Lord Don Pedro Castro de Quiñones, Archbishop of Seville, gave these instructions to his entire archdiocese, and everyone must observe these pious, serious, and wise instructions. The fathers of the Company of Jesus of the city of Cartagena told the archbishop about the conditions on the slave ships and the inadequate baptisms that slaves receive. The archbishop issued this edict to improve the way in which baptism, the route to eternal life, is administered. Along with the instructions, I will also include here the archbishop's short introductory edict. I quote his exact words because they are so sensible and easy to understand.

The Edict Is as Follows:

I, the Licentiate Don Gonzalo de Campo, Archdeacon of Niebla, Provisor Canon, official and General Vicar of Seville[54] and its archdiocese, speaking for the Most Illustrious Lordship Don Pedro de Castro y Quiñones, Archbishop of Seville, on the Council of His Majesty, etc.

I command the priests in cities, villas, and towns to find the black slaves in your districts so that they will be baptized according to these instructions. Publish an edict commanding all the masters to send their black slaves to the church so that all of them will learn the Christian doctrine, according to their capacity. The slaves must be examined. If necessary, they must be baptized according to the rules set down in this instruction. You [the priests] must prevent their masters from interfering in the examination of their black slaves. You must not let the slaves fear this matter. Question them alone, with only the examiner and examinee present. You must even question those who say they were baptized in Spain. Ask them if water was poured on them, because some have only received the ceremonial side of baptism or were baptized invalidly in their own land. You must carry this out. I decree a punishment of excommunication against anyone who disobeys. I command all clerics, notaries, and sacristans to be notified of this edict. Signed in Seville, on February 20, 1614, by the Licentiate D. Gonzalo de Campo, in the presence of Pedro Heriega de Valdez.

In order to execute this edict so that what his Lordship commanded will be put into practice with the most prudent and suitable methods, the archbishop gives the priests the following instruction:

---

54. These official titles recognize the authority of Gonzalo de Campo, the person who actually issued the edict in the name of Archbishop Quiñones.

Instruction to help ensure that the blacks who come from Guinea, Angola, and other provinces of that coast of Africa have been baptized.

This important matter requires an effective remedy. Direct and trustworthy information proves that many blacks from various nations of Africa are not baptized, and many others are baptized invalidly. This causes two fundamental problems, along with many other lesser concerns. First, many souls lack salvation, because they do not receive the most basic preparation for the attrition of sins, even if they do not need contrition.[55] They are denied the divine help and goodness that come from sacred baptism. Second, later on, these people receive the other sacraments even though they are completely incapable of receiving them. This is sacrilege. It cannot be excused by ignorance. There are so many blacks, and, by virtue of divine grace, they are so well disposed to the faith, that it is a great shame that they die without the sacrament of baptism even when they live among an abundance of priests who frequently perform the sacraments.

CENSUS

1. All priests must take a census, or make a list of all the black men and women, free or enslaved, in their parishes. They must note down their names and note if they are free or enslaved and, if they are slaves, the names of their masters. Most importantly, the priest must record if the slave was baptized in Spain or not, and if he is married.

   Note: indicate if the slave is *bozal* or *ladino*. If someone is well educated with a very good knowledge of some language of his nation, he can serve as an interpreter for the *bozales* of his language. Note what languages they speak.

2. Add a marginal note to this list, indicating the black men or women who are sick, so that one can more easily tell which individuals more urgently need immediate spiritual help. The priest must go quickly to the sick and help them receive baptism preceded by catechism as is described below.

3. The priests of the Sagrario of Saint Mary the Great[56] must do more work because they must look for and list all the blacks, vagabonds, or foreigners who do not have a set abode or parish but instead go to the main church. They must

---

55. See note 41.

56. The Sagrario refers to a chapel in the central cathedral of Seville; in Sandoval's time the term referred to the cathedral itself. As stated, people who attended the main church might be wanderers. Instead of attending a parish church tied to a certain neighborhood, they were considered the responsibility of the Sagrario priests.

describe how and where these vagabonds can be found. They must take special care with these souls.

4. The priests of the Sagrario must provide spiritual help for those on the slave ships, asking His Most Illustrious Lordship for the necessary help.

Gentleness of the Spiritual Father

5. The priests, examiners, and catechists or whatever other ministers are involved must try to work as much as possible with divine grace, charity, patience, and gentleness, mixed with fatherly authority, in order to gain the goodwill of both the slaves and their masters, because it is easier to help these souls when their masters do not resist.

Examination

6. Four essential questions must be asked in the examination. First, in the slaves' land or upon leaving the port, did someone pour water on them while saying the words of baptism? Second, did someone, by means of an interpreter who knew their language and ours, tell them the purpose, usefulness, or meaning of baptism? Third, did they understand anything that was said to them, even roughly or crudely, conforming to their capacity? Fourth, did they give their free consent and willingly receive what their masters and the priest tried to give them with that corporeal washing, or did they only endure it as an order from their masters, not showing any exterior sign of contradiction? Did they pretend that they willingly received baptism while rejecting in their hearts? Or did they say to themselves that they did not consent to receiving it?

7. As a general rule, if the slaves do not agree to one of these essential points, whichever it is, even if they agree to the rest, they must be rebaptized. If they do not agree to more than one of the points, they should be baptized unconditionally.

8. If it is certain that they agree to all of these points, they should not be baptized but only given the additional Church ceremonies, if they have not already received them. Write down their names and their masters' names in separate lists, and note down that they only need additional baptism ceremonies.

9. During the examination, make a note of those who come from the nations of Guinea, Wolof, and Mandingo, as well as others who embark from the port of Cacheu. Almost all of these people come here without valid baptisms. They are told nothing of baptism or the Christian faith or religion. They understand nothing, and therefore they must be baptized unconditionally. Sometimes slaves come from Cacheu with valid baptisms, including the necessary instruction and consent. People must be examined individually to determine who are exceptions, and who received valid baptisms.

10. Slaves from Congo and Angola usually receive some form of instruction and have been asked their consent for baptism. This means they need more questioning in order to determine if their baptism is valid. Some come late and miss part of the ceremony; others are too far away to hear the instruction or are distracted. All of these individuals must be baptized unconditionally. Others arrive on time and hear and understand what is taught, so they must be asked the questions noted in number 6, making sure they do not disagree with any of these points. These rules also apply to the small number of black slaves who come from other ports.

11. The examiner asks first from which land or nation the black slave comes, in what port of Africa did the merchants that brought him to Spain buy him, and if he was present when the other blacks were baptized in his slave ship. Also ask if someone told him in his own language why they washed his head with water, and if he understood what they said to him, and if he willingly accepted the law of the whites who baptized him and agreed to worship their God.

12. Depending on the responses to these questions, the slave will require more or different questions. This cannot be explained in a general rule and is left to the examiner's judgment and the inner advice he receives from the Holy Spirit.

13. After sufficient questioning, if the individual agrees to all four essential points from number 6, note down this person's name, whether they are free or enslaved, the name of their parish, and the date of the exam that determined that the baptism was valid and that there is no sufficient reason to doubt it.

14. If the questions and answers show some disagreement in the four essential points, note down the slave's name, his master and his parish, and that after questioning, his baptism was found to be invalid and that he must be baptized unconditionally.

15. If the examiner could not tell if the individual received a valid baptism or not, even if it seems more probable that he was baptized, note down that the examination indicated that this individual should be baptized conditionally, because there is some doubt if his baptism was valid.

16. The examiner is warned that neglecting to baptize is more dangerous than baptizing conditionally when a person is already baptized. The opinion of one examiner is sometimes not enough to determine if someone has not been baptized. Another person should be consulted. If both agree that an individual is already validly baptized, do not baptize him. If they disagree, baptize the person conditionally.

17. If there are further doubts, the examiners can and should ask advice of wise theologians, especially the fathers of the Company of Jesus of the College of San Hermenegildo. The illustrious archbishop has given them the job of providing information on the nation or language of any black slave, because sometimes it is very difficult to find this out.

18. This examination must be done secretly, particularly when examining *ladinos,* because they often need baptism even though they have lived so long with Christians.

19. Due to the above point, the examiner must reassure the individual examined that he must tell the truth and that answers will be kept secret, and that baptism can take place secretly, without anyone else knowing other than the examiner or another priest who will faithfully guard that secret. If the examination shows that the individual must be baptized, but the individual refuses public baptism, the examiner must go to one of the fathers of the Company of Jesus from the College of San Hermenegildo, who are in charge of this matter, so that they will order that the baptism be done secretly.

20. If the master causes problems by publicizing the baptism or complaining of the cost, the person baptized can be reassured that the baptism will cost nothing, as stated in number 33.

21. In the examination, one must proceed slowly and patiently, giving the examinees time to think about their answers, because they usually feel agitated and confused and rush to respond yes or no without knowing what they are saying. They must be advised that their salvation depends on their speaking the truth and to disregard their petty vain honor that makes them tell lies. Do not rush them or distress them, but do not be content if they say once or twice that they are already baptized and that they understood it and wanted it. After moderate and gentle questioning, if you are still not sure, put them among those that must be baptized conditionally.

22. Sometimes, when questioned about their baptism, the slaves give answers based on what they have learned or their desires coming from time spent here, not from what they knew before they were baptized or at the time they were baptized. Make clear that they must explain what they understood about baptism before coming here. If they do not respond correctly or cannot understand the difference, baptize them conditionally.

23. In order to examine or catechize the black *bozales* who do not understand our language, priests must find interpreters. It is very important that the interpreter be very *ladino* and behave honestly and correctly. The interpreters should be rewarded and well treated, because otherwise they will translate any way they want to or shorten their translations according to their whim.

24. The above instructions are for those slaves who left their lands when they were older than seven years. Those who say they were baptized in their lands before they were seven years old do not have to be examined any further but should be listed among the baptized ones. If you doubt whether they left their lands at age seven or not, or if they had the use of reason or not when they were baptized in their land, baptize them conditionally.

Catechism

25. Those that have to be baptized conditionally or unconditionally must first be catechized and prepared to express regret for their sins and a desire to amend them.

26. The fundamental mysteries that they must learn and understand according to their individual potential are the following: that there is only one God, creator of all things; the mystery of the Holy Trinity, Father, Son, and Holy Spirit, three persons and one God; that the Son of God was made man to save us; that he died, was resurrected, and is in glory in heaven; that there is another life, and it is eternal joy or eternal torture; that they cannot be saved without baptism and without the law of Our Lord Jesus Christ; that all Christians believe this, because God Our Lord taught it; that it is not possible to deceive us, and for this reason all the saints and wise men that have ever existed believe it and protect it. Tell them they must believe these things.

27. Usually only priests are involved in the catechism, but many others can help them. It is appropriate for masters to teach their slaves prayers, although they do not need to memorize them. This will help them a great deal.

28. On the day of their baptism, just before their baptism, urge them to feel regret for their sins. Tell them that without this they will lose out on glory and deserve eternal torment and that it is evil to offend those that care for us, sustain us, and do us so much good. It is appropriate to make them say some words to show that they regret their sins, feel a strong desire to protect the law of Our Lord, and never want to sin again. At this time, tell the most *bozal* individuals that the water that they want poured on their heads is the water of God, so that they will be children of God and go to heaven with Our Lord Jesus Christ. In this way, you ensure that they freely and knowingly receive what the other Christians receive.

29. Do not say too much about these things, but instead explain them briefly and simply and repeat them many times, giving them time and space to understand.

The Sick

All of the above must be done more quickly for the sick, especially when they are dangerously ill.

30. Some of the sick will undoubtedly be very weak and in need of bodily help. In such cases, there is a strong obligation to give them some kind of gift so that both their bodies and their souls will be cured. Priests can use donations from their parish, the archbishop, or a pious person to fund this charitable act, which will help gain the consent of the sick and encourage them to seek salvation.

31. Make a note of those who had to be baptized in their houses due to their sickness so that if Our Lord heals them later on they will go to the church and have the complete ceremony.

32. The holy sacrament of the viaticum [communion] must be given to the sick when they are baptized, if they are able to receive it without irreverence. Give the sacrament of penance to those who were baptized conditionally beforehand.

Manner of Baptism

33. Healthy people should always be baptized in their parish church, with all the solemnity and ceremonies that that Holy Mother Church commands. Priests must always do these baptisms.

34. Neither a priest nor anyone else who does the baptism should take payment or offerings for baptizing the poor.

35. Take care that the baptism water does not remain only in their hair, but that it at least bathes the skin of the head and face. If they want it to bathe more of the body, do this with all possible decency and decorum.

36. Say these words in a conditional baptism: *Si es baptizatus, non te baptizo; si autem non es baptizatus, ego te baptizo in nominee Patris, et Filii, et Spiritus Sancti. Amen* [If you are baptized, I do not baptize you; If you are not baptized, I baptize you in the name of the Father, Son, and Holy Ghost. Amen]. Pour the water during the final words.

37. Carefully and completely note down the adult baptisms in the book of baptisms, especially recording if they were done conditionally or unconditionally, because this will affect how other sacraments are done.

Black Women Who Serve Nuns

38. Black women who serve in convents of nuns are subject to whatever priest oversees the convent. If the convents are overseen by a religious order, the order must also obediently assure the salvation and baptism of the black women who serve in the convents.

Sacrament of Penance

39. When those who are baptized unconditionally confess after baptism, they only have to confess the sins that they committed after baptism.

40. Those baptized conditionally will not receive penance until the confessor examines them on the sins they have committed since their previous baptism. Then the confessor must examine the sins that were committed since their last confession until the most recent baptism and absolve them in the customary manner, unconditionally, with the intention that the absolution applies to all the sins committed since the last baptism.[57]

---

57. See Chapter 19.

41. For those who are dangerously ill and baptized conditionally, question them about the sins committed since their last confession. Absolve them by saying: *Si es capax absolutionis, ego te absolve* [If you are capable of absolution, I absolve you].

Confirmation

42. If they have been confirmed and need conditional baptism, the confirmation is invalid. If they were baptized unconditionally, they can be confirmed.[58]

Matrimony

43. When two individuals are married, and one is newly baptized unconditionally and the other does not need to be baptized, even conditionally, they should restate their consent to the matrimony and understand that they can freely reject the marriage but that it is best to agree to it again. The execution of the marriage is entrusted to the priest, if he does not find any just cause for divorce. This should be done as quickly as possible, because the matrimony is legal. When one or both of the spouses are baptized conditionally, explain that it is better for them to restate their consent to the marriage. However, they are not free of the bonds of matrimony, even if they do not want to consent to it. When both individuals are baptized unconditionally, it is not necessary to revalidate the matrimony.

44. In the other towns of the archdiocese, the vicar of each district will give the order so that all of the above, other than the examinations, are carried out by priests, because there are fewer well-educated priests outside Seville.

45. Outside Seville, choose well-educated, discreet, wise, pious men, priests, friars, or seculars to help in the examinations and catechisms described above, and ask their advice on appropriate topics.

46. Do this for the principal towns in the jurisdiction, and go personally to the other towns in the jurisdiction and do the same. If this is impossible for a legitimate reason, send a religious professional or a very trustworthy secular priest to carry out this important matter.

47. Upon carrying out this plan, the vicars should tell His Most Illustrious Lordship the individuals they have chosen to help in the examinations and catechisms. If anyone impedes this work, let the bishop know, and also tell him anything good that happens in connection to this matter.

The above is the instruction.

---

58. A sacrament given to young adults to confirm their commitment to the Catholic Church. The point here is that if a person received an invalid baptism, his or her confirmation ceremony is also invalid.

In order to show the holiness of His Most Illustrious Lordship the Archbishop, I quote a few lines from a letter that describes the results of these efforts. Each day those who work in the archbishop's holy ministry experience great rewards. This success is inspirational because of the many apparently insurmountable difficulties that have been overcome. The letter comes from Father Mateo Rodríguez, a well-known scholar in sacred theology in Seville. He writes from Seville on October 14, 1615:

> I wrote a letter to Your Reverence congratulating you for the charity you did in sending me the letter about confirming the black slaves' baptisms. I sent the letter with the last fleet, but as sending letters to the Indies is so uncertain, I want to again congratulate Your Reverence because the simple information that you sent led to great glory for Our Lord and did much good to a great number of souls. Before we did not know how the slaves were risking eternal condemnation. Other dioceses should make the same efforts. I have already tried to encourage this by sending some information to various places. All of this will greatly benefit these unfortunate people. Your Reverence should be very grateful to Our Lord for making you the instrument of such work. Continue it and you will continue these good results, even if some oppose it. In the end, truth will conquer. The methods that Your Reverence relates seem very suited to their urgent needs and the lack of time. Trust in Our Lord to continue this mission with great results.

This ends the letter. This letter and other statements show that great results came from the edict issued by the archbishop of Seville. He was not satisfied that this work should only be done in his archdiocese; he also wanted the pope to send the same commands to other places that have slaves with similar needs. The pope commands that all receive the water of the holy sacrament, and thus he wrote the letter that we have mentioned in the second book.

Above is the edict of Seville, carried out in this entire archdiocese. This edict confirms, with great authority, almost all contained in this third book. It should be the rule applied to all the churches in Spain and the Indies, because it is so effective and fruitful.

END OF THE THIRD BOOK.

BOOK 4

THE GREAT ESTEEM THAT THE COMPANY OF JESUS HAS ALWAYS HAD FOR THE BLACKS, AS CAN BE SEEN IN THE SPIRITUAL GOOD DEEDS IT HAS DONE AND ITS GLORIOUS WORK IN THE CONVERSION OF THESE SOULS.

As he states in the argument below, in Book 4 Sandoval targets readers within the Company of Jesus. Aimed at this very specific audience, this book is the most philosophical and theological part of the work, so this translation only includes a small selection. Many of the chapters are briefly summarized here. However, these summaries are important for guiding readers through the complete development of De instauranda's *argument, especially in terms of interpreting Sandoval's thinking on race and justifying European imperialism through Jesuit-led worldwide missions. The chapters that are presented in a more complete form focus on Sandoval's reports of his personal experiences.*

In Book 4 Sandoval broadens the label "Ethiopian" to encompass nearly the entire world's non-Christian population—at least those peoples whom Sandoval could loosely categorize as darker skinned than Europeans. This theme carries through all of De instauranda: *a careful reading of the book reveals how Sandoval began discussing Africans and Christianity in Book 1, with a concentration on African history itself, and then changed the focus to the African diaspora in both the Americas and Spain in Books 2 and 3. If readers trace the specifics of this development throughout* De instauranda, *they can further explore the overwhelming evidence of how Sandoval engages a sense of Christian and European superiority with paternalistic racism. In Book 4 the concept of "Ethiopian" becomes as broad as possible, moving beyond the reach of the African slave trade and its slave ships to absorb a potentially global Catholic empire. Why does Sandoval have to make potential converts "Ethiopian" in order to make them possible colonial subjects?*

In Sandoval's vision, the entire world becomes a colonial subject, he hopes under the moral and spiritual guidance of the Jesuits, as he connects his mission in Cartagena to Jesuit missions around the world—in India, Ethiopia and other parts of Africa, the Philippines, and the New World. By doing this he also gives his own efforts legitimacy within the Company of Jesus. He emphasizes this legitimacy by including numerous positive letters from Jesuit leaders who praise his work. He also seeks to motivate Jesuits to move into this global realm, to accept what might be in his mind the most important role on earth: soldiers spreading the Christian mission to all corners of the earth, in a sense taking advantage of the great opportunities presented by the unconquered, un-Christian peoples of the world. Sandoval even pushes the Jesuits into a metaphysical domain that surpasses the confines of the earth itself, by exploring a detailed metaphor of Ignatius Loyola and Francis Xavier as the sun and the moon.

Argument of the Fourth Book

My primary intent in this discussion is nothing else than to motivate the fathers of the Company and point out how much the blacks need our spiritual guidance. I hope I might inspire the fathers to take time from their other good, praiseworthy, and holy occupations and employ themselves in this endeavor, since it is so appropriate for priests and so connected to the goals of the Company of Jesus. In the first three books I felt obligated to show how beneficial this ministry is for anyone who takes part in it. However, I do not want to neglect my central goal, so this book targets my fellow brothers and fathers in the Company. Here I emphasize how much value our sacred Company has always given to working with these nations [Ethiopians in the broadest sense]. I also discuss the glorious work it has done traveling to the nations themselves. Many Jesuit fathers have dedicated themselves to this work and have earned great rewards, although personal gain was not their most important motivation. However, these rewards motivate and inspire us to strive to glorify God and help these poor, abandoned people. I offer this book to His Divine Majesty in the hopes that I will succeed in achieving my goals.

Chapter 1. How the ministry to the blacks is proper work for the Company of Jesus.

In this chapter Sandoval links Portuguese seafaring voyages in the late 1400s to the birth of men who would later create the Company of Jesus. Even if his dates are a few years off, how does he intertwine the spread of Christianity and European imperialism?

Some scholars read De instauranda *as a response to the accusation that Jesuits concentrated too much on educating European elites; perhaps this chapter most reveals Sandoval's defensiveness in response to this kind of accusation.[1] What are the general contours and specific details of Sandoval's argument against this accusation? In order to defend the Jesuits from accusations that they catered to the elite, Sandoval must share his accusers' conception of a dichotomy between those at the pinnacle of society (the Spanish) and the absolute bottom (African slaves), so his defense must be paternalistic and engage with the racial, national, and social hierarchies of his time. In this chapter*

---

1. Note how Sandoval returns to this discussion in Chapter 15 and how he shifts the focus to other religious orders and more deeply explores racial and social hierarchies in the colonial world.

he also tries to encourage other Jesuits to take on the task of missionizing Africans. As always, he looks to examples from the past to inspire contemporary Jesuits to fulfill the goals and examples of their predecessors. How does he tie this mission to the early leaders of the Jesuit order? How do the details of their behavior and opinions presented here provide models for Jesuits who might read this book? How does Sandoval use Loyola's vision and Xavier's dream to further defend the Company and inspire his colleagues? How does the vision of Christ not carrying weapons or symbols of power contradict the parallel destinies shared by European expanding monarchies and the Jesuits, as described in the first paragraph of this chapter?

Wherever I observe the history and achievements of our sacred Company, I see that we were founded to help these poor blacks. No one else helps them, so they desperately need us, and we are obligated to attempt to aid them. God elected to found this Company at the same time that the most serene kings of Portugal received concessions and licenses to take slave ships to western Ethiopia. At this time many obscure black Guinean nations began to communicate with us, and now they nearly number more here [in Latin America] than we Spaniards. This is no surprise, because a great number of black slaves came here from the beginning [of the Spanish presence in the Americas]. I have it on good authority that in 1554 there were so many blacks in Peru that they took part in the early uprisings and formed a force of more than three hundred harquebusiers. In early July 1497 the Portuguese discovered India, leading to the discovery of many Ethiopian kingdoms and provinces, including Mozambique, Melinde [Malindi, coastal Kenya], Socotora [the island of Socotra, off the coast of Somalia, in the Indian Ocean], the Paravas [coastal India], the Cape of Comorin [on the southern tip of India], Malucos [the islands of Maluku in Indonesia], and Malabar [coastal India]. In precisely the same year, the holy father Francis Xavier was born in Navarre.[2] It is understood that God gave Xavier the destiny of bringing the Gospel and the faith to these extensive regions, especially those black nations that I have just named. But first, Portuguese arms and commerce opened the way and leveled the field. The king of Portugal undertook an enterprise that foreigners and even many of his own people did not believe to be correct and that they called unwise. It seems that God himself said: "These men that are being born right now are destined to help these people, and these people will be helped by the glorious labor of these men." The founding of the Company of Jesus and the opening of communication with the Ethiopians are like twins born in the same womb: the Company was born as an instrument of

---

2. This date is confusing. Ignatius Loyola was born in 1491 and Francis Xavier in 1506. Vasco de Gama arrived on the southwest coast of India in 1498. See Book 1 for more references to the places Sandoval mentions here. This list of places corresponds to the journeys of Francis Xavier.

their salvation. God gave the Company the goal of bringing them salvation as well as helping others in Rome, Italy, Spain, or Europe, and in all the rest of the world. God calls us to be soldiers in the Company of Jesus to wander through these barbarous and remote black nations, to save the people, and to bring them into his service. Our destiny is to teach the doctrine to humble, low, crude people and care for them as if they were children.

The first Jesuit fathers provide us with inspiring examples. Our holy father Ignatius often took on the sacred task of preaching to the poor. Father Diego Laynez, while attending the holy Council of Trent along with many great Church leaders and scholars, stated that he believed that the vilest and lowest people must be taught the doctrine in the public city plazas.[3] The brother and father Francisco de Borja, duke of Gandia and third general of our religion, taught us to walk the streets of cities, towns, and villages ringing a little bell.[4] The holy father Francis Xavier embraced this task and shouldered this burden as if God Our Lord had given it to him alone. He taught the doctrine to children, slaves, and crude people on the land and sea, in churches, plazas, streets, fields, and beaches, on ships and boats, night and day. His letters show us that he was incredibly enthusiastic and determined. In 1544 he wrote to our holy father Ignatius from the Cape of Comorin. In the letter he described the way in which he taught the doctrine to the black Paravas. He said he taught them for four hours a day, two in the morning and two in the afternoon, often until he lost his voice.

Xavier considered this holy labor part of his position of authority. He composed a book to instruct other brothers of the Company in teaching the doctrine to the poor. He once wrote the father rector of the college in Goa,[5] saying: "Your Reverence must teach the doctrine to the Portuguese boys in Goa as well as the slaves and other ignorant and crude people. You must do this task yourself and

---

3. Diego Laynez or Lainez was a Jesuit theologian born around 1512. He attended the Council of Trent and became the second general of the order after Loyola died. The Council of Trent met from 1545 to 1563, as a response to the Protestant Reformation. It standardized Catholic doctrine and practice. Some view the Jesuits as "soldiers of the Counter-Reformation" (note Sandoval uses the term "soldier" in this chapter) because much of their work supported the goals of the Council of Trent in strengthening Catholicism against Protestantism.

4. Francisco de Borja lived from 1510 to 1572. He was a very powerful Spanish nobleman connected to the court of Emperor Charles V, and he became a Jesuit after his wife died in 1546. A handful of popes in the late 1400s and 1500s were part of the Borja family.

5. A Jesuit college was established in Goa in southern India in the 1540s. Xavier had some conflicts with the Jesuit leaders in Goa. The purposes of the college in Goa was not only to convert the indigenous people but also to work with the Portuguese who had settled there.

not trust it to others." Later on he continued: "Every Sunday and holiday, ring the bell after noon. Teach the doctrine in the church, Your Reverence, to the slaves, servants, and Portuguese children." He also says that the rector must not neglect instructing children and other ignorant people in the catechism in order to do other works of piety. He strongly states, "Do not waste time instructing the old Christians, because there are plenty of new ones who need more help." Our sacred Company was founded to do this holy ministry and has always valued it. We have always showed fervent, apostolic enthusiasm for helping miserable people. All we need is a simple ministry instructing people in the Christian doctrine. We do not need chairs, pulpits, or complicated resolutions of cases of conscience.

Among all characteristics of the Company of Jesus, its name best indicates its central goal of aiding the poor. Father Ignatius was inspired by heaven to give us this name, and the Council of Trent confirmed it. Father Ignatius said that we are called the Company of Jesus to show that we are nothing more than that and that we can do nothing more than serve in his Company. This name gives us a burden and obligation that we must honor carefully. We carry out three tasks similar to the burdens given to people in the Old Testament who had the name "Jesus":[6] we fight battles in the New World, destroy idolatry, and encourage religion through teaching the doctrine. Because our name is "the Jesuits" or "the Company of Jesus," and Jesus means "savior," our name means "companions" or "those who help save." This name shows our obligations, especially to the poor blacks, who die in great numbers without anyone to help them with their pain or to pity their certain and eternal condemnation. You are to be savior, Lord and Jesus, not only for reasonable, civilized men but also for bestial, *bozal*, fierce, and barbaric men. You do not die just to save noble and free white men but also black slaves. Your Jesuit companions and fellow soldiers also have this obligation, that is, to save whites and blacks; they help everyone, from the highest to the lowest, the brightest and the darkest, because all are children of God and souls redeemed with his precious blood. Thus we do not seek the stars, the Spanish Christians that already have the light of faith. Instead we look for the black slaves, trampled grains of sand. After we teach them about Christ our Redeemer and his faith, they are no longer grains of sand on earth but stars in the heavens. God made us his companions and called on us to help him save them, and he wanted us to help this nation and others like it that are poor and abandoned, who have no one else to help them. He did not ask us to help white

---

6. The name "Jesus" or "Joshua" is used a handful of times in the Old Testament, referring to ancestors of the Jesus of the New Testament. However, Sandoval cites the apocryphal writer Abdias for his information. The Hebrew word *Jehoshua*, one version of the name "Jesus," literally means "Jehovah is salvation."

nations that already have many who help them. I can best prove my point by
telling the story of how God Our Lord gave the Company the name of "Jesuits," indicating that our job is to save souls.

Christ Our Lord gave our saintly father Ignatius this name when he
appeared to Ignatius on the road to Rome [in 1537], appointing him to found
this Company.[7] Christ our Savior chose him as the captain of this group of sav-
iors. Christ did not appear like a glorious king carrying his crown and scepter,
because he did not want us to work with kings. He did not carry a general's
baton, because he did not want us to fight battles and wars. He did not hold an
orb symbolizing the globe, because he did not want us to be concerned with
earthly matters. He did not appear as we see him in paintings, with his hand
raised to give blessings, because he did not want us to hold church offices.
Finally, he did not come with his hands crossed, because he did not want us to
be idle. He came with the cross on his shoulders, because this is how he wanted
us to be: not carrying harquebuses or lances, engaged in territorial conquests,
but only holding a cross, the weapon he used to save us by sacrificing himself.
The cross heals humankind. He calls us to save people: not those that praise us
and give us material rewards but instead people who make us suffer with their
cruelty, barbarity, and crudeness. Xavier, that great apostle to the blacks,
dreamed that he carried a black man on his shoulders. This burden was so heavy
that he could not breathe or sleep. Xavier was called to be a Jesuit to save these
people. Jesus called Xavier to follow him by carrying a cross on his shoulders.
Xavier worked hard, traveled, and suffered persecution and hardship to save the
souls of rude, barbaric, and slow black people. They gave him no earthly reward
other than hope and more work. He received no praise, only humiliation. This
is our cross; this is our vocation; this is one of our principal ministries. And for-
tunately, this is the main reason that Christ Our Lord gave our sacred Company
the name "Jesus," in honor of his own coat of arms: the cross. The name of Jesus
and the burden of the cross are always joined, and for this reason our father
Ignatius gave us this cross and this name.

Chapter 2. In which the authority or prophesy of the prophet Isaiah proves the argument of the preceding chapter.

*In this chapter Sandoval discusses Isaiah 18:1, "Vae terrae cymbalo alarum, quae est
transflumina Aethiopiae" [Woe to the land of whirring wings beyond the rivers of Ethi-
opia]. He refers to these lines from the Bible to show that there is a divine plan for Africa*

---

7. Loyola chose the name for his new religious order at this time: the Company of Jesus,
implying a group of soldiers led by Jesus. The official papal foundation documents called
it a society.

and to indicate how the Jesuits play a role in carrying out divine will. Using Isaiah's words, Sandoval seeks to inspire his colleagues by describing how earlier Jesuits fulfilled Isaiah's words when they ventured to African nations, after the Portuguese began exploration there, armed with only a few clothes and their prayer books. Sandoval argues that the Jesuit's freedom from material concerns and prestigious positions in the church hierarchy makes them seem like angels, although he does claim that the Jesuits are welcomed by African leaders, such as in Congo, and joyfully received by the regular populace. Sandoval also encourages his fellow missionaries to read more about the lives of earlier heroic Jesuits who risked their lives preaching around the world from Africa to the Philippines.

Chapter 3. The great appreciation and esteem that the Company of Jesus has had for the Ethiopians' salvation.

This chapter discusses the challenges faced by Jesuits in their missions to the various groups of people Sandoval labels as "blacks," including people from islands in the Indian Ocean and from Japan. Most important of all is the work of Xavier in India in the earliest days of the Company. Contrary to statements in the last chapter and Jesuit regulations, Sandoval reveals here that the Jesuits did accept ecclesiastical offices connected to their worldwide missions under papal or royal compulsion and in hopes of advancing their goals, although he says that these positions led to hardships and labor, not wealth and acclaim. Sandoval also tells the story of several Jesuit martyrs, including some killed in Ethiopia and India, to prove his point that the Jesuits will sacrifice their lives for their missionary work. He points out that Jesuits in Cartagena can do the same but with less risk of death.

Chapter 4. That our father Saint Ignatius was the sun, most especially in this ministry to the blacks.

This chapter, perhaps the theoretical core of the book, explores a very complex metaphor. In it Sandoval presents his vision of a symbolic Jesuit cosmology with Ignatius in the position of the sun. Sandoval outlines all the properties of the sun and shows how Ignatius represents these elements. For example, Ignatius shines in the darkness of Lutheran heresy; like the sun, he is in constant, perfect motion, traveling everywhere and illuminating everything without diminishing his own light; nothing can affect or corrupt the essence of his nature, as the sun's rays do not lose their purity by shining in dark places. The persecution he faced was like the clouds and rain that temporarily darken the sun, but from which the sun creates bountiful harvests. Like the sun is perfectly round, Ignatius was perfect, and the Company of Jesus is more perfect than all other religious orders because of their vow to be missionaries to all the world's infidels. Sandoval compares Ignatius's early Jesuit followers Francis Xavier and Francis Borja to the sun's rays, because they extend the essence of the founder over the entire world.

*Nothing can block the rays of the sun; it will shine through a tiny crack. Similarly, like
the sun, Ignatius could shine through tiny cracks to bring his message even to those who
completely shut him out. Ignatius gave off spiritual illumination and clarity in darkness, as the sun gives off life-sustaining light and heat. According to the last words in
the chapter, translated below, what characteristics, according to Sandoval, does Ignatius
share with the sun, and how does this symbolism argue for Sandoval's vision for the
Jesuits?*

. . . These are the properties and effects of the sun. Because we found all of them
most perfectly in Ignatius, we say that Ignatius is our sun. Our glorious and
holy father, you are a bright and resplendent sun from birth: in your name,
shape, movement, rays, communication, illumination, radiation; in creating
day and night; in unmaking clouds. You are a happy sun that enlightens the
wise and strengthens the martyrs. You give confessors patience, make virgins
pure, and make the Church triumphant. You illuminate and destroy the darkness of ignorance, the errors of idolatry, and the fallacies of heresy. Your courageous Company, your sons and rays, have conquered and surrender their
conquests at the feet of the vicar of Jesus Christ, by consoling the sad, administering sacraments, confuting heresies, and facing hard labor, difficulties, pilgrimages by sea and land, persecutions, martyrdom, and atrocious deaths to
spread the Holy Gospel and hoist the divine standard of Jesus, in the most isolated and hidden kingdoms in the East and West Indies and in all of unseen and
remote Africa. We are happy to do this, because we are your rays, and we work
to join in spreading your light and heat.

Chapter 5. How this most excellent sun improved this ministry to the blacks through the moon, our holy father Francisco Xavier, who spread the ministry through most of Africa and all of Guinea.

*In Chapters 5, 6, 7, and 8 Sandoval continues his extended metaphor of Loyola rep-
resenting the sun by comparing Francis Xavier to the moon, because he illuminated
what Sandoval sees as the darkness of infidelity in Africa, India, Japan, and China,
while Ignatius, "the greater luminary," spent his life in Europe. Sandoval cites the sta-
tistic of Francis Xavier's performing six hundred thousand baptisms in his travels and
points out that, like the moon, all Xavier's light came from the brighter light of the sun,
Ignatius. Sandoval briefly mentions some of Francis Xavier's experiences, after leaving
Europe in 1541 to undertake missions to Mozambique, Malindi, Kenya, the island of
Socotra, and finally Goa in 1542. Sandoval tries to further connect the work of his
potential readers to Xavier's efforts by asserting that the natives of eastern India and the
islands where Xavier preached must be viewed as "blacks" or "Ethiopians." Sandoval
argues that he has seen people from these lands in Peru and Cartagena, and they do*

*indeed have very dark skin, "as black as Guineans, although their hair is straighter."
The fact that Xavier also traveled within Africa itself provides more proof, in Sandoval's
opinion, that the Jesuits must focus their efforts on Africans and all people worldwide
who fit under the broad umbrella of "black," as Sandoval defines it.*

Chapter 9. How this most excellent sun also improved this ministry to the blacks through the brilliant stars that are the innumerable apostolic men of our sacred religion, especially in Asia.

*In this chapter Sandoval argues that if Ignatius is the sun and Xavier is the moon, then
all of the Jesuits are the stars, because they are like "angels on earth, celestial men"
looking always toward heaven and spiritual goals. As stars, they illuminate the darkness
of the lives of non-Christians. Sandoval continues the metaphor by describing the
achievements of some heroic Jesuits who worked as missionaries in India and the Philippines so that they "can provide a shining example to motivate their fellow Jesuits
reading this book." The Jesuits began to work in the Philippines in 1580, and Sandoval includes this project under the umbrella of converting the black races of the world and
ranking the different peoples of the Philippines according to the color of their skin and
his perception of their level of civilization.*

Chapter 10. Continuing with the same material, giving illustrious examples of how many other apostolic men of our sacred religion have dedicated themselves to the conversion of the Ethiopians in the kingdoms and provinces of all Africa.

*Sandoval begins by mentioning that five Jesuits died on the Cape Verde Islands, before
they even reached the mainland. The surviving priest from this company of missionaries
traveled along the coast to Sierra Leone and also preached inland. Twelve more Jesuits
were sent from Portugal to Sierra Leone in 1600 to establish churches and schools
there, while the Portuguese gained material wealth from trade in this region. Sandoval
emphasizes that the Portuguese must not neglect the spiritual needs of those they
enslave in Africa, and if they do, only the Jesuits can help. He also points out that the
Moors have taken advantage of the weakness of Christianity in West Africa and have
enthusiastically spread Islam there, a point he returns to in Chapter 15. Sandoval also
mentions how five Jesuits, sent by the king of Portugal, were initially well received by
the king of Congo, and they founded a school there with six hundred students who
learned reading, writing, and Christianity. However, Sandoval admits that the king
soon "went bad and lived in a manner unsuitable for a Christian, as did the rest of the
kingdom, twisting the Gospel to their appetites and whims." On the other hand, Sandoval professes Congo to be a Christian nation to the present day due to the efforts of*

the clergy. Efforts to convert the king of Angola did not go as well. The king asked the Jesuits to come there, but then he imprisoned them. However, Sandoval has hopes for this kingdom because the Jesuits established a college in the Angolan port of Luanda. Sandoval also relates the experiences of a martyred Jesuit working in Mozambique in the 1560s. He concludes the chapter with a repetition of all the challenges and hardships these heroes of the Company faced in converting Africans. Sandoval suggests that Jesuits in the Americas have just the same opportunities for self-sacrifice and labor when they commit to working with the large number of Africans in the New World, some of whom might be easy to convert, others more challenging.

Chapter 11. The esteem that the superiors of the Company beyond this province have shown to have for this ministry in their letters.

In this chapter and in Chapter 12, Sandoval includes quotations from letters sent to him by his superiors in the Company of Jesus as another way to motivate his colleagues and give the stamp of approval to his efforts. Sandoval received many letters praising his "efforts with such abandoned souls . . . spending so much time working with the blacks and having so much patience with the bozales, *suffering their odor and their poverty and nudity," words taken from a letter from Juan Sebastián, the Jesuit provincial in Peru, who had known Sandoval since his days as a student in the Lima Jesuit college. Sebastián writes that Sandoval's successes show that he is especially favored by God, fulfilling the hopes and prayers of the writer, who was his mentor at the college, and Sebastián encourages him to continue. Several other Jesuit leaders in the Americas also praise Sandoval's efforts, some mentioning that they will pass on what he has written them to other American church leaders. Sandoval also cites several other letters that encourage him and praise his work, saying that he is "earning his crown in heaven." Sandoval concludes this section of quotations from letters by saying that these words alleviate the discouragement he feels from trying to overcome so many problems and working constantly, and he hopes that they will do the same for others who read them.*

Chapter 13. Some particular incidents that have happened in this ministry in connection with the sacrament of baptism.

Sandoval begins this chapter by citing sacred texts that encourage preachers to publish accounts of "the work done to preach the Gospel, so that others can be inspired by its example and bring greater glory to the celestial Father." He takes his own advice: Chapters 13 and 14 focus on his personal experiences. Sandoval's anecdotes provide further evidence for his attitude of pious paternalism and his belief that Christianity and baptism are the most positive things to happen to slaves. His proof comes from the signs he witnesses indicating that he has divine favor and that the slaves themselves desire baptism. From his perspective, he is a witness to not only great suffering but also redemption, which justifies the suffering. It is useful to keep in mind that many of Sandoval's experiences have been filtered through his interpreters' words. In the first story about the moleque, why does the boy want baptism, and what do his fellow slaves do about it? Who would have told Sandoval this story and given it this particular angle? How might the slaves included in these anecdotes be behaving according to what they believe Sandoval expects? Why? What motivates the master in the third story to baptize his slave? How is the connection between slavery, disease, and death presented here? How does divine intervention help Sandoval negotiate language difficulties, according to the anecdotes in this chapter? How does the penultimate example show how the slaves' African origins continue to play a role in their lives in America? In the last anecdote, how does Sandoval's outburst relate to the criticisms he directs toward slave owners throughout De instauranda? *In this case, it turns out that his criticism was unjustified—but only through the intervention of what two forces?*

One day while I was working on the slave ships, I met a twelve-year-old boy. His ship arrived when the sun had already set, and he was very sick, so I decided to postpone questioning him about his baptism for another day. When I went back, I passed most of the day confessing, examining, and baptizing others who I felt were the neediest. When I returned to the boy's ship, I was very saddened to hear that the *moleque* (what boys are called) was already dead. I wanted to see him, and when I found him I saw that he had not yet passed away, although he was on the brink of entering the next world. He was swollen like a wineskin because he had eaten a poisonous forest fruit that is similar to a cherry. They told me that he had been shouting all night long in his own language, demanding baptism and that water be poured on his head so that he could be like the whites and all the rest of his companions. Because he was so persistent, the other slaves baptized him. Soon I had to return to the college because it was late in the day. But I began to worry, thinking that perhaps they had made important errors in this baptism. I returned to the port feeling distressed. I found that the slaves were waiting for me to do another confession, so I began to confess them. They were the most obedient and willing listeners. This gave me relief from my fears and worries. When I looked around for the boy, the slaves told me they had not given him a complete baptism but had had a sailor do it. The sailor saw that he had committed an error and confessed it. I then baptized the boy correctly, because he was already unconscious. He soon died, but he will live forever. After this, I baptized another sick woman, and she received the gift of eternal salvation with great contrition.

A woman from the port of Cacheu gave birth after I baptized her. I did not baptize the infant, taking a risk that the baby might die without being baptized. I hoped the woman would baptize her son in the Church, because he was a Creole born here in Cartagena. But the woman got sick when she was on the road with the slavers and had to return to Cartagena. When she had to leave again, she assumed I had already baptized the child, which was why she did not ask me about it. I realized the risk she might be taking and called her back. When I baptized her son, she embraced me a thousand times, indicating how happy she was to see him Christian. She knew what being a Christian meant, since I had catechized her before I baptized her.

Once I went to attend to an important matter at the house of a prominent Cartagena man. At the door I encountered an extremely thin girl who was five or six years old. Finishing my business, I told the gentleman that there was another important issue for me to deal with at his house. I asked him if the child had been baptized. The gentleman listened to what I said, not surprised that I would bring this up. He responded that even if she was thought to be Christian, she should be examined, because she came from the rivers of Guinea [where Sandoval says few slaves receive valid baptisms]. He hoped that I would question her, believing that her reputation would suffer if she was not examined. He asked his wife and others in the house if they knew anything about her baptism, but no one did. He even questioned other people outside his house, and many of them said that she had never been baptized. He gave thanks to the Lord, praising his divine providence, that he had been diligent in saving a soul. He had the girl baptized in the church with great ceremony to make up for his oversight.

I will now discuss how important it is that we go quickly to the ships when black slaves are disembarking, in order to help them as much as possible. Many arrive here already very ill and near death, as the story I am about to tell indicates. A ship full of black slaves arrived from Cape Verde plagued with smallpox, measles, and typhoid. The authorities did not permit the slaves to enter the city, which meant more work for us when we tried to help them. Our interpreters did not want to travel out to the ship or go among people with such diseases. However, a few charitable interpreters went with me. On the ship many people were very sick. The ones that were swollen up with disease seemed the most at risk of dying, but first I catechized and baptized three individuals suffering from diarrhea. Each one was from a different nation and caste. The next morning, returning to visit the new Christians and Christianize the rest, I found out that two of those I had baptized had already died, and the third died in my presence. I could describe many other cases like this one, because slave ships arrive every day full of very sick people, but I have already discussed this in Book 3. In this case, the most important help came from my faithful interpreters. I depend on them constantly and I use them very carefully. The following cases will touch on this issue.

One day, having finished doing baptisms on some large slave ships, a difficult task, I walked home, passing by the church of Saint Augustine. I said to my companion:[8] "Brother, it is said that the holy father Luis Beltrán[9] once said to his companion, as they walked by the church of Saint Catherine Martyr,[10] 'What thirsty man will pass by a fountain and not drink?' This made them enter the church, where they prayed deeply, then proceeded along their way, exiting through another door. We should do the same." So we entered and, after commending ourselves to God, we left by another door, imitating the story I had just told about Fray Luis Beltrán. In the doorway I met a black man of the Caravali[11] caste. I had been looking for this man for two months in order to baptize him. I had already given up on him and decided to tell his master that he was not Christian and his soul was in great danger. We went together to search for an interpreter. In a little while, we entered the house of a *ladina* black woman. She came from a very different caste than he did, but he understood her speech. I catechized him and found that he was not Christian, so I planned to baptize him that afternoon. I decided that, because the *ladina* black woman came from a remote land and probably was not baptized, I should question her and find out. Heaven and the work of God made it clear to me that she was not Christian, although she had participated in the ceremony of having oil and chrism poured on her. Although she was so *ladina* and spoke well, she had rarely taken communion or made confession. I told her that her soul was in grave danger and need. She fell on her knees, and with tears in her eyes, she asked me to baptize her. She prepared for it and received it with the greatest joy that she had ever felt in her life. She also thanked the Lord for what he had done for her relative, the man I had met earlier in the church. He was also baptized that afternoon and felt very comforted.

Once we had been working to baptize more than three hundred slaves and only two were left. These final two were of the Zape caste,[12] but they spoke an obscure language. After an entire month of looking, we could not find an interpreter that understood their language. The only word we understood was *boloncho*, which they said in trying to tell us their caste among the Zapes. We could not find anyone of this caste. Their ship was about to embark for Portobello, and I was very sad that these two souls, alone among so many, were in danger. I

---

8. Possibly another reference to Pedro Claver.

9. A Dominican saint who lived from 1526 to 1581. He preached for several years in Colombia.

10. An early Christian beheaded by the Roman emperor Maximus, after she destroyed a wheel that was meant to torture her to death.

11. A person from Calabar on the West African coast.

12. Zapes came from coastal Sierra Leone. As can be seen in this paragraph, this label encompasses several more complex divisions.

was afraid that this ship also would sink, as had been the case for another ship that had sunk one day after it left Cartagena on the way to Portobello. This ship had carried 25 Spaniards and 120 black slaves. My feelings of compassion inspired me to keep working, but I was at the end of my human resources and capabilities, so I sought divine help. I said a Mass for Our Lady [the Virgin Mary] and dedicated it to finding a translator or interpreter to help those poor unfortunate slaves. After the Mass I felt very confident. In the first house I entered I found the interpreter who I had been seeking for a month. The Great Lady in heaven sent me a black Zape man. I asked him about the Bolonchos, and he said this was a type of Zape. He said the Zapes were divided into various language groups, including Cooli, Limba, Baca, Lindagozo, Zozo, Pelicoya, Baga, and Boloncho. He said he knew of a *ladina* black woman, who spoke Boloncho, living on a farm outside the city. I gave thanks to God and to the most holy Mother for the mercy I received. My two catechumens [assistants in teaching the catechism] walked outside the town, and I found her, but she was too sick to serve as a translator. However, the most holy Virgin continued to help me by making another black man appear at the woman's house. He had come to see the sick woman and was from the same nation and caste. He was a clear and speedy translator, so the Bolonchos were baptized easily. I brought them back to their master, who took them to the port, and they embarked as Christians and had a happy voyage.

The most holy Virgin not only helps the Bolonchos but also protects all the other black nations. Every day she helps them in some way similar to the example I have just given and this next one. One day I was dressed to go say Mass, and a very sad man arrived. He asked me to baptize a black *bozal* man who was about to die without being baptized. He said that the man had gone unconscious two days ago before, and now he could not eat or drink. I said to him that it seemed like the best thing to do would be to pray for God's help, so I would say a Mass for him and for the sick man. This good man asked for a Mass in praise of the most holy Virgin. I said the Mass, and when it was finished we went to the *bozal* and found him openmouthed, ejecting matter through his mouth, with the whites of his eyes showing and his hands clutching his head. When I saw him, I said to his master, "Now that he is dead, you ask to have him baptized? You might as well throw him in the sea or bury him in the dung heap." The poor man was distressed, and taking his pulse, he said: "He still lives." I then touched a relic of our father Saint Ignatius to his head, said the Gospel to him, and left the relic there. I left to baptize ten or twelve people whom I had already instructed in the catechism. When I finished this job, I returned to the sick man. On the way, I encountered his master in the road. He had come running to find me, shouting that the sick man had sat up and spoken and that he could hear and see. I returned quickly for an interpreter who spoke the Fulupe language. The Virgin found him for me. Finally, I instructed

the slave very carefully and then baptized him. He died soon after, but we faithfully believe that he achieved glory in heaven by the merits of the blood of Jesus
Christ, received through the special favor of his most holy Mother.

Chapter 14. Other cases that have occurred while administering the sacrament of baptism in this holy ministry.

*This chapter offers Sandoval his final opportunity to relate his personal experiences
working with the slaves in Cartagena; why does he choose these particular stories? He
provides a short introductory paragraph: does the chapter carry out the theme set out in
this introduction? In the first example, Sandoval sums up the last few traumatic days of
a man's life. How would the slave have described these moments? How do the first few
paragraphs of this chapter target a specifically Jesuit audience? How does Sandoval
explain the death and suffering described in this chapter?*

*Sandoval revisits the theme of discreetly baptizing those slaves who, having spent
some time in the Americas, had a general reputation of being Christian, suggesting the
double-edged sword experienced by Africans who felt pressured into baptism. This sense
of pressure from authority figures such as Sandoval conflicted with their fears that their
peers and relatives would realize they had lived among Christians so long without baptism. Sandoval considers his own role in preserving the slaves' sense of personal reputation and wants to help by baptizing them. For him, baptism is the only solution, and
he does not understand how he, as an authority figure convinced that they must be baptized, contributes to their internal conflicts. How does this chapter show the limits of
Sandoval's empathy for African slaves?*

Working for the salvation of the black slaves, we encounter many disgusting,
horrible things, but beneath the vile surface are indescribable delights and joy.
This comes from experiencing daily examples of God's immense mercy in filling
a soul with great happiness and peace. This chapter will describe this type of
occurrence.

Once a black man was given the name of Alonso at baptism, but he did not
want to be called anything but Ignatius, because Ignatius is like a light guiding
the blind. He was correct to choose this name, because those named after Ignatius are happy. In another case, I struggled many days to instruct an evil and
unreasonable person. Even if I ignored all my concerns and doubts about him, I
still did not dare baptize him. One day I passed by his house and heard someone shouting: "For the love of God, baptize this black man, even if he does not
understand anything, because he is like an evil child and he runs the risk of
dying without baptism." In the doorway of his house he met his salvation,
because an African of his own nation called Ignatius happened to pass. I had
baptized this person years ago. After the man called Ignatius passed, we went to
a quiet place where I baptized the man calmly and quietly. As I spoke to him, it

seemed that he woke up from a deep dream and saw his own bestial nature that before had prevented me from baptizing him. Now he understood the interpreter, although he had not comprehended him before. If the Lord had not granted him this comprehension, it would have been impossible to baptize him. His godfather decided that he should be baptized with the name of Ignatius. Three days later, he met me in the street. He approached me, grabbed my hand, and embraced me joyfully. The next day, they found him dead but staring upward, where his soul had without doubt flown to meet God.

On the day celebrating the Jesuit Saint Luis Gonzaga,[13] I experienced a very mysterious and happy catechism and baptism. I baptized one man with the name Luis and another whom, in reverence to our holy father, I called Ignatius. On the very same day Luis died, and on the next day Ignatius also died, but both went to be with their two saints in heaven. Comforted by this thought, I continued working. In another house, I found a dead woman rolled in a filthy mat. I presumed she died without baptism, because they did not call me in time to help her. Even if we carefully inspect the ships, we sometimes do not immediately go to those who need us most, because we do not know about them. I did not suffer very long for this, because the Lord alleviated my pain with works of his mercy. A very sick black man told me, while I was absolving him with the last rites, that he saw many beautiful children gathered around a very pale lady, and this made him very happy and comforted him. He believed this vision was a favor from heaven. I believed him, because the blacks do not deceive us or make up stories like other people do. Later I baptized a black woman and then moved on to confess another black man in the same house. I was told that the black woman I had just baptized was about to expire. Another woman spoke through the interpreter: "If that woman was not Christian, from what she said, I am not Christian either, because the same things happened to me as did to her. Baptize me later, because I am not near death like she is." Following her request, I baptized her after thoroughly questioning her. She did not die; instead the Lord gave her many years of life to do many good works.

One day I was out looking for an interpreter in order to give confession to a very sick black woman. In the hall of a house I saw a dead body, the corpse of a person who had not received the sacraments because he was a *bozal*. This hurt me, but it is a common, ordinary, and hopeless occurrence, because the masters do not tell us when their slaves are dying. I asked if anyone else inside the house was sick, to find out if I could do anything to make up for the neglect and carelessness inflicted upon the person who had already died. They responded yes. I entered and found that there was not one but a dozen sick people packed

---

13. Gonzaga lived from 1568 to 1591, when he died of the plague in Rome.

together in a small room. They were thin and dangerously ill with diarrhea, emitting a very bad odor due to their sickness and the closeness and discomfort of the place. I determined that they were all deathly ill and in extreme need. I did not dare leave them until I examined them to see if they had been baptized, and I catechized them with the help of a skillful and faithful interpreter of the Arda[14] caste that I found in the same house. I took the confession of everyone I had baptized. By then it was very late. Only one of all these people survived. All the rest died one by one, including the first one I knew about and for whom I looked for a translator when I encountered the dead body. I did not find the translator that night, and in the morning, when I went to see the woman who originally needed the translator, she had already died. This shows us that no one can comprehend the high and secret judgments of God, who chooses some and condemns others, according to his plan and divine wisdom. His divine kindness is a rule, and we are punished if we ignore his divine inspirations and vocations.

Once the archbishop of Goa, Don Francisco Alejo de Meneses, had to rebaptize an entire large town because he found out that many errors had been made when the people were first baptized. He secretly went to each house individually, because it would cause great scandal if he administered the baptisms publicly. We must also observe this kind of discretion. We must help the slaves with great care, not only those who have just arrived but especially those who are already *ladino* and have been here a long time. Some of them are thought to be Christian and take all the holy sacraments, although they are not really Christian. I will end this chapter with a few happy examples of these kinds of cases.

A black woman of the Bañona caste came to beg me various times to baptize a sister of hers that she knew for certain was not Christian, although she had lived ten years among Christians and everyone believed she was Christian. I asked her how she knew her sister was not Christian. She responded that she had often heard me questioning other slaves, with the help of interpreters and translators, to find out if they were Christians. (My work was that well known and people discussed it, showing great enthusiasm and love, even those who did not understand it. I have said many times that this was a special gift from the Holy Spirit.) I had always judged her sister to not be Christian, due to the answers she gave me. With this in mind I went to look for the sister. I examined her at length and determined that her sister said the truth. Even if she would surrender to the church, she did not, because she was concerned about what was respectful and suitable to the glory of God. Thus, I prepared her the best that I

---

14. Or Allada, an important kingdom on the slave coast of Lower Guinea. See Book I, note 19.

could. Her sister was her godmother because she had done so much to help her. I baptized her, entrusting her masters to arrange for oil to be poured on her. I never found out what the masters did, because they died and I could not learn what had happened to their slave, nor could I ask her sister, because she went to Spain with her masters.

Another black woman I knew was also a *ladina* who had lived for a long time in Spanish lands but was originally from Angola. Everyone, including me, thought she was Christian. Therefore, even if I was baptizing many other slaves that lived in her house, I had not insisted on examining her. One day, inspired by her companions' baptisms, she said was not baptized and asked me to baptize her. I told her to calm down because she had been baptized, being from Angola. She remained quiet for four or five months, but then she came to see me and insisted that she was not baptized. I told her I was on my way out to meet a slave ship that had just arrived. I would have to examine her afterward. When I finished, she returned and insisted for the third time that she was not baptized. I examined her, and after a rigorous examination, it turned out that she was right; she really was not Christian, even if they had thrown water on her in the port with the rest of her companions. This was because she had been in prison and was only released just before the priest poured water on the other slaves. Thus she did not receive the catechism and instruction normally given to these people before they are baptized. (The fact that catechism is taught at all is very different from the situation in the rivers of Guinea and the port of Cacheu.) Therefore, she did not understand anything about why they had freed the prisoners and washed their heads and then returned them to prison. When she came to the whites' lands, she heard that I poured water on those who had not understood what was happening when water had been poured on them. This led her to persistently ask me to baptize her, and I did it (having the holy oils ready). This gave great comfort both to her and to me.

Once, at ten o'clock in the evening, a certain black man's masters called me to confess him. I found the man to be very *bozal*. I needed an interpreter, so I asked him what caste he was, in order to find one as soon as possible. They said he was Bran. I left and found my interpreter, but he did not understand her because he was Banhun. I realized it would be difficult to find an interpreter at that hour, but the sick man was dying. I left, trying to feel inspired by the challenge. The Lord helped me and I quickly found the interpreter that I needed. But when we returned, he could not speak. I tried very hard to make him understand, but he did not regain consciousness. I requested a glass of water to see if that would rouse him. Finally, as I pleaded to the Lord, he spoke, and he understood the interpreter very well. He gave his confession and contrition. With this part secure, it was most important to absolve him quickly. I began to catechize him in the faith. I did this as well as I could, considering the urgent rush and his dire need. I asked him about his baptism. His answers showed his baptism was suspect. I could not leave him without trying to help him. To find out more, I wanted to ask his master if he knew anything about the baptism of his slave. This only disturbed the slave, so I tried to calm him down. I quickly instructed him in the catechism and the meaning of baptism. I had asked for the water to revive him, but instead I baptized him with it and then I conditionally absolved him. I made them give him the holy oil, and upon receiving it, he died. Luckily, it took less than one hour to find him two different interpreters. In that time, he had been catechized, baptized, and confessed, had received the holy oil, and died. His soul entered heaven, bathed in innocent grace. After so many years, he returned to the blood of the good Jesus fresh, pure, and beautiful, like a newborn infant just leaving the baptismal font.

One day by chance I was called to confess a black woman from the Mandinga nation. When I found her, she was so fatigued that if she were not so *ladina,* I could not have understood her. Even so, it was difficult because she confessed very slowly. But I understood her and she confessed as if she were a Spanish or Creole woman, so I did not examine her baptism, assuming that she must be baptized. However, I realized that she was from Guinea, so then I examined her and came to believe with utter certainty that she was not Christian. Although they poured oil on her and gave her confirmation, and she confessed and communicated here ten or twelve times a year, long ago her masters had been careless and this oversight had not been corrected. I felt great consolation from the Lord's mercy for this poor little woman. I warned her that she was in great danger of eternal condemnation if she was not baptized. She reacted happily, asking me not to wait a second longer to baptize her. But she begged me that, if possible, no one should know that she had never been baptized. She feared that if she survived her illness, she would be ashamed in front of those who knew her situation. I took a flagon of water from a box that I always brought with me in case of emergencies. I showed her the flagon, explaining baptism and how it would help her. I prepared her as well as I could, with acts of love and true comfort, and then poured the water on her, raising her head to heaven. As I put my hands on her head I said: "Blessed is the Lord." I have experienced many cases similar to this one, where I had to baptize very *ladino* people who were understood to be Christians but told me that they were not.

These are a few situations that I have experienced while performing the sacrament of baptism. I will not repeat other very mysterious cases I have experienced while performing the other sacraments. This ministry has baptized fifty thousand blacks in this city. Those who work in this mission will not give up until it can be said confidently that fifty thousand people have been saved from every single one of all the innumerable nations and languages of Ethiopia. The Lord gives great mercy in conceding the world's most humble and limited talents for such a holy and divine ministry. One and all give glory to God.

Chapter 15. The motives and reasons why the Company of Jesus has, in the Indies, devoted itself to the salvation of the blacks.

In this final chapter, what is Sandoval's interpretation of several key themes central to colonial Latin American history? How does he contrast indigenous Americans and African slaves? Sandoval's extensive metaphors in this chapter highlight his perception of the clash between spiritual idealism and materialism in the expanding world economy, and between Christianity and commercialization. Race plays a role in the expanding global market, whether the "products" being bought and sold are slaves, gold, silver, jewels, cloth, or souls. What is the interplay between race and Christianity in the metaphor of the Jesuits as pearl divers? How and why does Sandoval rank the products sold by the merchants and shopkeepers, both literally and symbolically, in the Indies? Why would Sandoval, in a final effort to spark the enthusiasm of his Jesuit readers, return to the issue of the expansion of Islam in his penultimate paragraph, reinserting contemporary African issues into a discussion of preaching to African slaves in the Americas? What point is he making by juxtaposing his discussion of merchants with a paragraph on the successes of Islam? How does emphasizing the threat of Islam strengthen the points made in the first paragraph of this chapter? Perhaps the mention of continuing Islamic expansion even underscores his sense that converting African slaves is both a struggle for world domination and an otherworldly battle for souls. Of course, Sandoval is confident that he is on the right side of this battle, and thus he can assert the rightness of his morality and belief in the global hierarchy of races, civilizations, and religions.

It is very true that our principal function in the Indies is to work with Indians, as stated in our constitutions. But it is also absolutely certain that very important work must be done for the black slaves that serve us in these parts. Without doubt, the purpose of the Company of Jesus here is to help the natives, but we should also help the blacks, especially in the places where there are no Indians. After all, black slaves came here to supplement the lack of Indians to serve us here on earth. They are also here for us to help them spiritually. They are our slaves and not free people like the Indians. Therefore, we must make a greater effort to help them because, as I have clearly shown, the blacks are in much greater need than the Indians. It is more difficult to instruct the blacks than the Indians, and thus they offer the hope of a greater reward. Our sacred Company has already truthfully declared that it equally values working for the salvation of both the blacks and the Indians, and all the ecclesiastical privileges that are conceded to the Indians are also conceded to the blacks and vice versa.

Our mission is to go to diverse parts of the world looking for souls in need. We wonder at and envy our brothers who are sent from Naples, Genoa, even Rome itself, and the other cities of Italy to work in the distant kingdoms and provinces of the Ethiopians. They joyfully and determinedly cross the Alps and the Pyrenees of Savoy, France, and Spain, happily in the company of other

Jesuits. They leave from Lisbon, heading to many remote black empires, kingdoms, and provinces in the Cape of Good Hope, Africa, Ethiopia, and India. They do not fear furious hurricanes or shipwrecks, although many of their brothers have perished on voyages in those tempestuous seas. I hope that God Our Lord and the letters I have included here help inspire our Company's brothers so that no one will ever be able to stop them in working for the glory of God himself. They have had such success in their travels and pilgrimages, conquering so many challenges and doing so much work to implant the Gospel around the world. They have gathered such a copious harvest from the Ethiopians. I hope that what I relate here is only the prologue or short introduction to a very long and impressive chapter in the history of the Church.

Our brothers' deeds undoubtedly inspire all of us who live in these remote places to follow their example. We make a vow to share this mission. We must follow through on this vow when we see with our eyes and touch with our hands the perdition and condemnation of the souls of so many black *bozales* and *ladinos,* utterly lacking anyone to help them. With our help and hard work, they can be saved. To help them we endure traveling, long roads, deserts, rivers, seas, and great and extraordinary effort, as do our brothers, but we will not leave until we bring them spiritual health. These challenges promise us great successes, especially considering how great the harvest is and how few are the workers.

There is another reason why the Company should hurry to help save the blacks. The Indies are dominated by merchants, and merchants concern themselves only with worldly goods. Our great King, who trades only in the Gospel, wants to acquire the most valuable pearls of the Orient and the West: souls redeemed by his blood. These pearls come from the coarse and ugly shells of black and Indian bodies. To get this bounty, he sends religious people to the Indies so that they will dive into the deepest sea to gather the pearls. The Company of Jesus is not the least important or the least agile among these divers who bring His Majesty what he deserves: the finest and longest strings of pearls.

Spanish merchants discovered the Indies and made it their granary. They send their cargo ships, soldiers, and officials, with the sole purpose of taking away gold, silver, pearls, and precious stones. Christ, the reigning merchant, also discovered the Indies, but he desired to enrich his court with a more precious kind of gold, silver, and jewels: the souls of the natives and the blacks. For this reason he sent *his* agents, overseers, and officials to this land. These are the members of the religious orders, who carry virtue, sanctity, and learning. Seeing that the riches were many and his ministers few, he created a Company with the goal of going to the most remote parts of the world to find souls and give him the profits. His Majesty wants all the glory of this work for himself, but he also gives the workers all the benefits. This Company is the Company of Jesus, and we are very happy companions in it. My fathers, we all work for the greatest of all merchants, and our stock overflows with souls for the greater glory of His

Majesty and our own gain. In a land where all are merchants, we have no excuse not to deal in the most fruitful product of the region.

If a rich and powerful merchant sent many clerks to the Indies to carefully manage his shops in order to increase his fortune, the clerks would sell both the best-quality and the worst-quality products to profit the merchant, not caring if they were mocked for selling cheaper goods. I observe that my companions sell precious silks, linens, and brocades, but I can try to make even the coarsest fabrics look appealing, even if they look down on me for trying to sell them. I know a merchant would appreciate my efforts. God Our Lord also has stores in the New World. He stocks them with rich merchandise: cloth of gold, brocade, velvet, satin, and damask. These rich fabrics represent the prominent and rich men, modest maidens, married matrons, and noble ladies. But his well-stocked store also deals in iron goods, combs, canvas, fish, and so on. These cheaper goods are the Indians, mestizos, mulattos, and *bozal* blacks. He also sends fleets full of cashiers and clerks to profit from his primary investment—the several religious orders of his holy Church. Almost all of them deal only in the rich fabrics, brocade, velvet, damask, and satin, for the benefit of the white, noble, prominent people, the lord viceroys, judges, bishops, and archbishops. These goods bring great profits to the sciences, the pulpit, and the press. But this great Lord also has coarser goods on offer, although they give an even greater return on investment. One of his storekeepers might go to him and say: "Lord, I do not lack fine merchandise, in ministering to the whites, but I prefer to invest in the common goods, the black *bozales,* vile and low in the eyes of men, because they will bring you greater profit for a cost similar to the rest. I will try to indoctrinate, catechize, instruct, examine, and baptize them. I will confess them if they need it, and give them communion if they are capable of receiving it. I will prepare them for death with extreme unction, and you will profit from them because they will be saved and not lost." Who could doubt that this servant, this religious person who is so careful to help his Lord and increase the return on his investment, will not be more valued than the rest? He will at least be praised as much as the others. This will bring him joy and happiness. God says: "Be glad and rejoice, be happy and satisfied, son of the Company of Jesus, my faithful companion in such great and agreeable work. By giving me happiness and loving me, you do work that men do not value but that I consider very important. For this, you will come to my palace in heaven." Who does not hope to please this great merchant? Who could reject and disdain the riches of the merchants of the Indies?

What most shames me (and I believe also shames any son of the Company) is the care and work that the Moors give to perverting these black nations with their false Mohammed. Just recently, and before our very eyes, they have introduced the Mohammedan sect in four more important and populous Guinean kingdoms: those of the Berbers, the Mandingas, the Wolofs, and the Matomos, as well as probably in many others. To carry out their goals, they create schools where they teach the people to read and write, telling them that this will help them in negotiations all over the world and in doing business with all the merchants. The Moors preach their cursed sect on the Ethiopian coasts. They brave the scalding sands of Libya and endure such hunger and thirst that they have to kill their camels and suck their blood in order to not die on the road. The Moors endure so many dangers and risks for such a worldly, corrupt reward, but we as Christians, especially those who are religious professionals, and most especially brothers of the Company of Jesus, should run toward the greatest eternal prize. How shameful for the sons of this century to be defeated by those who eagerly run to their death, more quickly than we run to embrace life. We have to do so little to receive so much. They ask so little from us, compared to what they give us.

Ignorant men sacrifice themselves for their diabolic superstitions, so we should do everything we can for the sake of Christ's faith and the cross on which he died. He saved us and gives us blessed, unending life. The Eternal Father sent us a message when he appeared before our holy father Ignatius, in the company of Jesus Christ, his Son and Our Lord, carrying his cross on his shoulders. His cross symbolized immense labors and rigorous penitence. The Eternal Father told his Son that he entrusted him to the care of Ignatius and his Company. The Son appeared pleased and happy with this, and he leaned forward and gave his cross to Ignatius. As he put it on Ignatius's shoulders, he said: "Ignatius, I will favor and protect you throughout the world so that you and your Company will have the burden of carrying my cross. You must seek perfection in your own souls but also in the souls of your neighbors and brothers, wherever they are throughout the world." The unique and precious gift of Christ's cross shows that he greatly values our holy father Ignatius and all the apostolic men of our sacred religion. They work together to embrace the cross, caring for it in order to fulfill the demands of their vocation. They not only carry the cross constantly but also bring it to others and suffer martyrdom on it. And thus I seek the health of my soul and the souls of my brothers.

END OF THE FOURTH BOOK.

Published in Seville by Francisco de Lyra, printer of books, 1627.

GLOSSARY

Acosta, José de: A very influential Jesuit who lived from 1540 to 1600. His publications are among the most important early European commentaries on the Americas. Acosta's *De procuranda Indorum salute [On Procuring Indian Spiritual Health],* written in 1576 and published in 1588, inspired the title of Sandoval's book.

Arda, Ararae, Axarae: All of these words refer to Allada, an important kingdom in Lower Guinea, an area that includes southern Ghana, Benin, Togo, and Nigeria; also known as the "slave coast."

attrition: While contrition means truly hate sins out of love for God, attrition means regretting sins out of the fear of punishment, so attrition is sometimes called "imperfect contrition." Catholic doctrine as defined by the Council of Trent stated that attrition was enough to allow for an effective confession and absolution, where the priest absolves a person's sins, helping the soul on its journey to heaven.

Bañona, Banhun, Banune, Banuune: All of these words refer to an ethnic group from the Senegambia/Guinea-Bissau region.

Bantu: A large family of languages spoken in Central Africa.

Biafra: A common ethnic designation for Senegambians sent to the Americas as slaves in the 1500s.

Biojo: An ethnic group living in the Senegambia/Guinea-Bissau region.

Black Atlantic: The idea of the Black Atlantic privileges the African diaspora experience, not the histories of nation states in the Atlantic basin.

bozal: Rough or crude. Spaniards used this derogatory term for non-Spanish-speaking slaves who had recently arrived in the Americas from Africa.

Bran: A common ethnic designation among slaves in Latin America, used to describe Africans from the Cacheu River.

Cacheu: A port city in Guinea-Bissau.

Cafre: "Cafre" derives from an Arabic word that Muslims used to refer to South Africans who were not Islamic. These people were often sold as slaves to the Portuguese, who began to use the term as an ethnic designation.

Caravali: An ethnic designation commonly used for Africans in Latin America. The name comes from the coastal port of Elem Calabar and refers broadly to Igbo-speaking people from this region.

Cartagena de Indias: A Spanish port city founded in the 1530s on the Caribbean coast of what is now the country of Colombia.

casta: A Spanish colonial term for nonwhite, usually implying a person of mixed racial ancestry and fairly low social status.

catechism: In this book, basic Christian doctrine taught to African slaves.

circum-Caribbean: A geographic region including the Caribbean islands, parts of coastal Mexico, Central America, Venezuela, and Colombia.

Claver, Peter: A Jesuit who lived from 1581 to 1654, Claver worked closely with Sandoval. In 1888, Claver was canonized by the Catholic Church.

contrition: To Catholics, contrition means that a person despises what he has done that goes against Christian rules, and he strives to avoid this behavior in the future.

Council of Trent: The Catholic council that met from 1545 to 1563 to codify Catholic doctrine, beliefs, and practices as a reaction to the Protestant Reformation.

creole: The word creole, or *criollo* in Spanish, comes from the Spanish verb *criar,* "to nurse or breed." In this book, Sandoval generally uses "creole" to refer to slaves born in the Americas.

encomenderos: From the Spanish verb *encomendar,* or entrust. *Encomenderos* were Spaniards who received royal grants of Amerindians as laborers, in exchange for their military successes in the conquest.

Ethiopia: Sandoval uses this word to mean all of Africa. He also refers to dark-skinned people around the world as Ethiopians.

extreme unction: Last rites, a Catholic sacrament involving confession and absolution, done to prepare people for death and the afterlife.

Fulupe/Fulo/Fulopa: The Fulbe people of Senegal.

gentile: By gentile, Sandoval means non-Christian or pagan.

Inquisition: In the late 1400s, the Spanish monarchs Ferdinand and Isabella were granted papal permission to activate a court to seek out and examine dissenters from accepted Catholic beliefs and practices. Each region of Spain had its own Inquisition tribunal and, by the 1600s, the court also had branches in Lima, Mexico City, and Cartagena de Indias. For the first few decades of its existence, the inquisitors focused on uncovering Jewish practices among recent converts to Christianity, but they later persecuted Protestants and other non-Catholic Christians as well as individuals who allegedly engaged in sorcery or pacts with the devil.

ladino: An African or Native American person who speaks Spanish or Portuguese and behaves in a manner that shows knowledge of Iberian culture and the Catholic religion. Usually *ladinos* had lived among Europeans for most of their lives. *Ladino* is often used to mean the opposite of *bozal.*

limpieza de sangre: This term means "cleanliness of blood," and refers to an early modern Spanish obsession with lineage. Those individuals who had *limpieza de sangre* had no traceable non-Christian or non-European ancestors. Those without *limpieza* were officially excluded from attending universities or practicing certain professions.

Loyola, Saint Ignatius: Ignatius Loyola was born in the Basque region of Spain in 1491 and died in 1556. Until age 30, he served as a soldier in the service of one of his noble relatives. He changed the path of his life after sustaining a wound in battle. For several years Loyola spent time in pilgrimages and spiritual awakening. He described his system of self-exploration in his book *Spiritual Exercises,* which lays out a thirty-day plan of meditation toward greater understanding of an individual's connection to God. He spent several years as a student in Spain and Paris, gathering followers but also suffering persecution. He founded the Company of Jesus in 1534, when he met with six other men from the University of Paris to retreat into a practice of his *Spiritual Exercises.* The Jesuits received official approval from Pope Paul III in 1540. Loyola spent the final years of his life organizing and governing the Society of Jesus.

Lucumi: A Yoruba-speaking people from the region of modern-day Benin.

Mandingo: A West African civilization, also called Mande. Some Mandes called Mandinka or Manding founded the great Mali empire, which flourished from the 1200s to the 1400s.

mestizo: A Spanish colonial term referring to people with both indigenous American and Spanish ancestors.

moleques: A term used in the Atlantic slave trade to refer to African children.

nación: Literally, *nación* means nation, but in early modern Spanish, this term referred to a person's regional or ethnic origins.

Nalu: An African ethnicity from southern Guinea-Bissau.

palenques: A Spanish word for rebel slave communities in Spain's American colonies.

Pliny: Sandoval refers to Pliny the Elder, who lived from 23 to 79 C.E. and wrote an encyclopedic work that collected most of the knowledge of his time. Sandoval often cites Pliny for his information on Africa.

quilombo: This word, derived from the Central African term *kilombo,* refers to rebel slave communities in Brazil.

reales: A small unit of currency in the Spanish American empire. Eight *reales* equaled one *peso.*

Soninke: A Mande-speaking people from West Africa.

Xavier, Saint Francis: Francis Xavier was born in 1506 to noble parents in a Basque-influenced area of Navarre, now a province of northern Spain. He shared a room with Ignatius Loyola at the University of Paris and later took the original Jesuit vows in 1534. While the Jesuits were working in Portugal in 1540, King John III asked them to help bring Christianity to his new subjects in Asia. After arriving in Goa in 1542, Xavier worked among the Parava people on the southeastern coast of India. He died on an island off the coast of China in 1552.

Wolof: The Wolof empire was an influential confederacy in the region of Senegal and Gambia from the 1300s to the 1500s.

Zape: An overarching label for diverse peoples from coastal Sierra Leone. Sandoval says that further divisions among the Zape include Cooli, Limba, Baca, Lindagozo, Zozo, Pelicoya, Baga, and Boloncho.

SELECTED BIBLIOGRAPHY

AFRICA

Clarke, Peter B. *West Africa and Islam: A Study of Religious Development from the Eighth to the Twentieth Century.* London: Edward Arnold, 1982.

Curtin, Philip. *Economic Change in Pre-colonial Africa: Senegambia in the Era of the Slave Trade.* Madison: University of Wisconsin Press, 1975.

Ehret, Christopher. *The Civilizations of Africa: A History to 1800.* Charlottesville: University of Virginia Press, 2002.

Hastings, Adrian. *The Church in Africa, 1450–1950.* Oxford: Clarendon Press, 1994.

Kalu, Ogbu U., ed. *African Christianity: An African Story.* Pretoria, South Africa: Department of Church History, 2005.

Law, Robin. *The Slave Coast of West Africa.* Oxford: Oxford University Press, 1990.

Thornton, John. *Africa and Africans in the Making of the Atlantic World, 1400–1680.* Cambridge: Cambridge University Press, 1992.

———. *The Kongolese Saint Anthony: Dona Beatriz Kimpa Vita and the Antonian Movement, 1684–1706.* Cambridge: Cambridge University Press, 1998.

———. *Warfare in Atlantic Africa, 1500–1800.* London: Routledge, 1999.

SLAVE TRADE

Blackburn, Robin. *The Making of New World Slavery: From the Baroque to the Modern, 1492–1800.* London: Verso, 1997.

Boxer, C. R. *The Portuguese Seaborne Empire, 1415–1825.* New York: Knopf, 1969.

Chandler, David L. "Health Conditions in the Slave Trade of Colonial New Granada." In *Slavery and Race Relations in Latin America,* edited by Robert Brent Toplin. Westport, CT: Greenwood, 1974.

Curtin, Philip. *The Atlantic Slave Trade: A Census.* Madison: University of Wisconsin Press, 1969.

Hair, P. E. H. *The Atlantic Slave Trade and Black Africa*. London: Historical Association, 1978.

———. *The Founding of the Castelo de San Jorge da Mina*. Madison: University of Wisconsin Press, 1994.

Klein, Herbert. *The Middle Passage*. Princeton: Princeton University Press, 1978.

Rawley, James A. *The Transatlantic Slave Trade: A History*. New York: Norton, 1981.

Thomas, Hugh. *The Slave Trade: The Story of the Atlantic Slave Trade, 1440–1870*. New York: Simon and Schuster, 1997.

Toplin, Robert Brent, ed. *Slavery and Race Relations in Latin America*. Westport, CT: Greenwood, 1974.

Walvin, James. *Atlas of Slavery*. London: Pearson Longman, 2006.

GENERAL WORKS ON AFRICANS IN LATIN AMERICA

Andrews, George Reid. *Afro-Latin America, 1800–2000*. New York: Oxford University Press, 2004.

Bowser, Frederick. *The African Slave in Colonial Peru*. Stanford: Stanford University Press, 1972.

Klein, Herbert S. *African Slavery in Latin America and the Caribbean*. New York: Oxford University Press, 1986.

Lipski, John. *A History of Afro-Hispanic Languages: Five Centuries, Five Continents*. Cambridge: Cambridge University Press, 2005.

Rout, Leslie. *The African Experience in Latin America*. Cambridge: Cambridge University Press, 1976.

Schwartz, Stuart. *Sugar Plantations in the Formation of Brazilian Society, Bahia, 1550–1835*. Cambridge: Cambridge University Press, 1985.

Sweet, James. *Recreating Africa: Culture, Kinship, and Religion in the African-Portuguese World, 1441–1770*. Chapel Hill: University of North Carolina Press, 2003.

Von Germeten, Nicole. *Black Blood Brothers*. Gainesville: University Press of Florida, 2006.

COMPANY OF JESUS

Acosta, José de. *Natural and Moral History of the Indies,* edited by Jane E. Mangan, translated by Frances López-Morillas, with an Introduction by Walter D. Mignolo. Durham, N.C.: Duke University Press, 2002.

Alden, Dauril. *The Making of an Enterprise: The Society of Jesus in Portugal, Its Empire, and Beyond, 1540–1750.* Stanford, Calif.: Stanford University Press, 1996.

Bangert, William. *A History of the Society of Jesus.* St. Louis: Institute of Jesuit Sources, 1972.

Burgaleta, Claudio M. *José de Acosta, S.J. (1540–1600): His Life and Thought.* Chicago: Loyola Press, 1999.

Cushner, Nicholas P. *Lords of the Land: Sugar, Wine, and Jesuit Estates of Coastal Peru.* Albany: State University of New York Press, 1980.

———. *Soldiers of God: The Jesuits in Colonial America, 1565–1767.* Buffalo: Language Communications, 2002.

Donnelly, John Patrick, ed. and trans. *Jesuit Writings of the Early Modern Period, 1540–1640.* Indianapolis: Hackett, 2006.

Franklin, Vincent P. "Alonso de Sandoval and the Jesuit Conception of the Negro." *Journal of Negro History* 58, no. 3 (July 1973): 349–60.

Hyland, Sabine. *The Jesuit and the Incas: The Extraordinary Life of Padre Blas Valera, S.J.* Ann Arbor: University of Michigan Press, 2003.

Konrad, Herman W. *A Jesuit Hacienda in Colonial México: Santa Lucia, 1576–1767.* Stanford, Calif.: Stanford University Press, 1980.

MacCormack, Sabine. *On the Wings of Time: Rome, the Incas, Spain, and Peru.* Princeton, N.J.: Princeton University Press, 2007.

Morgan, Ronald J. "Jesuit Confessors, African Slaves and the Practice of Confession in Seventeenth-Century Cartagena." In *Penitence in the Age of Reformations,* edited by Katharine Jackson Lualdi and Anne T. Thayer. Aldershot, U.K.: Ashgate, 2000, 222–239.

Morner, Magnus, ed. *The Expulsion of the Jesuits from Latin America.* New York: Knopf, 1965.

Olsen, Margaret M. *Slavery and Salvation in Colonial Cartagena de Indias.* Gainesville: University Press of Florida, 2004.

O'Malley, John W. *The First Jesuits.* Cambridge, Mass.: Harvard University Press, 1993.

Pérez de Ribas, Andrés. *History of the Triumphs of Our Holy Faith Amongst the Most Barbarous and Fierce Peoples of the New World,* translated by Daniel T. Reff, Maureen Ahern, and Richard K. Danford. Tucson: University of Arizona Press, 1999.

Reff, Daniel. *Plagues, Priests, and Demons: Sacred Narratives and the Rise of Christianity in the Old World and the New.* Cambridge: Cambridge University Press, 2004.

Valtierra, Angel. *Peter Claver: Saint of the Slaves.* Westminster, Md.: Newman Press, 1960.

Von Germeten, Nicole. "Promoting Saint Peter Claver and Catholicism to African Americans." *American Catholic Studies* 116, no. 3 (Fall 2005): 23–38.

Wright, Jonathan. *God's Soldiers.* London: HarperCollins, 2004.

Zupanov, Ines G. *Missionary Tropics: The Catholic frontier in India (Sixteenth and Seventeenth Centuries).* Ann Arbor: University of Michigan Press, 2005.

RACE IN THE AMERICAS

Baptist, Edward, and Stephanie Camp, eds. *New Studies in the History of American Slavery.* Athens: University of Georgia Press, 2006.

Gomez, Michael. *Exchanging Our Country Marks: The Transformation of African Identities in the Colonial and Antebellum South.* Chapel Hill: University of North Carolina Press, 1998.

Hall, Gwendolyn Midlo. *Slavery and African Ethnicities in the Americas: Restoring the Links.* Chapel Hill: University of North Carolina Press, 2005.

Johnson, Walter, ed. *The Chattel Principle: Internal Slave Trades in the Americas.* New Haven, Conn.: Yale University Press, 2004.

Landers, Jane, and Barry Robinson, eds. *Slaves, Subjects, and Subversives: Blacks in Colonial Latin America.* Albuquerque: University of New Mexico Press, 2006.

Lovejoy, Paul, ed. *Identity in the Shadow of Slavery.* London: Verso, 2000.

Lovejoy, Paul, and David Trotman, eds. *Transatlantic Dimensions of Ethnicity in the African Diaspora.* London: Verso, 2004.

INDEX

and parental approval, 123–124
and sickness, 100–102, 161, 165,
  180, 182–183
and women, 108, 122–123, 166
before death, 49, 58, 94, 124, 132,
  137, 152, 179–180, 184–185,
  186–187
conditional baptism, 115, 125,
  130, 131, 143, 147, 151
examinations, 126–128, 146–148,
  160, 162–164
godparents, 109, 142, 144, 149
in churches, 145, 147, 166
masters discouraging or preventing,
  72, 147, 150
metaphors of water, 128–129, 141,
  142
misunderstandings of, 116, 118–
  121, 125
necessary education before, 118,
  131, 133–137, 151, 165
of infants, 117, 122–124, 152,
  179–180
use of amulets and medals, 141,
  143, 144–145
use of interpreters, 131–132
variety in African ports, 111, 130,
  162–163, 186
voluntary, 114, 115, 117–120, 122,
  162–163
Baroque Christianity, xix, xxiii
Beltrán, Luis, 81, 181
Benin, 14, 18, 34
Bogotá, 3, 4, 83
Bontemps, Alex, 106
Borja, Francis, 172, 175
bozales
as a derogatory term, 69
incorrectly baptized, 82, 113–114
need for interpreters, 103, 146,
  161, 164
not understanding baptism, 151

potential to be Christians, 72, 74,
  108–110, 173
sickness and death, 182, 184–185,
  186
Brazil, 12, 41, 51, 60, 80–81, 159

Cacheu [Guinea-Bissau], 13, 25,
  45–46, 50, 53, 112–114, 116, 130,
  162, 179, 186
Cape Verde islands,
  baptisms in, 51, 121, 127
  ethnicities in region, 12–15, 43–
    44, 46–47
  slave trading port, 50, 180
Cartagena de Indias [Colombia],
  African festivals in, xii–xiii, 155
  Africans in, xi–xii, 54
  slave trading port, xi, 46–48, 52
Casamance River, 13, 25
Catholic beliefs,
  absolution, 109, 153–154, 156,
    166–167
  and "whites", 116, 118, 119–121,
    131, 134, 163, 179
  attrition, 142, 155–156, 161
  contrition, 137–139, 142, 151,
    153, 155–156, 161
  damnation, 31, 58,
  devil, 6–7, 23, 30, 32, 33, 67, 72,
    78, 85, 92, 131, 134, 145
  gospel, 56, 79, 84, 90, 92, 96, 106,
    171, 189
  grace, 7, 75, 108–109, 134, 137,
    141, 143
  heaven, 8, 72, 133, 135–136, 151,
    156, 165, 173, 184
  hell, 31, 94, 134–136, 139–140,
    154, 156
  Holy Spirit, 71, 131, 135, 143, 185
  Jesus Christ, 66, 82, 93, 108, 134–
    135, 165, 191
  last judgment, 76, 136

Molina, Luis de, xx, 50
Mompox, 19
Mozambique, 15, 80, 171, 176, 178

naciones, 45–49
Arda, 14, 17, 34–35, 47, 60, 103, 147, 185
Berbers, 12, 25, 28, 32, 44, 53, 190
Biafra, 13–14, 26, 29, 44, 45–46, 53, 104
Bran, 13, 26, 29–30, 32, 33, 45, 118, 186
Caravali, 14–15, 47, 48, 111, 127, 147, 155, 181
Fulo, 13, 18, 25, 44–45
Lucumi, 14, 17, 35–36, 47–48, 111, 127, 147
Mandingo, 13, 25, 26, 44–45, 103, 118, 162, 187, 190
Mina, 12, 14, 47, 127
Nubia, 87

Oveido, Andrés de, 89

palenques, xi, xxviii
Paraguay, 115
Pérez de Ribas, Andrés, xvi–xvii
Peru, ix, 46, 110, 146, 171
Pliny, xvii, 17, 23, 59, 61–62, 102–103
Portugal and the Portuguese
imperial expansion, 171, 175, 177
in Africa, 25, 26, 38–39
in Goa, 171–172
interaction with African leaders, 36, 40–41, 87
language, 47, 91
slave traders, xi, 11, 14, 53
Porto Bello, Panama, x, 181–182

Prester John, 16, 59
priests,
committing sacrilege, 133, 148–149
giving incorrect baptisms in Africa, 115–116, 118–119, 121
responsible for slaves in America, 146, 149

Quilombo, 19
Quito, 110

race,
and beauty, 16–17, 19, 21, 22, 85, 97
and climate, 20
and color, xxiv–xxv, 6–8, 12, 16–21, 31, 44, 79, 85
and inheritance, 17–20
black images of the Virgin Mary, 82
curse of Ham, 17, 20
hair and skin, 18–21, 44
historical and biblical sources on, 17–18, 20
labels, 18
mestizos, xxvi, 190
Reff, Daniel, xvii, xvii n. 20, xx n. 28, 3 n. 1, 8 n. 9, 57 n. 79

Sandoval, Alonso de
education, ix–x, xv
family, ix
Jesuit intellectual influence on, xvi–xix
perceptions of Africans, xv
publications, xviii, xxix–xxx
Sâo Tomé,
baptisms in, 51, 103, 111, 116, 121, 127–128
priests in, 14, 38
slave trading port, 44, 47–48, 50

Senegal River, 24–25
Seville, ix, x, 25, 113, 114, 146,
159–161, 167–168
Sierra Leone, 14–15, 23–24, 26,
28–29, 177
slavery
and African leaders, 50–52, 53–55
and Christian morality, 67, 75–78
and Christianity, 49–51, 55–56,
71–78
and death, 55, 58
and disease, 57–58, 100–101
and freedom, 49, 51, 53–54, 158
as a judicial punishment, 26, 53, 55
caused by war, 15, 53
in the Bible, 76–78
masters, 50, 67, 68–72, 75–78,
141, 158
paternalistic view of, 68, 71, 74–78
ports, see port names
punishments and abuse, 68–70, 75
traders in Africa, 52–53
work routines, 69–70
slaves
as Christians, xiv, 75, 110
branding, 120, 136
burials, 58, 68, 70–71, 96
dehumanizing and objectifying, 43,
66, 67, 102
fair treatment, 75–78
intelligence, 67, 72–73, 105–109,
137–138, 157–158
marriage, 73, 167
replacing Amerindians, 66, 70, 188
sadness, 8, 56, 75, 95, 108–109,
119, 126, 129

sexuality, 102, 137, 139, 153–155
souls, 8, 56, 58, 67, 77, 78, 81, 85
their desire for baptism, 74, 107–
109, 129, 178–179
slave ships, x, xvii, 6
baptism on, 73, 111–116, 118–
121, 148, 160, 186
conditions on, 55–58
overcrowding, 52, 56
shipwrecks, 52, 150, 182
sickness, 57–58, 126, 151–152,
179–180
thirst, 96, 126, 128–129
slave traders,
guilt, 50–54
testimonies of shipboard baptisms,
113–115
Socotra, 16, 171, 176
Spiritual Exercises, xvi, xviii

Vieira, Antonio, xxiv

Wolof, xxviii, 12–13, 25, 28, 32, 44,
53, 162, 190

Xavier, Francis, xviii–xiv, 23, 89,
91, 92, 141–142, 145, 171–172,
174–177

Zape, 14, 24, 26, 44, 46, 48, 181–
182